Australian Signpost MATHS 3

Mentals

Alan McSeveny
Diane McSeveny-Foster
Rachel McSeveny

Pearson Australia
(a division of Pearson Australia Group Pty Ltd)
459–471 Church Street, Level 1, Building B, Richmond, Victoria 3121
PO Box 23360, Melbourne, Victoria 8012
www.pearson.com.au

First published 2018 by Pearson Australia
2025 2024 2023 2022
10 9 8 7 6 5 4 3 2 1

Content and Learning Specialist: Sophie Matta
Project Manager: Shelly Wang
Production Manager: Elizabeth Gosman
Editor: Sally Woollett
Designers: Anne Donald & Jennifer Johnston
Cover Designer: Jennifer Johnston
Rights & Permissions Editor: Samantha Russell-Tulip
Senior Publishing Services Analyst: Rob Currulli
Cover art: Michael Barter
Cover background: rf_vector/Shutterstock.com
Illustrators: Michael Barter, Wendy Gorton, John Winter

Printed in Australia by Pegasus Media and Logistics

ISBN 978 1 4886 2183 3

Pearson Australia Group Pty Ltd ABN 40 004 245 943

Introduction

Using the Mentals Books

Each unit of the Mentals Book is programmed to review Student Book content for the previous two weeks (based on the Suggested Program in the Teacher's Book). For example, Unit 15 of the Mentals Book can be set as homework to review weeks 13 and 14 of the Student Book while week 15 is being taught.

Presentation

- The content of the strands Number and Algebra, Measurement and Geometry, and Statistics and Probability is covered thoroughly.
- Essential skills are explained.
- Language, problem solving, graphs and tables are given a high profile.
- Mathematics is applied to real-life situations wherever possible.
- The **Arithmetic Card** (page 5) is an exciting teaching tool for practising basic number skills.
- **ID Cards** (pages 6 and 7) review the terms essential to success in the course.
- **Measurement standards and examples** (pages 8 and 9) are provided so that students can estimate effectively.

Mixed-topic Questions

The units present questions in a mixed-topic format.

- This is essential for thorough understanding and continuous review.
- In real life, similar questions don't often occur together.
- It allows the teacher to discover weaknesses that could otherwise pass unnoticed.
- It provides a real test of understanding.

Graded Questions

- Column 1: easier
- Columns 2 and 3: harder
- Column 4: Extension and Challenge

Motivation

- Cartoons make mathematics more appealing.
- There are two lizards hidden on each page for students to find.

Extra Activities

- Problem-solving **strategies** are introduced in a carefully planned sequence throughout the series.

- Important concepts from **Number and Algebra** and **Measurement and Geometry** are explored.

- **Measurement** concepts and activities are introduced and investigated.

- **Statistics and Probability** concepts are presented for revision and extension.

- A **tables** program for each of addition, subtraction and multiplication is included.
- It is important for students to try to learn addition and multiplication tables by heart.

3 Contents

Arithmetic Card 5

ID Cards 6–7

Tables of Number and Measurement 8

Examples of Measurements 9

Units 10–83

How Would You Name the Lizards? 84

Answers A1–A12 (middle pages)

Unit Activities

Unit	Content	Extra Activity	Unit	Content	Extra Activity
1:1/2 **1:3/4**	+ 1, − 1 Personal measures	+/− tables Measure	**20:1/2** **20:3/4**	Chance Language	Chance ID Card A
2:1/2 **2:3/4**	Australian money Looking for tens	Concept Concept	**21:1/2** **21:3/4**	13 −, 14 − Time in minutes	− tables Measure
3:1/2 **3:3/4**	Australian money + 1, − 1	Concept +/− tables	**22:1/2** **22:3/4**	+ 8, + 9 Addition grid	+ tables + tables
4:1/2 **4:3/4**	Time Chance	Measure Chance	**23:1/2** **23:3/4**	× 5 Perimeter	× tables Measure
5:1/2 **5:3/4**	Skip counting Language	× tables ID Card B	**24:1/2** **24:3/4**	− 10, − 10 Rounding (nearest 100)	− tables Concept
6:1/2 **6:3/4**	× 2, × 4 Problem solving	× tables Strategy time	**25:1/2** **25:3/4**	24 +, 32 + Language	+ tables ID Card B
7:1/2 **7:3/4**	Rows of, groups of Skip counting	× tables × tables	**26:1/2** **26:3/4**	15 −, 16 − Linking + and −	− tables Concept
8:1/2 **8:3/4**	+ 2, + 3 Subtracting 9	+ tables Concept	**27:1/2** **27:3/4**	+ 3, + 5 Rounding (nearest 10)	+ tables Concept
9:1/2 **9:3/4**	× 10 × 5	× tables × tables	**28:1/2** **28:3/4**	+ 4, + 6 Using number lines	+ tables − tables
10:1/2 **10:3/4**	× 5, × 0 Language	× tables ID Card B	**29:1/2** **29:3/4**	− 2, − 4 + 7, + 9	− tables + tables
11:1/2 **11:3/4**	+ 3, + 4 Lots of, groups of	+ tables Concept	**30:1/2** **30:3/4**	Chance Language	Chance ID Card A
12:1/2 **12:3/4**	× 3 7 −, 8 −	× tables − tables	**31:1/2** **31:3/4**	Writing fractions Near doubling	Concept Concept
13:1/2 **13:3/4**	11 −, 12 − × 3	− tables × tables	**32:1/2** **32:3/4**	Chance Fractions	Chance Concept
14:1/2 **14:3/4**	Chance Adding with blocks	Chance Concept	**33:1/2** **33:3/4**	Subtraction Language	Concept ID Card B
15:1/2 **15:3/4**	× 1, × 10 Language	× tables ID Card B	**34:1/2** **34:3/4**	Problem solving Linking + and −	Strategy time Concept
16:1/2 **16:3/4**	+ 5 Roman numerals	+ tables Concept	**35:1/2** **35:3/4**	+ 8 Language	+ tables ID Card A
17:1/2 **17:3/4**	+ 6, + 7 Combinations to 10 & 13	+ tables Concept	**36:1/2** **36:3/4**	Language Problem solving	ID Card A Strategy time
18:1/2 **18:3/4**	Chance 13 −, 14 −	Chance − tables	**37:1/2** **37:3/4**	Rounding (nearest 5) Personal measures	Concept Measure
19:1/2 **19:3/4**	Chance + 10, + 10	Chance + tables	**Answers**	These can be found in the middle of this book on pages A1 to A12.	

 ISBN 978 1 4886 2183 3

Arithmetic Card

	A	B	C	D	E	F	G	H	I	J
1	11	3	7	20	4	2	7	50	37	$6
2	17	7	4	16	25	10	11	80	93	$1
3	14	1	10	12	64	14	3	20	16	$7
4	19	5	3	17	16	4	15	70	55	$3
5	16	8	5	13	81	12	19	40	100	$8
6	12	6	8	18	1	16	1	60	71	$5
7	18	10	2	11	36	8	9	100	48	$9
8	15	4	6	14	9	20	17	30	82	$2
9	20	9	1	19	100	18	5	90	64	$10
10	13	2	9	15	49	6	13	10	29	$4

How to Use This Card

If students were told to "subtract B from A", they would write:

1. 11 – 3 = 8
2. 17 – 7 = 10
3. 14 – 1 = 13
4. 19 – 5 = 14
5. 16 – 8 = 8
6. 12 – 6 = 6
7. 18 – 10 = 8
8. 15 – 4 = 11
9. 20 – 9 = 11
10. 13 – 2 = 11

Other instructions might be:

- **Multiply column B by 5.**
- **Subtract column F from column I.**
- **Halve column F.**
- **What multiplied by 10 gives column H?**
- **What is left from $30 if I spend the amount in column J?**
- **Double column C.**
- **Add column B and C.**
- **Subtract 10 from column I.**
- **Add 10 to column E.**
- **What must be added to column D to make 20?**

The applications of this card are endless.

ID Card A

Do not write on this card.

1 **m** stands for m ________

2 **cm** stands for c ________

3 **L** stands for l ________

4 **g** stands for g ________

5 **kg** stands for k ________

6 **min** stands for m ________

7 **1, 2, 3, ...** are the c ________ numbers

8 **2, 4, 6,...** are the e ________ numbers

9 **1, 3, 5,...** are the o ________ numbers

10 **1st, 2nd, ...** are the o ________ numbers

11 **Another name for '0'** is z ________

12 **816** has 3 d ________

13 **6 groups of 2** means 6 ______ 2

14 **4 rows of 10** means 4 ______ 10

15 **8 lots of 10** means 8 ______ 10

16 **share between** means d ________

17 **how many groups of?** means d ________

18 **=** means is e ________ to

19

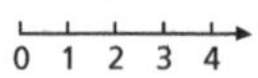

n ________
l ________

20 **7 + 9 = 16** is a n ________ s ________

21

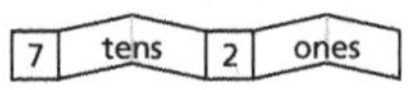

is a n ________ expander

22

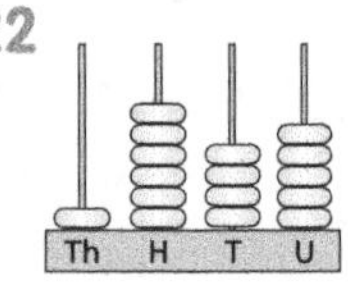

a ________

23

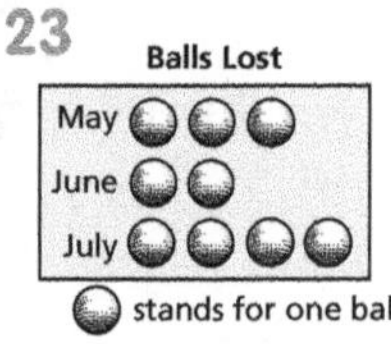

p ______ graph

24

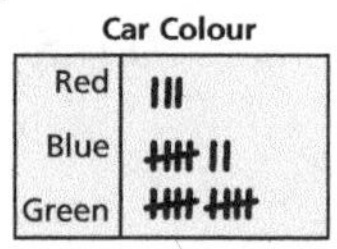

t ________

25

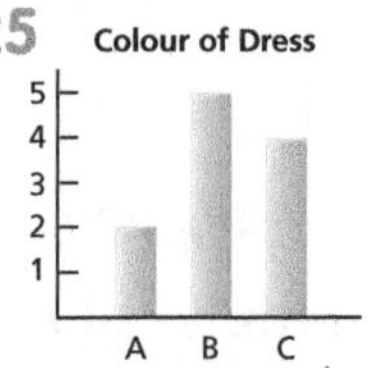

c ______ graph

26

Animals	
birds	7
monkeys	5
lions	4

t ________

27

d ________ watch

28

a ________ clock

29

February

Sun	Mon	Tues	Wed	Thurs	Fri	Sat
1	2	3	4	5	6	7
8	9	10	11	12	13	14
15	16	17	18	19	20	21
22	23	24	25	26	27	28

c ________

30

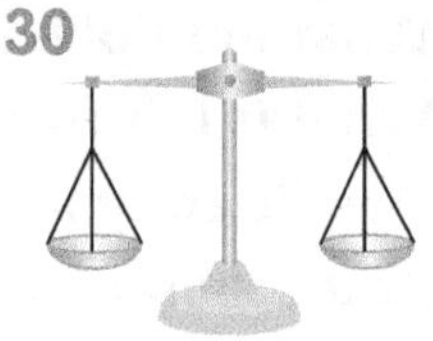

b ________ scales

See page A1 for answers.

ID Card B

Do not write on this card.

1

c ________ line

2

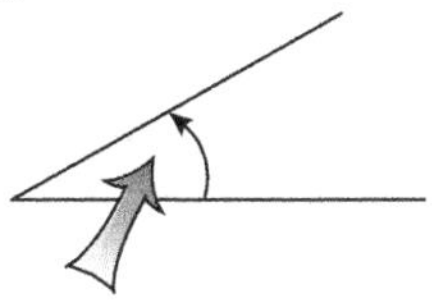

a ________

3

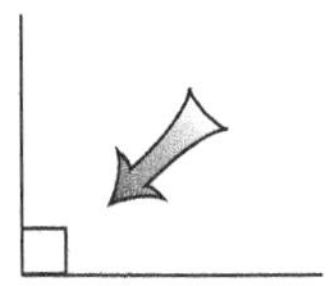

r ________ angle

4

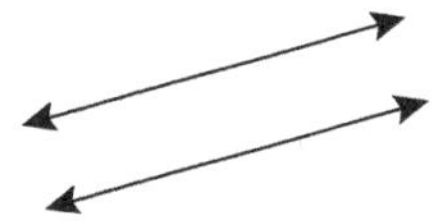

p ________ lines

5

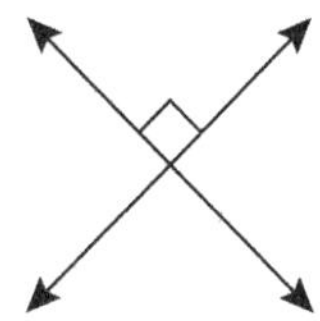

p ________ lines

6

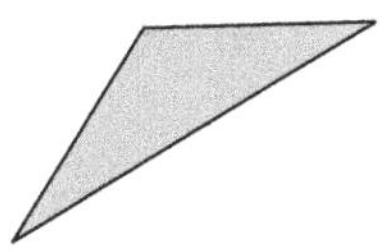

t ________

7

s ________

8

r ________

9

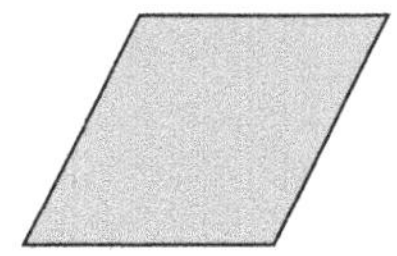

d ____ or r ____

10

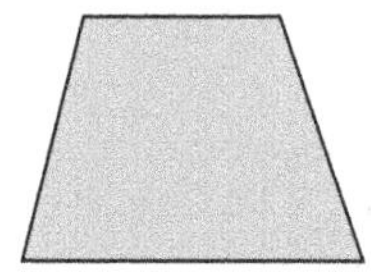

t ________

11

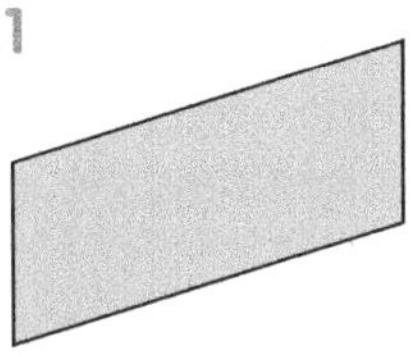

p ________

12

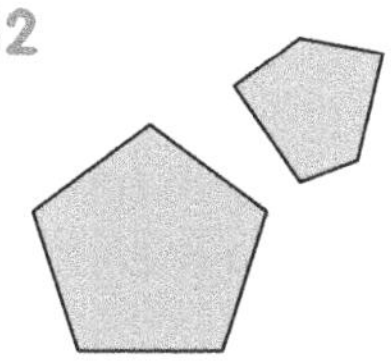

p ________

13

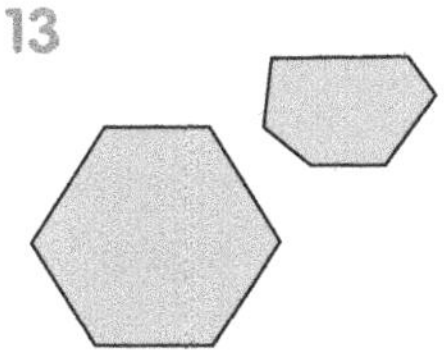

h ________

14

c ________

15

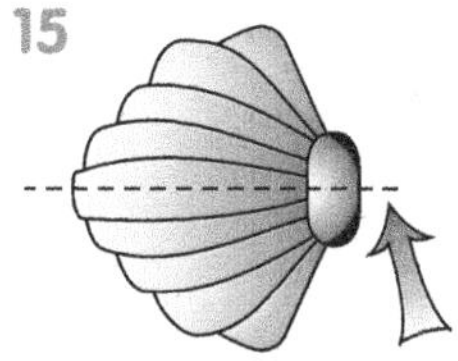

line of s ________

16

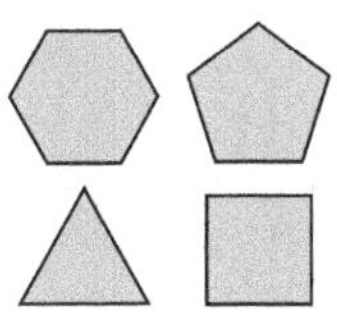

r ________ shapes

17

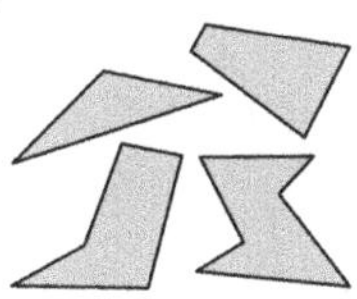

i ________ shapes

18

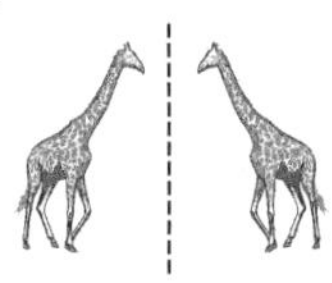

f ________

19

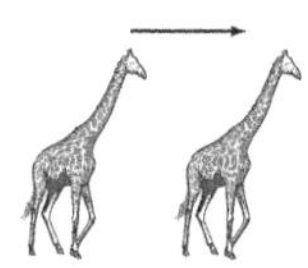

s ________

20

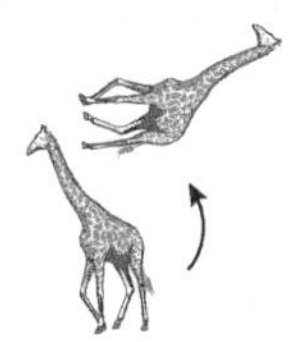

t ________

21

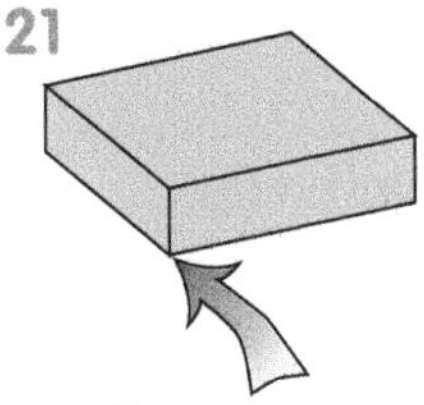

c ________

22

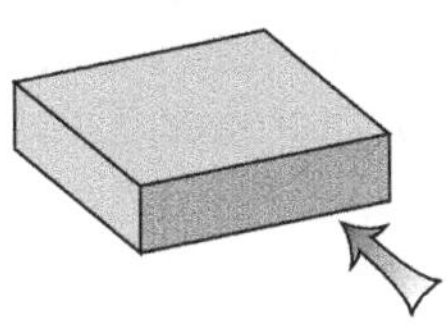

e ________

23

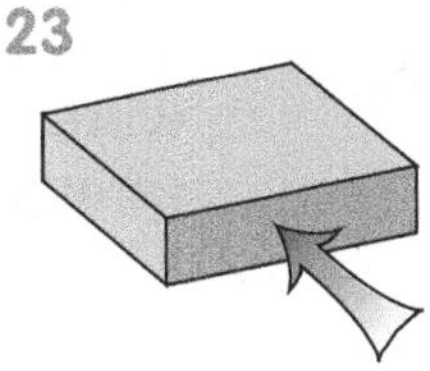

f ________

24

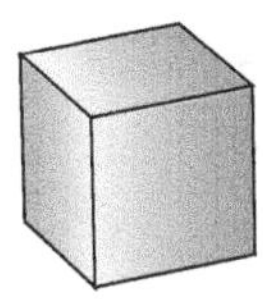

c ________

25

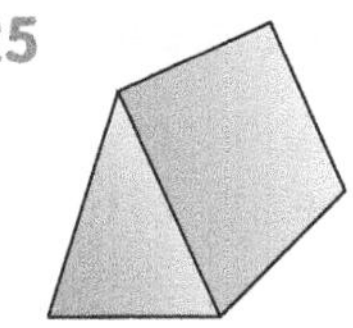

p ________

26

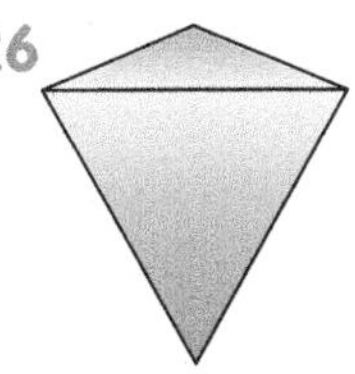

p ________

27

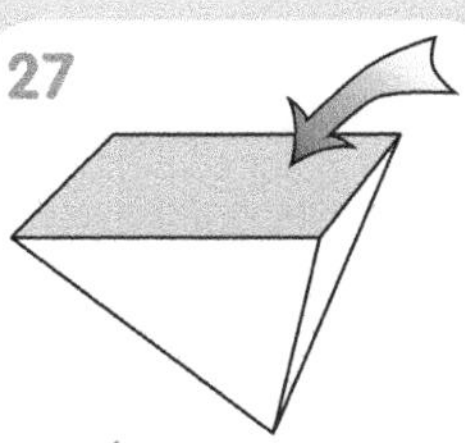

b ________

28

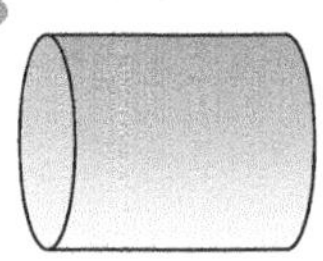

c ________

29

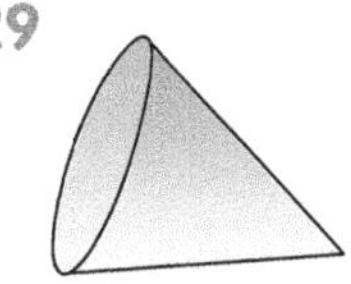

c ________

30

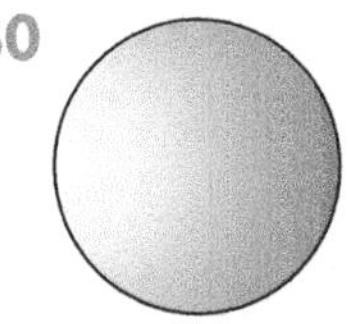

s ________

See page A1 for answers.

Tables of Number and Measurement

Length

1 centimetre = 10 millimetres
1 metre = 100 centimetres
1 kilometre = 1 000 metres

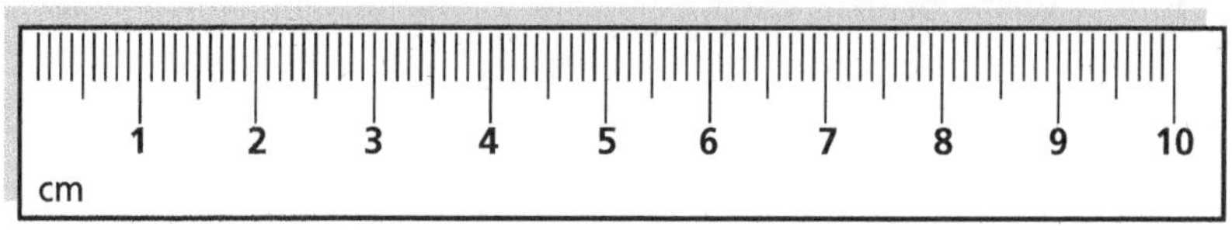

Mass

1 kilogram = 1 000 grams

Capacity and Volume

1 litre = 1 000 millilitres

A carton of milk holds 1L.

A teaspoon holds about 5 mL.

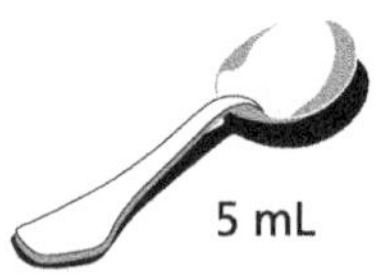

Time

1 minute = 60 seconds
1 hour = 60 minutes
1 day = 24 hours
1 week = 7 days
1 fortnight = 2 weeks
1 year = 52 weeks
1 year = 365 days
1 leap year = 366 days
1 decade = 10 years
1 century = 100 years

am stands for **ante meridiem**.
am means **before midday**.

pm stands for **post meridiem**.
pm means **after midday**.

The **freezing point** of water is **0°C**.
The **boiling point** of water is **100°C**.

A temperature of **5°C** is **a cold day**.
A temperature of **35°C** is **a hot day**.

Roman Numerals

1 = I	**6** = VI	**20** = XX	**90** = XC
2 = II	**7** = VII	**30** = XXX	**100** = C
3 = III	**8** = VIII	**40** = XL	**200** = CC
4 = IV	**9** = IX	**50** = L	**500** = D
5 = V	**10** = X	**60** = LX	**1 000** = M

Months of the Year

Thirty days have September, April, June and November. All the rest have thirty-one, except February alone, which has twenty-eight days clear and twenty-nine days each leap year.

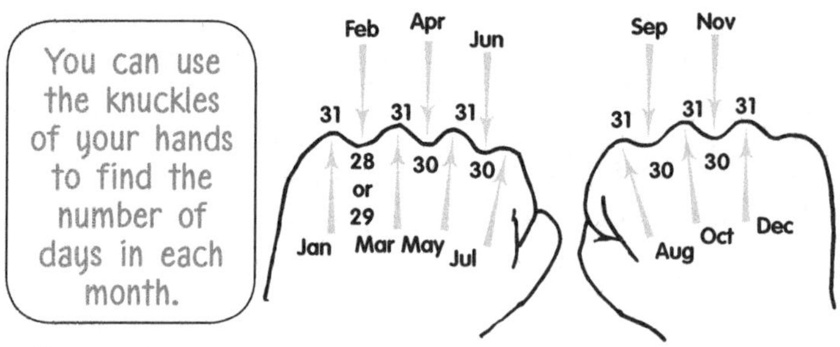

Seasons

summer: December, January, February
autumn: March, April, May
winter: June, July, August
spring: September, October, November

Multiplication Tables

1 × 2 = 2	1 × 3 = 3	1 × 4 = 4	1 × 5 = 5	1 × 6 = 6	1 × 7 = 7	1 × 8 = 8	1 × 9 = 9	1 × 10 = 10
2 × 2 = 4	2 × 3 = 6	2 × 4 = 8	2 × 5 = 10	2 × 6 = 12	2 × 7 = 14	2 × 8 = 16	2 × 9 = 18	2 × 10 = 20
3 × 2 = 6	3 × 3 = 9	3 × 4 = 12	3 × 5 = 15	3 × 6 = 18	3 × 7 = 21	3 × 8 = 24	3 × 9 = 27	3 × 10 = 30
4 × 2 = 8	4 × 3 = 12	4 × 4 = 16	4 × 5 = 20	4 × 6 = 24	4 × 7 = 28	4 × 8 = 32	4 × 9 = 36	4 × 10 = 40
5 × 2 = 10	5 × 3 = 15	5 × 4 = 20	5 × 5 = 25	5 × 6 = 30	5 × 7 = 35	5 × 8 = 40	5 × 9 = 45	5 × 10 = 50
6 × 2 = 12	6 × 3 = 18	6 × 4 = 24	6 × 5 = 30	6 × 6 = 36	6 × 7 = 42	6 × 8 = 48	6 × 9 = 54	6 × 10 = 60
7 × 2 = 14	7 × 3 = 21	7 × 4 = 28	7 × 5 = 35	7 × 6 = 42	7 × 7 = 49	7 × 8 = 56	7 × 9 = 63	7 × 10 = 70
8 × 2 = 16	8 × 3 = 24	8 × 4 = 32	8 × 5 = 40	8 × 6 = 48	8 × 7 = 56	8 × 8 = 64	8 × 9 = 72	8 × 10 = 80
9 × 2 = 18	9 × 3 = 27	9 × 4 = 36	9 × 5 = 45	9 × 6 = 54	9 × 7 = 63	9 × 8 = 72	9 × 9 = 81	9 × 10 = 90
10 × 2 = 20	10 × 3 = 30	10 × 4 = 40	10 × 5 = 50	10 × 6 = 60	10 × 7 = 70	10 × 8 = 80	10 × 9 = 90	10 × 10 = 100

 • *AUSTRALIAN SIGNPOST MATHS 3 MENTALS* • ISBN 978 1 4886 2183 3

Examples of Measurements

1

2

3

4

5

6

1
- The width of your finger is about 1 cm.
- The length of a place-value tens block is 10 cm.

2
- The height of the girl is a little more than 1 m.

3
- The container of milk holds 2 L.
- The can of Fizz holds 375 mL.
- The teaspoon holds 5 mL.

4
- The boy has a mass of 40 kg.
- The margarine has a mass of 500 g.

5
- The area of the newspaper is about the same as the table.

6
- 30°C is a hot day.
- 3°C is a very cold day.

Use the pictures above to estimate the answers to these questions.

1 a How high is the glass?
b How wide is the table?

2 a How wide is the clothes line?
b How tall is the woman?

3 a How much will the bucket hold?
b How much will the cup hold?

4 a What is the mass of the dog?
b What is the mass of 2 L of milk?

5 a How many sheets of newspaper would cover the area of the window?
b How many place-value ones would cover the area of the top of the matchbox?

6 a What is the temperature on a very hot day?
b What is the temperature on a cool day?

1:1 ☐ out of 8

1 In **a** to **h**, write the number modelled.

a 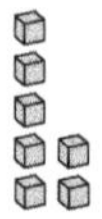 ______	**b** 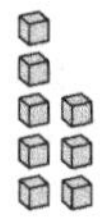 ______
c 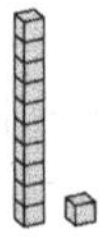 ______	**d** 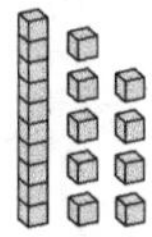 ______
e 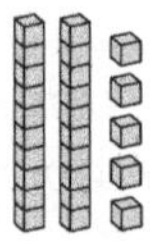 ______	**f** 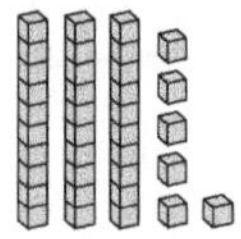 ______
g 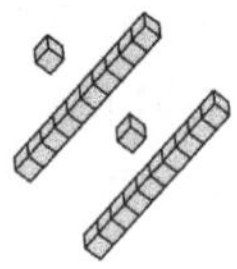 ______	**h** 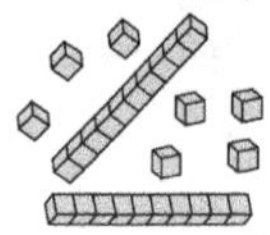 ______

2 How many place-value ones blocks make one tens block? ______

3 = means "is e ______ to".

4 Complete the pattern.

2, 4, ______, ______, 10, 12

5 **a** ~~||||~~ || stands for: ______

b 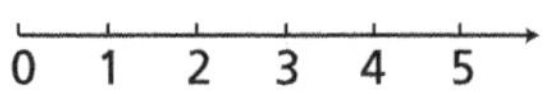

This is a n______ l______.

6 The numeral for nine. ______

7 How many digits in 13? ______

8 Josh had 5 toy trucks and was given 4 more by his Pa. How many has he now? ______

1:2 ☐ out of 15

1 2 + 8 ______

2 7 + 3 ______

3 10 − 5 ______

4 10 − 7 ______

5 $\begin{array}{r} 3 \\ +\ 3 \\ \hline \end{array}$

6 Digits in 184. ______

7 \$7 + \$7 ______

8 7, 9, 11, ______

9 Take 5 from 15. ______

10 $\begin{array}{r} 9 \\ -\ 4 \\ \hline \end{array}$

11 

The number sentence is:

8 − ______ = ______

12 Colour one half of this rectangle.

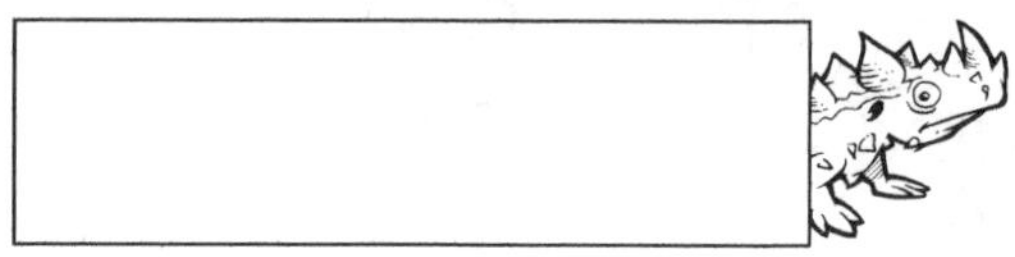

13 What time is shown?

a 

______ past ______

b 

______ past ______

14 Colour half of this group.

15 **a**  ______ **b** 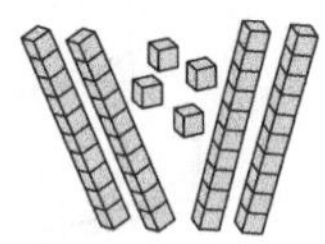 ______

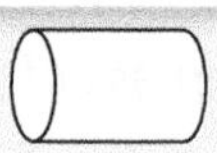

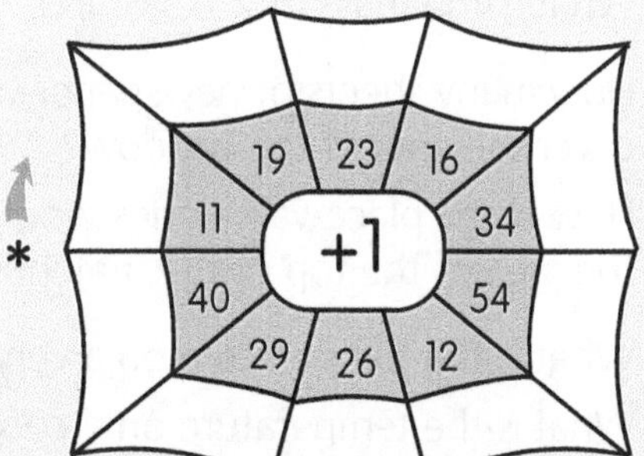

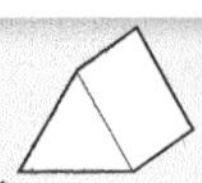

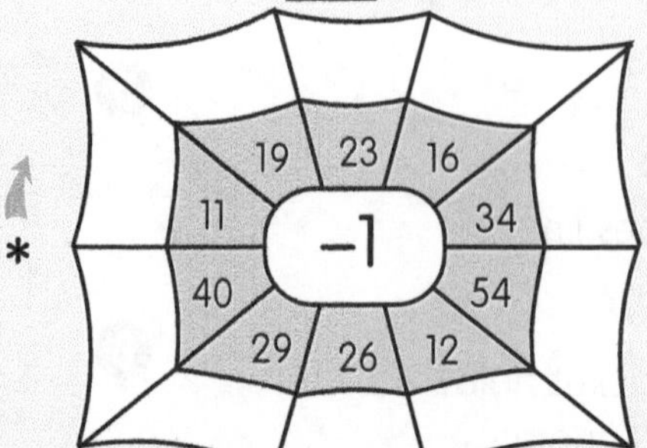

 ISBN 978 1 4886 2183 3

1:3 — out of 19

1. 14 − 10 ______
2. 8 + 4 ______
3. 15 − 4 ______
4. 7 + 6 ______
5. 13 plus 4. ______
6. 2, 4, 6, ______
7. Add 10 and 7. ______
8. 13 minus 4. ______
9. Write 19 in words. ______
10. 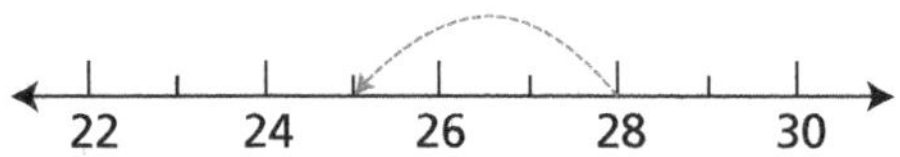

    a 28 – 3 ______ **b** 28 – 5 ______
11. 3 more than 17. ______
12. The numeral for fifty-two. ______
13. What month comes after December? ______
14. Fill in the ordinal numbers.

    1st, ____nd, ____rd, ____th, ____th
15. Four equal q________ make 1 whole. Colour one quarter. 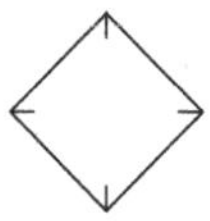
16. Wednesday is the ____th day of the week.
17. Complete this pattern.

    42, 44, 46, ____, ____
18. Colour one quarter of this group. 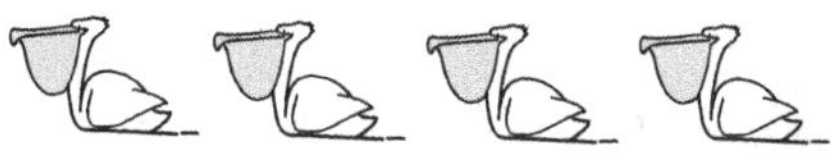
19. The value of these coins. 

    ______

1:4 — out of 5

Extension

1. 10 + ☐ = 16 ☐ = ______
2. 72, 62, 52, ____, ____, ____
3. How many in each box if we share the balls fairly? ______

    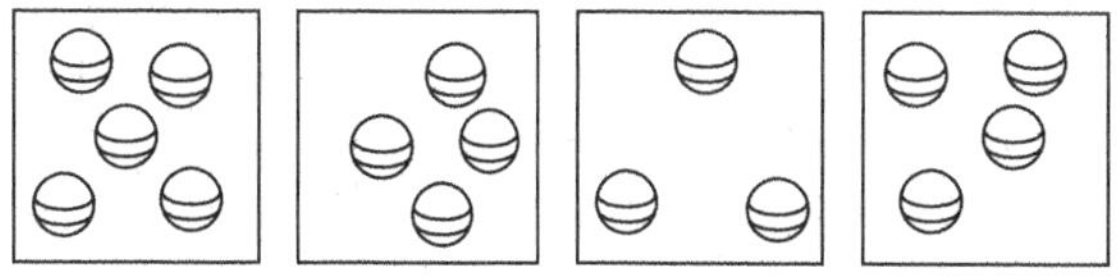
4. How many minutes in half an hour? 

    ______
5. What is to the: 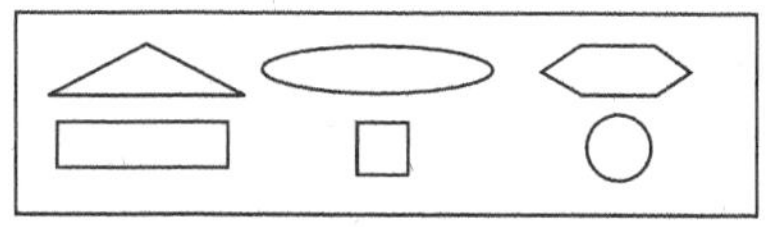

    a left of the hexagon? ______

    b right of the rectangle? ______

Challenge

Draw or write as many different patterns as you can fit in the space.

Fill out this table about yourself, a relative or a friend.

Name: ______ **Date:** ______

Age: ______	Mass: ______ kg	Shoe size: ______
Height: ______ cm	Waist: ______ cm	Neck size: ______ cm

2:1 ☐ out of 9

1. In **a** to **f**, write the number modelled.

a 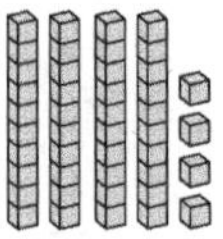 ______

b 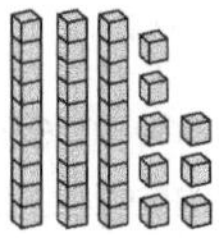 ______

c  ______

d  ______

e 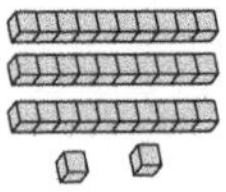 ______

f 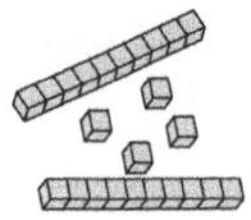 ______

2. **a** 6 + 4 = ______
   b 5 + 5 = ______

3. How many ones in 3 tens? ______
4. The numeral for eighteen. ______
5. True or false? 7 + 3 = 11 ______
6. Write the word for 7. ______
7. Does a 10-cent coin have a platypus on it? ______
8. Days in 1 week. ______
9. 

   Lauren had 6 rabbits but gave 2 away. How many did she have left? ______

2:2 ☐ out of 15

1. 14 − 1 ______
2. 10 − 4 ______
3. 10 + 8 ______
4. 9 + 6 ______
5. $\begin{array}{r} 2 \\ +\ 5 \\ \hline \end{array}$
6. 3 more than 11. ______
7. 17 plus zero. ______
8. $5 + $5 ______
9. 15, 14, 13, ______
10. $\begin{array}{r} 10c \\ -\ 5c \\ \hline \end{array}$
11. **a** The girls are standing ______ to ______.
    b The snake is coiled ______ the tree.

12. Colour one quarter.

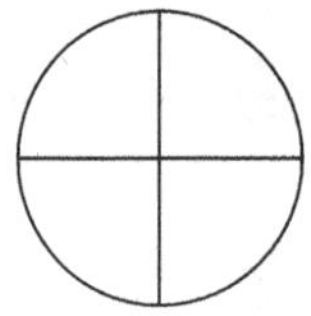

13. Write the value of each coin.

______ ______ ______

14. 
    A
    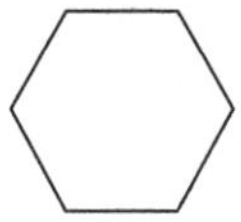
    B
    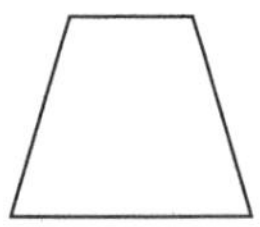
    C

    A is a ______.
    B is a ______.
    C is a ______.

15. Write the value of each note.

______ ______ ______

Australian Money

Write the value of each Australian coin.

20 cents ______ ______ ______ ______

2:3  out of 14

1. 16 − 3 ______
2. 20 − 4 ______
3. 10 + 10 ______
4. 9 + 8 ______
5. Four plus ten. ______
6. \$2 + \$8 + \$5 ______
7. 21, 23, ______, 27
8. 20 minus 2. ______
9. Write 17 in words. ______
10. 

    a 28 + 3 ______ b 28 + 7 ______
11. What is: 
    a behind the book? ______
    b in front of the jug? ______
12. I had 10 toy dinosaurs. I sold 6. How many were left? ______

13. Write a number story for this picture.

______

14. Circle the **heavier** object.

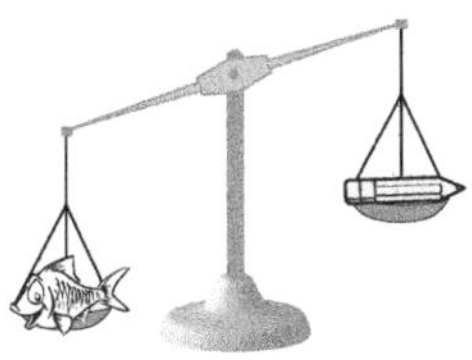

2:4 Extension out of 6

1. a 7 + ☐ = 15 ☐ = ______
   b ☐ + 16 = 24 ☐ = ______
2. In a race, I am 4th out of 5. How many are:
   a in front of me? ______
   b behind me? ______
3. Use the code to work out this message.

A	B	C	D	E	I	K	N	S
1	2	3	4	5	6	7	8	9

11 − 9	2 + 3

3 + 4	10 − 4	8 + 0	12 − 8

4. What is the time half an hour after quarter past three? ______
5. Colour one quarter of this shape.

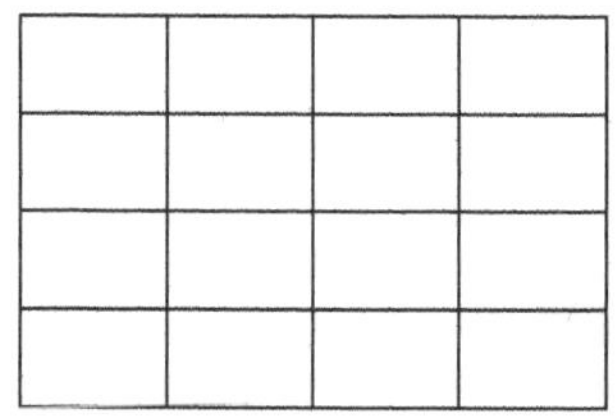

6. 2 + 8 + 3 + 7 + 1 + 9 ______

Challenge

Write different number sentences that equal 15.

______

______

______

Concept

Looking for Tens When Adding Numbers

That's 1 ten and 7.

4, 7, 6 — 17

1 + 9
5 + 5
8 + 2
3 + 7

a	**b**	**c**	**d**	**e**
1	4	5	2	6
8	3	5	6	4
9	7	2	8	9
f	**g**	**h**	**i**	**j**
8	7	3	9	7
9	8	5	4	7
1	2	5	6	3

3:1 ☐ out of 5

1. In **a** to **h**, write the number modelled.

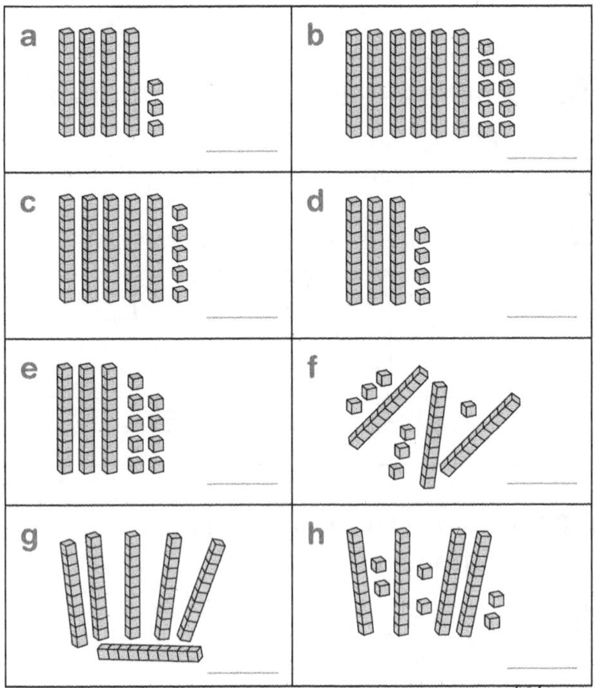

2. **a** 3, 6, 9, ____, ____, ____, ____

   b 4, 8, 12, ____, ____, ____, ____

   c 7, 14, 21, ____, ____, ____, ____

3. Complete:

   1st, 2nd, ____, ____

4. Ryan had $20 and spent $10 to buy a toy bear. How much does he have left? ____

5. **a** 1 + 9 = ____ **b** 9 + 1 = ____

   c 10 − 1 = ____ **d** 10 − 9 = ____

3:2 ☐ out of 15

1. 4 + 5 = ____
2. 7 + 8 = ____
3. 2 + 3 = ____
4. 8 + 9 = ____
5. 9 − 8 = ____
6. 8 and 4. ____
7. 9 plus six. ____
8. 7 add four. ____
9. 8 and 3. ____
10. 7 − 5 = ____

11. Each small cube stands for one child's choice. How many chose:

    a green? ____ **b** yellow? ____

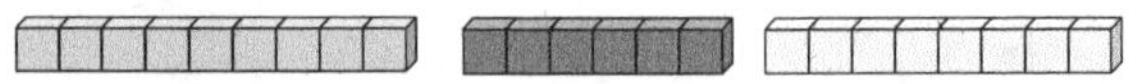

12. Draw a rectangle inside this oval, so that each corner touches the oval.

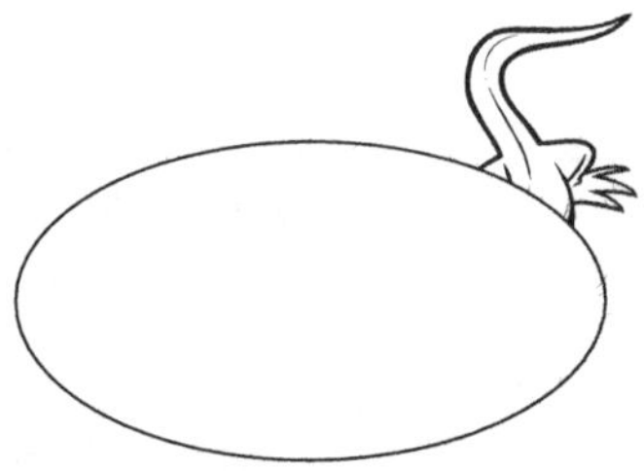

13. Write the value of each coin.

____ ____ ____

14. Complete these near doubles.

    3 + 4 ____ 7 + 8 ____ 9 + 8 ____

15. Use bridging to ten to find:

    9 + 5 ____ 8 + 6 ____ 9 + 3 ____

Australian Money

Write the value of each Australian note. Colour each note the correct colour.

10 dollars ____ ____ ____ ____

© PEARSON AUSTRALIA 2018 • *AUSTRALIAN SIGNPOST MATHS 3 MENTALS* • ISBN 978 1 4886 2183 3

3:3 out of 12

1. 4
   6
   + 2

2. 6
   3
   + 7

3. 8
   4
   + 2

4. 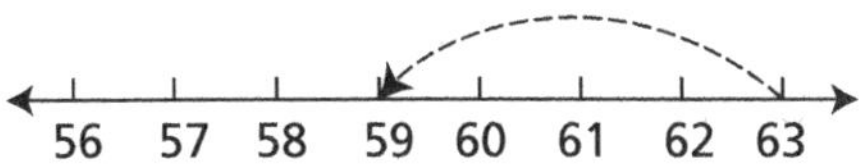

   a 63 − 4 ______ b 61 − 3 ______

5. Three quarters means:

   ______ out of ______

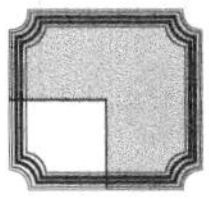

6. Fill in the ordinal numbers.

   1st ______ ______ ______ ______

7. Write 52 in words. ______

8. Another name for half past eleven. ______ : ______

9. What part has been circled?

   ______

10. ☐ + 14 = 21 ☐ = ______

11. Which coins have a value greater than 50 cents? ______

12. a 8 + 3 + 6 = ______

    b 5 + 3 + 1 = ______

    c 9 + 6 + 2 = ______

3:4 Extension out of 5

1. a 8 + 2 ______ b 7 + 3 ______
   c 1 + 9 ______ d 5 + 5 ______

2. This square is divided into four q______.

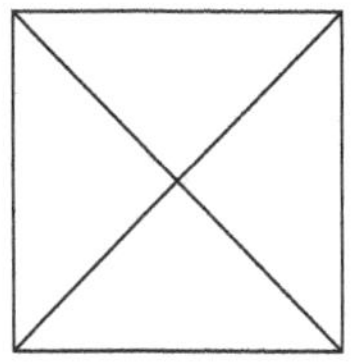

3. The total value of these coins. ______

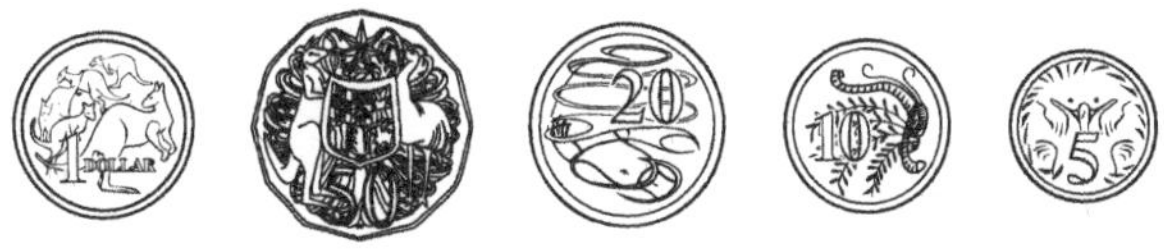

4. 50c + 20c + 10c + 5c ______

5. The difference between the value of the largest coin and the smallest coin in question 3. ______

Challenge

Show how you can make 50c in different ways.

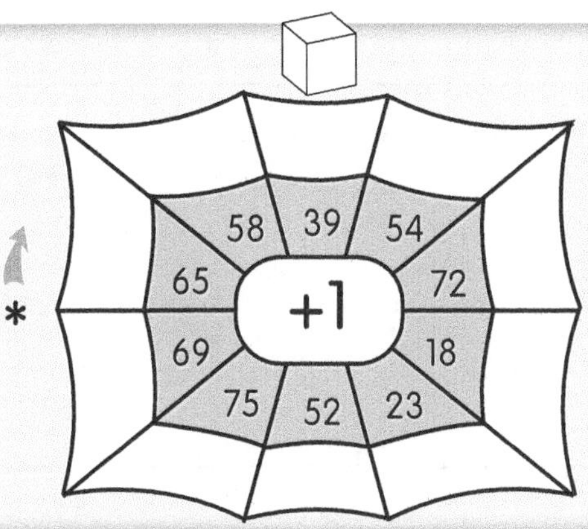

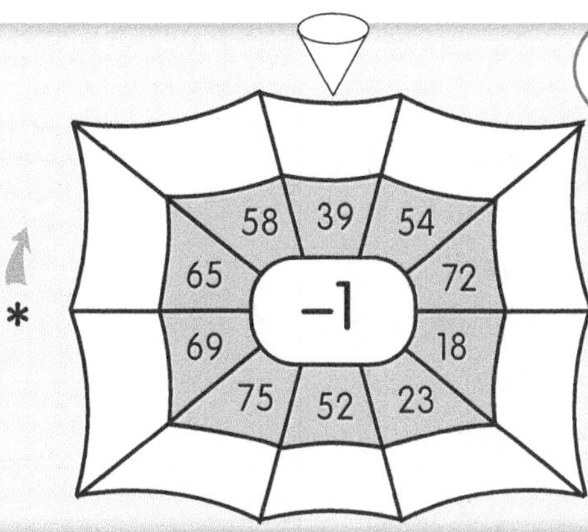

 • *AUSTRALIAN SIGNPOST MATHS 3 MENTALS* • ISBN 978 1 4886 2183 3

4:1 ☐ out of 7

1 In **a** to **f**, write the number modelled.

a  ______	**b**  ______
c 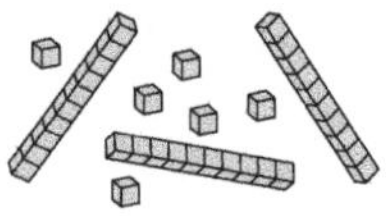 ______	**d**  ______
e 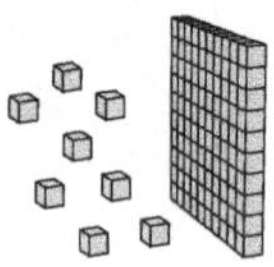 ______	**f** 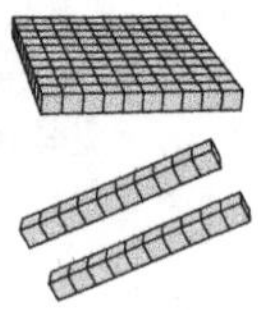 ______

2 Which number is larger, 62 or 39? ______

3 Which is heavier, a pen or a book? ______

4 Luke is now 8. How old will he be in:

a 3 years? ______

b 7 years? ______

c 9 years? ______

5 Circle the container that holds the most.

6 **a** 4 + 1 = ______ **b** 1 + 4 = ______

c 5 − 1 = ______ **d** 5 − 4 = ______

7 Jasmine has 4 plates, 4 cups and 4 spoons. How many altogether? ______

4:2 ☐ out of 15

1 17 − 5 ______

2 16 + 4 ______

3 12 × 2 ______

4 Halve 14. ______

5 $\begin{array}{r} 8 \\ -\ 6 \\ \hline \end{array}$

6 Sum of 8 and 7. ______

7 Take 3 from 12. ______

8 117, ______,119,120

9 20 cm + 10 cm ______

10 $\begin{array}{r} 5 \\ -\ 4 \\ \hline \end{array}$

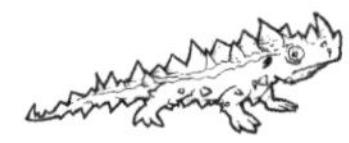

11 Is 6 an odd number? ______

12 Half of 16. ______

13 How many edges has this shape? ______

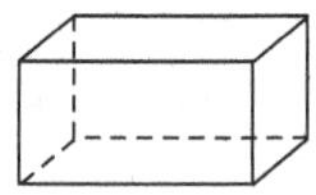

14 **a** 6, 12, 18, ______, ______, ______, ______

b 10, 20, 30, ______, ______, ______, ______

c 9, 18, 27, ______, ______, ______, ______

15

Swimming Attendance

Yuri		●		●	●	●		●
Sue	●	●	●		●			
Tan	●	●	●		●	●		●
Jess	●	●	●	●	●	●	●	
Greg	●	●	●	●	●	●	●	●
Mari	●		●	●	●	●	●	●
	Day 1	Day 2	Day 3	Day 4	Day 5	Day 6	Day 7	Day 8

a Who was never away? ______

b Who was away the most? ______

c How many days was Jess present? ______

Time

60 minutes = 1 hour
30 minutes = half an hour
7 days = 1 week
14 days = 1 fortnight
52 weeks = 1 year
12 months = 1 year

Write, in order, the seven days of the week.

S ______ M ______ T ______

W ______ T ______

F ______ S ______

4:3  ☐ out of 12

1
```
  8
  3
  2
+ 7
```

2
```
  5
  1
  9
+ 5
```

3
```
  8
  0
  9
+ 2
```

4 90, 80, 70, ______, ______, ______

5 | 6 | hundreds | 5 | tens | 3 | ones | = ______

6 

______ out of ______ are shaded.

7 How many curved surfaces has:

a a cone? ______ b a cube? ______

8 Count on to find:

a 17 + 2 ______ b 15 + 4 ______

9 Count back to find:

a 9 – 2 ______ b 15 – 3 ______

10 How many corners has this shape? 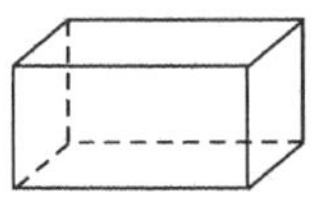 ______

11 What two shapes are used to make this pattern? 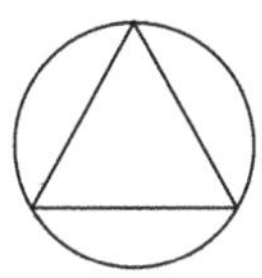

12

Favourite Colours

Red	Blue	Orange	Yellow
10	12	4	7

a The most popular colour was ______.

b The least popular colour was ______.

c How many people liked blue? ______

d How many people liked red? ______

4:4 Extension ☐ out of 5

1 Would a 4-digit number be bigger than a 3-digit number? ______

2 a ☐ – 13 = 4 ☐ = ______

b 20 – ☐ = 6 ☐ = ______

3 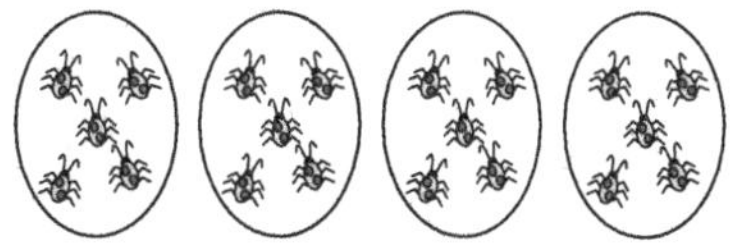

a How many bugs in 4 groups? ______

b How many bugs in 5 groups? ______

c How many bugs in 8 groups? ______

4 a The smallest area below. ______

b The largest area below. ______

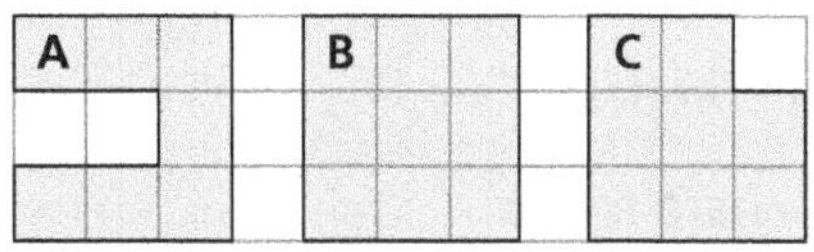

5 Flip, slide or turn? 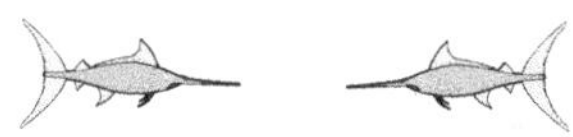

______

Challenge

23 – 6 = ______

Explain how you found your answer.

______

______

______

______

______

Answer each question with always (A), sometimes (S) or never (N).

a Do students go to school on Saturday? ______

b Do people walk from here to China? ______

c Does a dog give birth to a cat? ______

d Do people walk on the moon? ______

e Does the sun rise in the morning? ______

f Do boys beat men at running? ______

5:1 ☐ out of 11

1 In a to f, write the number modelled.

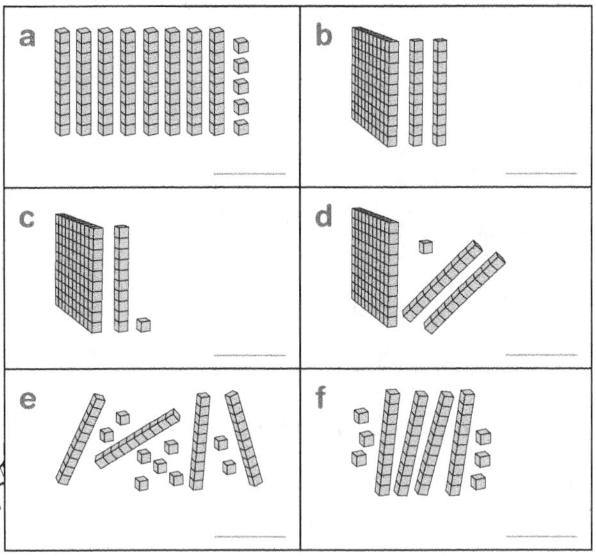

2 Is 7 an even number? ______

3 Is the whiteboard longer than your table? ______

4 The colour of a $2 coin. ______

5 a Draw a cross at the centre of this drum.
b Draw a zigzag line beside the drum.

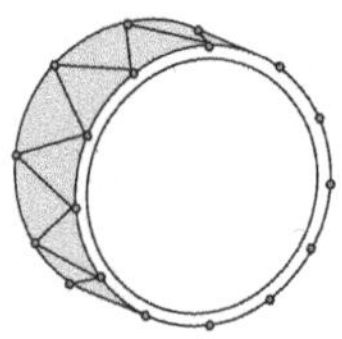

6 9 + 1 ______

7 How many ones in 9 tens? ______

8 Does a circle have any corners? ______

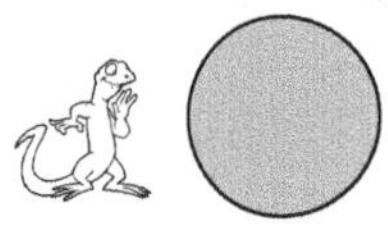

9 Write the number sixteen. ______

10 The colour of a 20 cent coin. ______

11 The season after summer. ______

5:2 ☐ out of 17

1 10 − 8 ______

2 9 + 6 ______

3 4 × 0 ______

4 2 × 8 ______

5 $\begin{array}{r} 6 \\ +\ 6 \\ \hline \end{array}$

6 7 plus 5. ______

7 Double 14. ______

8 $8 − $6 ______

9 13 minus 4. ______

10 $\begin{array}{r} 9 \\ +\ 9 \\ \hline \end{array}$

11 Order from smallest to largest.

391, 902, 535 ______, ______, ______

12 A
B
C

a The longest line. ______

b The shortest line. ______

13 Draw a line of symmetry on each picture.

14 30, 28, 26, ______, ______, ______

15 If there are 10 craft sticks in a bundle, write the number shown here. ______

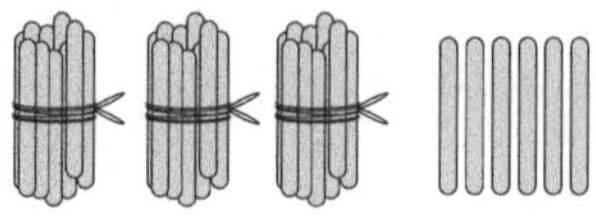

16 50 = ______ tens

17 Which shapes have only flat surfaces?

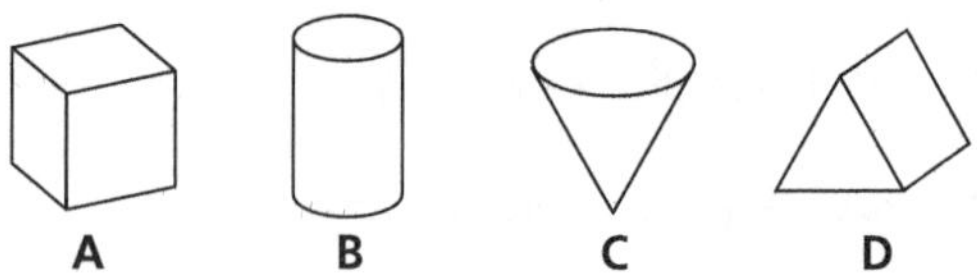

______

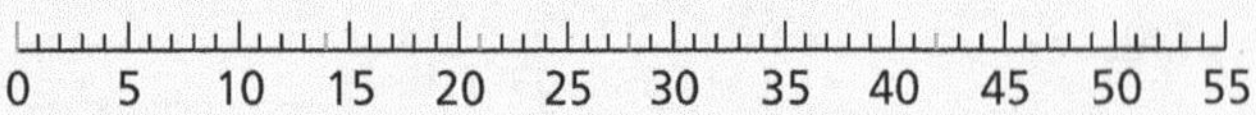

In each case, skip count, writing in the numbers as you go.
Use the number line to help you.

Skip count by 2.	2 →	4 →	→	→	→				
Skip count by 4.	4 →	8 →	→	→	→				
Skip count by 10.	10 →	→	→	→	→	→	→	→	

5:3 ☐ out of 9

1.
```
  6
  4
  7
+ 3
```

2.
```
  8
  9
  1
+ 2
```

3.
```
  3
  9
  7
+ 1
```

4. How much money is in the money box? ________

5. a The month before October. ________

   b Days in September. ________

6. Yoo-Jin had 5 pairs of shoes. How many shoes does he have altogether? ________

7. The next odd number after 13. ________

8. Name this solid.

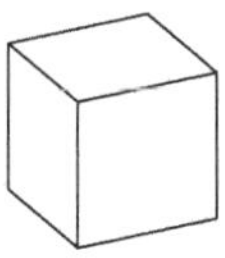

____

9. **Favourite Animal**

Bird	Dog	Cat	Mouse
7	13	4	1

a The most popular animal was a ________ .

b The least popular animal was a ________ .

c How many people liked dogs? ________

d How many people liked birds? ________

5:4 ☐ out of 7 **Extension**

1. Draw two lines of symmetry on this shape.

2. 9 + 1 + 8 + 2 + 10 + 0 ________

3. 40 − 4 − 4 − 4 − 4 − 4 ________

4. These ladybirds have the same number of dots on both sides. How many dots altogether? ________

5. If this wavy line were made 3 times as long, how many hills would be drawn? ________

6. Rachel saw the same number of koalas in 5 trees. There were 15 koalas. How many in each tree? ________

7. 17 + 3 + 16 + 4 + 15 + 5 ________

Challenge

Draw a 3D object and write everything you know about it.

Turn to ID Card B on page 7.
Give the answers for these numbers.

(6) ________ (7) ________

(8) ________ (9) ________

(13) ________ (14) ________

Which of these shapes has six sides? ________

6:1 ☐ out of 19

1. 6 − 5 ______
2. 3 + 2 ______
3. 9 − 4 ______
4. 3 + 3 ______
5. $\begin{array}{r} 9 \\ -\ 7 \\ \hline \end{array}$
6. Add 2 to 6. ______
7. 7 minus 4. ______
8. 10c + 10c ______
9. 1 ten = ______ ones
10. $\begin{array}{r} 10c \\ -\ 5c \\ \hline \end{array}$
11. What colour is a $1.00 coin? ______
12. I found 3 bugs in the bush. My son found 4 more. How many bugs did we find altogether? ______

13. Months in 1 year. ______
14. Cross the even numbers. Circle the odd numbers.

    12 4 15 21 18
15. Is 5 an even number? ______
16. How many rows of 10? ______

17. How many sides on:
    a 2 triangles? ______
    b 3 triangles? ______

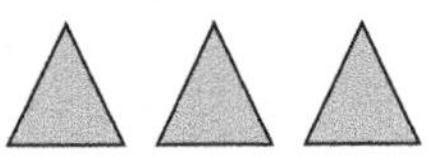

18. The numeral for sixty. ______
19. Show 3:00 on this clock face.

6:2 ☐ out of 16

1. 8 + 8 ______
2. 13 − 6 ______
3. 3 × 2 ______
4. 9 × 2 ______
5. $\begin{array}{r} 8 \\ +\ 8 \\ \hline \end{array}$
6. 12 take away 8. ______
7. Sum of 7 and 9. ______
8. 40c plus 20c. ______
9. 10 less than 13. ______
10. $\begin{array}{r} 5 \\ +\ 5 \\ \hline \end{array}$
11. The day before Tuesday. ______
12. Draw a line of symmetry on this picture.

13. Order from smallest to largest.

    857, 758, 875 ______, ______, ______
14. The number modelled. ______

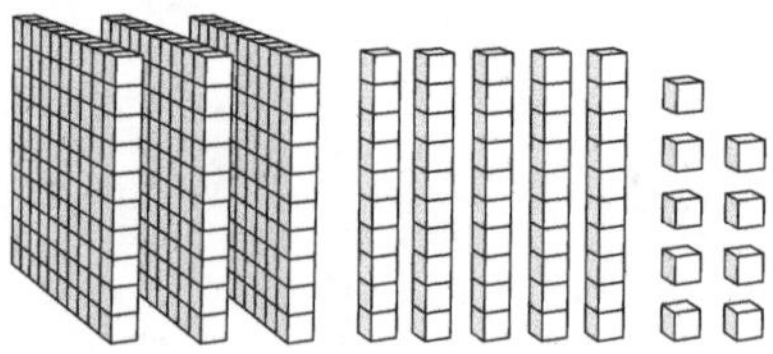

15. Finish these pictures using symmetry.

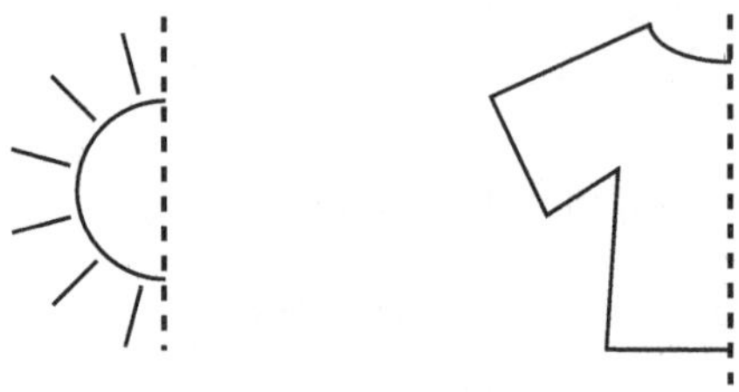

16. Is 10 an even number? ______

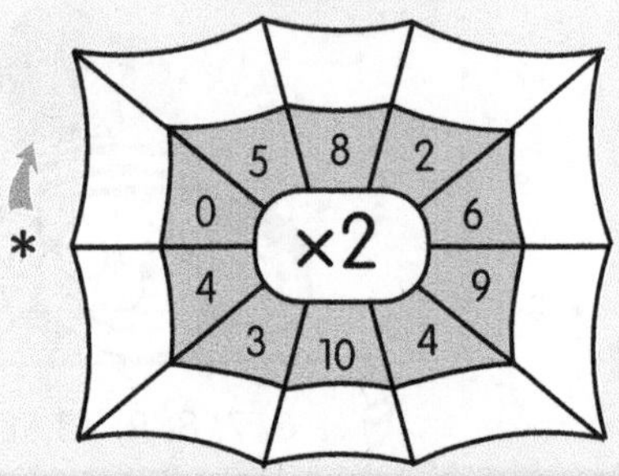

6 groups of 2 is the same as **3 rows of 4**.

	2	4	6	8	10
× 2					

	1	2	3	4	5
× 4					

6:3 out of 14

1. 15 − 2

2. 16 − 5

3. 17 − 4

4. What part is shaded?

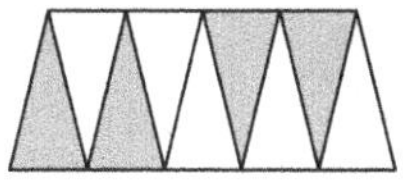

_____ ninths

5. How many 10 cent coins in $1? _____

6. 12:15 can also be called

_____ past _____.

7. Christmas is in the month of D_____.

8. Which line is the longest? _____

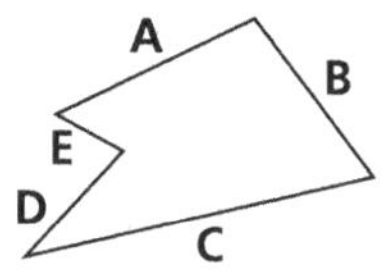

9. Write the digital time.

a [:] 3 o'clock

b [:] 11 o'clock

10. How many ones in 6 tens? _____

11. The numeral for eighty. _____

12. Write 40 in words. _____

13. How many faces (flat surfaces) has:

a **A**? _____

b **B**? _____

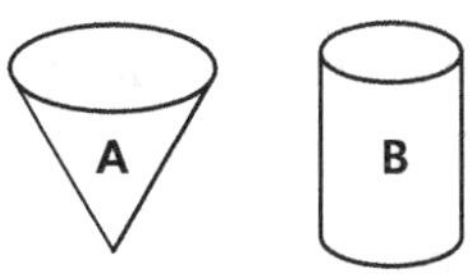

14. Draw the line of symmetry on this picture.

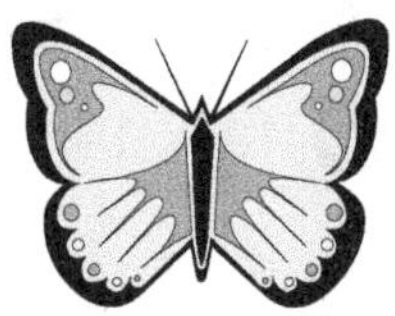

6:4 Extension out of 7

1. a ▢ − 13 = 10 ▢ = _____

b 24 − ▢ = 9 ▢ = _____

2. 92 = ▢ tens ▢ ones

3. Minutes in half an hour. _____

4. Weeks in 1 year. _____

5. Complete the pattern.

15, 12, 9, _____, _____

6. Can you work out the message?

Code

A	E	I	L	M	S	T
@	?	/	$	^	•	*

•	^	/	$	?	@	*	^	?

7. Complete:

a 20 + _____ = 100

b 100 − 20 = _____

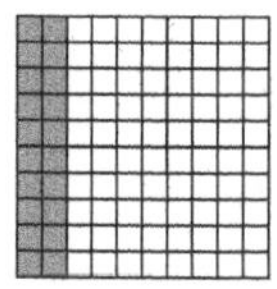

Challenge

Draw as many symmetrical letters, shapes and symbols as you can.

Strategy Time

a Which path is longest? _____

b Which path is shortest? _____

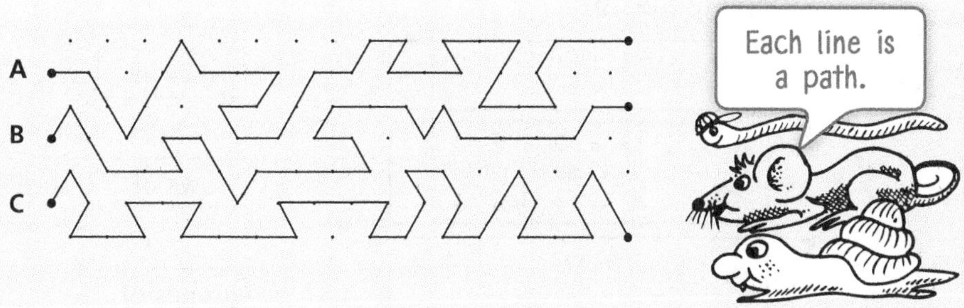

7:1 ☐ out of 17

1. 9 + 1 ____
2. 8 − 3 ____
3. 5 − 4 ____
4. 6 + 2 ____
5.
   4
   − 2
6. 7 plus 1. ____
7. 20c minus 10c. ____
8. 5 tens = ____ ones
9. 2 rows of 3. ____
10.
   5
   + 1

11. The number between 17 and 19. ____
12. Write the numeral shown on the abacus. ____

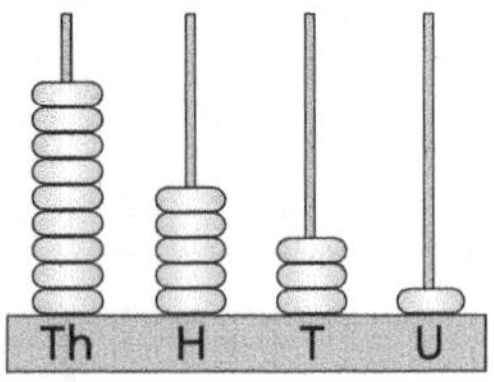

13. Which has the greater mass, a pillow or a chair? ____
14. Which months are in:
    a summer? ____
    b autumn? ____
15. Days in 1 fortnight. ____
16. Begin at 90 and join the dots to count backwards by tens.

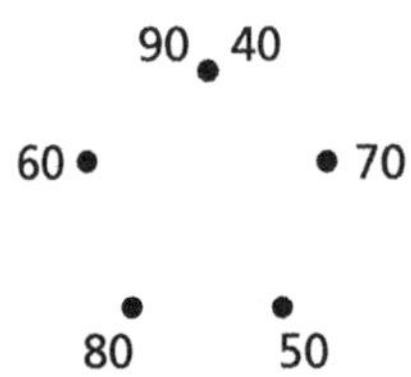

17. Write the number for sixty-seven and complete the numeral expander.

☐ tens ☐ ones

____

7:2 ☐ out of 19

1. 8 + 6 ____
2. 16 − 3 ____
3. 7 + 7 ____
4. 7 + 8 ____
5.
   3
   8
   + 2
6. 3 + 3 + 3 + 3 ____
7. Digits in 700. ____
8. 4, 8, 12, ____
9. 7 tens = ____ ones
10.
   5
   9
   + 5
11. Draw the line of symmetry.

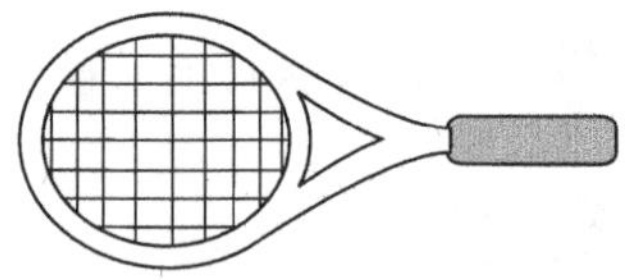

12. 3, 6, 9, ____,15, 18
13. How many sides has a triangle? ____
14. When the minute hand is on the numeral 12 it is called "o'clock".

    This time is: ____
15. Write 374 in words.
    ____
    ____
16. 24, 23, 22, ____, ____
17. Order from the smallest to largest.
    541, 398, 649 ____, ____, ____
18. Subtract zero from 30. ____
19. 18th, 19th, 20th, ____, ____

Complete the cards.

a 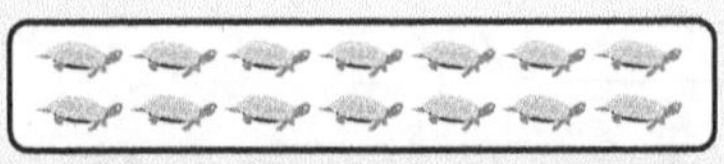 ____ rows of ____

b 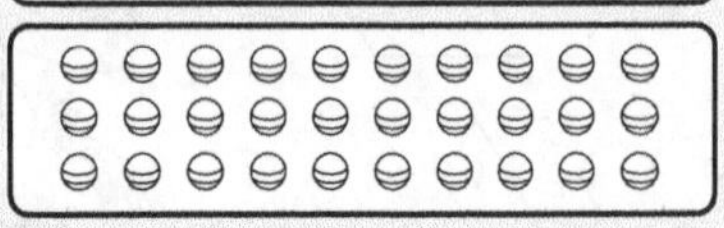 ____ rows of ____

c  ____ groups of ____

7:3 ☐ out of 11

1
```
   6
   2
   3
   4
   9
 + 1
```

2
```
   5
   4
   3
   2
   1
 + 6
```

3
```
   9
   2
   1
   8
   6
 + 2
```

4 Write the answer and fill in the numeral expander.

= ________

☐ hundreds	☐ tens	☐ ones

5 Write the number above in words.

____

____

6 Start at 117. Count by odd numbers.
117, ____, ____, ____, ____

7 □, ○, △, ■, ●, ▲, □, ____

8 Write the digital time.
a 6 o'clock [:] **b** 10 o'clock [:]

9 How many corners has a circle? ____

10 What coin has 12 sides? ____

11 Which shapes will roll?

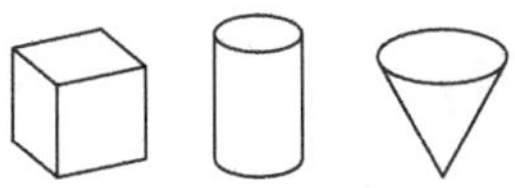

A B C

____

7:4 ☐ out of 9 Extension

1 **a** 46 + 5 ____ **b** 58 + 4 ____

2 30 + 3 − 3 + 5 − 5 + 1 − 1 ____

3 100 − 2 − 2 − 2 − 2 − 2 − 2 − 2 ____

4 57 + 3 + 3 + 3 + 3 + 3 + 3 + 3 ____

5 Complete this picture if the dotted line is a line of symmetry.

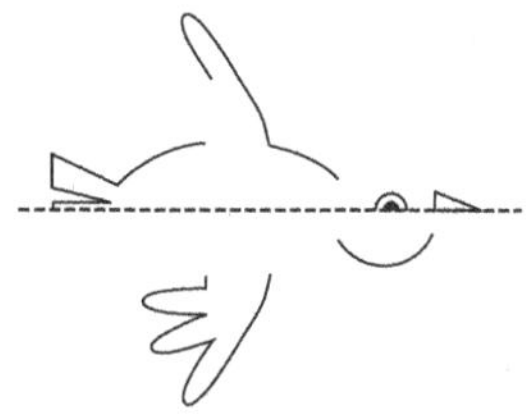

6 Write 342 in words. ________

____

7 Three different counting numbers that add to give 7. ____

8 How many days altogether in June and July? ____

9 Weeks in 4 fortnights. ____

Challenge

Draw a picture that has symmetry.

0 5 10 15 20 25 30 35 40 45 50 55

In each case, skip count, writing in the numbers as you go. Use the number line to help you.

Skip count by 3. [3] → [6] → [ ] → [ ] → [ ] → [ ] → [ ]

Skip count by 6. [6] → [12] → [ ] → [ ] → [ ] → [ ] → [ ]

Skip count by 8. [8] → [ ] → [ ] → [ ] → [ ] → [ ] → [ ] → [ ] → [ ]

8:1 out of 18

1. 3 + 8 ______
2. 10 − 5 ______
3. 5 + 6 ______
4. 8 − 1 ______
5.
$$\begin{array}{r} 5 \\ -\ 2 \\ \hline \end{array}$$

6. 4 more than 5. ______
7. Double 4. ______
8. 5c + 5c + 5c ______
9. 3 groups of 2. ______
10.
$$\begin{array}{r} 7 \\ +\ 1 \\ \hline \end{array}$$

11. 84 = ______ tens and ______ ones
12. Put these numbers in order from smallest to largest.

    212, 129, 76, 318, 236

    ____

13. The number modelled is ____________.

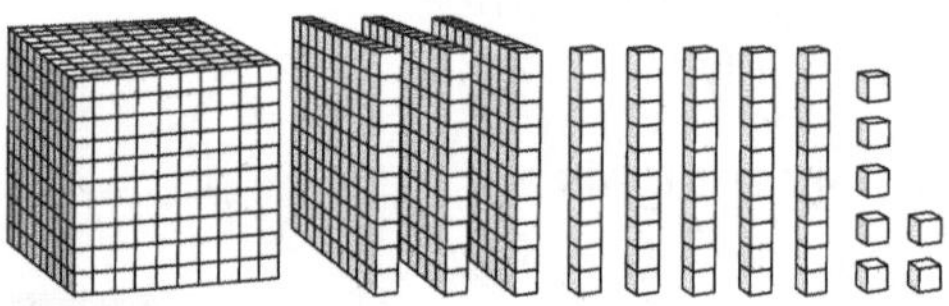

14. Write 44 in words.

    ____

15. Days in 1 week. ______
16. **a** 2, 4, 6, ______, ______, ______

    b 3, 6, 9, ______, ______, ______

    c 5, 10, 15, ______, ______, ______
17. Show 2:30 on this clock face.

18. 12, 14, 16, ______, ______

8:2 out of 20

1. 10 + 8 ______
2. 11 − 8 ______
3. 7 × 2 ______
4. 9 × 1 ______
5.
$$\begin{array}{r} 4 \\ 7 \\ +\ 6 \\ \hline \end{array}$$

6. Double 7. ______
7. Sum of 13 and 6. ______
8. 6 + 6 + 6 ______
9. 5,10, ▢, 20. ▢ = ______
10.
$$\begin{array}{r} 2 \\ 6 \\ +\ 8 \\ \hline \end{array}$$

11. How many sides has a triangle? ______
12. Write the word for 12. ______
13. Complete these patterns.

    a 13 − 5 = ______ **b** 16 − 7 = ______

    23 − 5 = ______ 26 − 7 = ______

    ___ − 5 = ______ ___ − 7 = ______
14. Does a line of symmetry cut a shape into two halves? ______
15. Write the numeral for three hundred and ninety-seven. ______

    ____
16. **a** The month before July. ______

    b Months in a year. ______
17. 732, 734, 736, ______, ______
18. Draw the axis of symmetry.

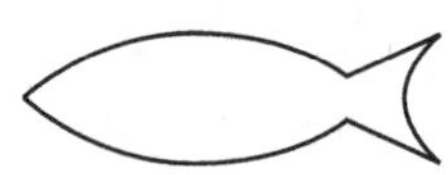

19. 5, 10, 15, 20, 25, ______, ______, ______
20. Make the biggest number you can using 3, 9 and 7. ______

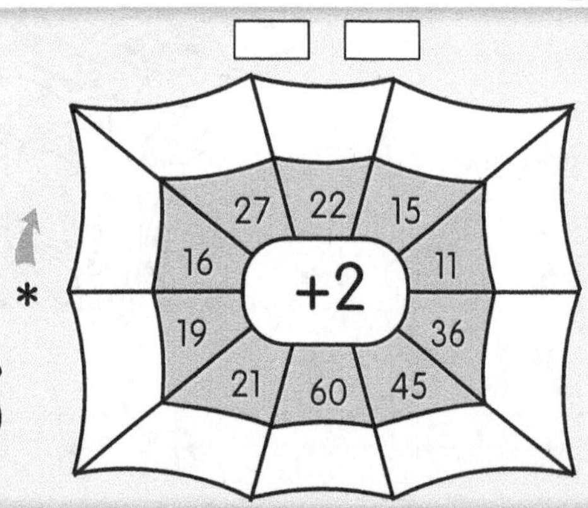

8:3 — ☐ out of 9

1
```
  3
  4
  8
  6
+ 9
```

2
```
  9
  2
  4
  1
+ 3
```

3
```
  8
  6
  2
  1
+ 4
```

4

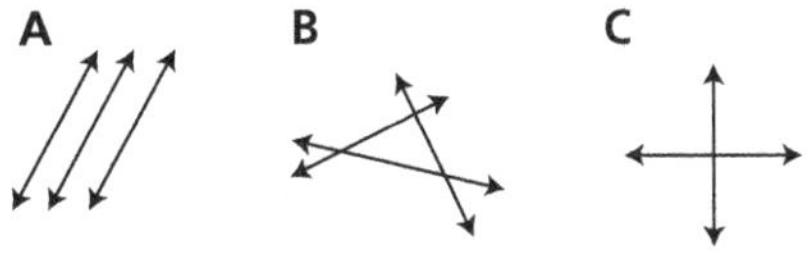

Which group shows parallel lines? ______

5

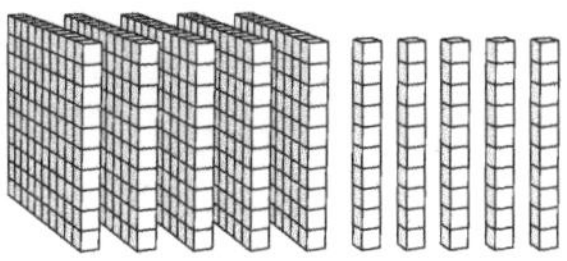

☐ hundreds ☐ tens ☐ ones

6 Name the months in spring. ______

______

7 The next even number after 68. ______

8 Write the number eight hundred and forty-six. ______

9

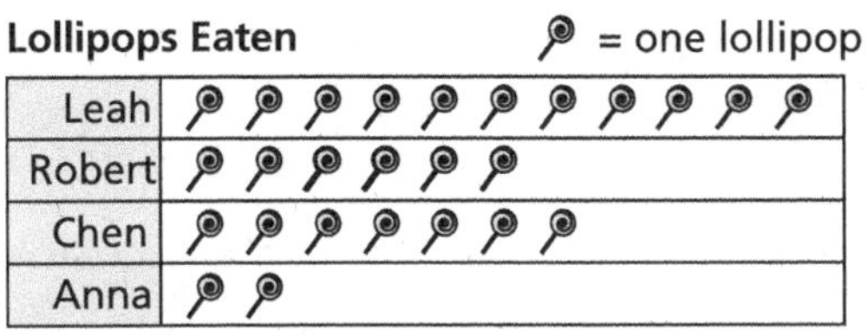

a Who ate the most lollipops? ______

b Who ate the least lollipops? ______

c How many did Chen eat? ______

d How many lollipops were eaten altogether? ______

8:4 — Extension — ☐ out of 9

1 How many different arrangements can you make?

______

2 7 + 13 + 12 + 8 + 1 + 9 ______

3 28 − 4 − 4 − 4 − 4 − 4 ______

4 If 2 non-parallel lines are drawn to cross these parallel lines, at how many points would lines cross altogether? ______

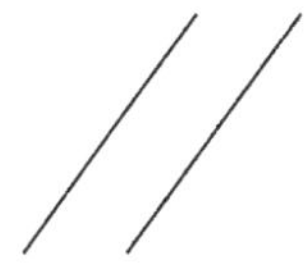

5 Minutes in 1 hour. ______

6 August is the ______ th month of the year.

7 Days in one fortnight. ______

8 Complete this picture if the broken line is a line of symmetry.

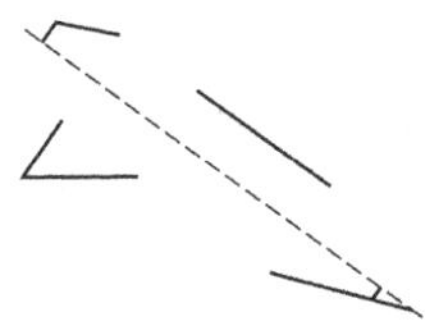

9 5 hundreds 3 tens 1 ones

= ______ tens and ______ one

Challenge

Write as many number sentences as you can linking 5, 6 and 11.

______

______

______

Subtracting 9

	29	50	64	37	82	48	73	96	101	129
−10										
−9										

	31	78	80	65	52	66	27	94	113	139
−9										

9:1 ☐ out of 19

1. 5 − 1 ____
2. 2 + 6 ____
3. 7 + 3 ____
4. 8 − 6 ____
5. $\begin{array}{r} 9 \\ -\ 6 \\ \hline \end{array}$
6. 8 m + 2 m ____
7. To 0 add 9. ____
8. 5 less than 10. ____
9. 2 lots of 4. ____
10. $\begin{array}{r} 4 \\ +\ 4 \\ \hline \end{array}$
11. The product of 2 and 8. ____
12. Show 8:00 on the clock face.

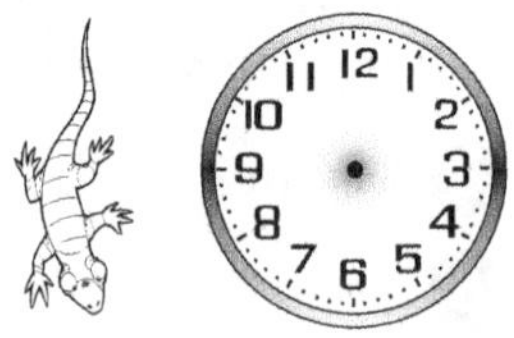

13. Circle the abbreviation for metres.
    A M **B** ms **C** m **D** MS
14. Show 725 on this numeral expander.

	hundreds		tens		ones

15. The odd numbers between 10 and 20.
    ____, ____, ____, ____, ____
16. Which is larger, fifty or fifteen? ____
17. The months in autumn. ____
    ____
18. Which is longer, 1 week or 1 month? ____
19.

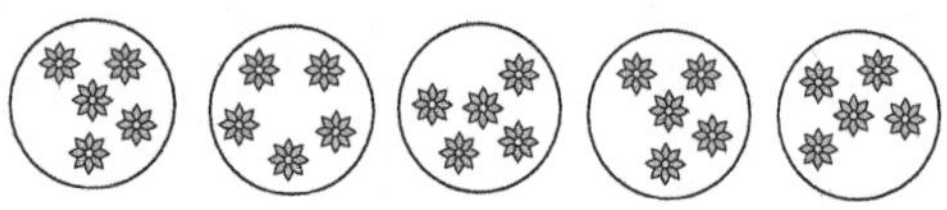

____ groups of ____ = ____

9:2 ☐ out of 18

1. 10 + 9 ____
2. 16 − 0 ____
3. 0 × 0 ____
4. 3 × 10 ____
5. $\begin{array}{r} 2 \\ \times\ 2 \\ \hline \end{array}$
6. Nine plus seven. ____
7. 9 × tens = ____ ones
8. 68, ____, 72, 74
9. Six more than ten. ____
10. $\begin{array}{r} 2 \\ \times\ 4 \\ \hline \end{array}$ This means "4 times 2".
11. 5, 10, 15, 20, ____, ____
12. This shows:

____ groups of ____
13. Write the digital time for:
    a six-oh-eight ☐ :
    b seven fifteen ☐ :
14. 472, 482, 492, ____, ____
15. What number comes after 999? ____
16. Which picture shows lines that are:

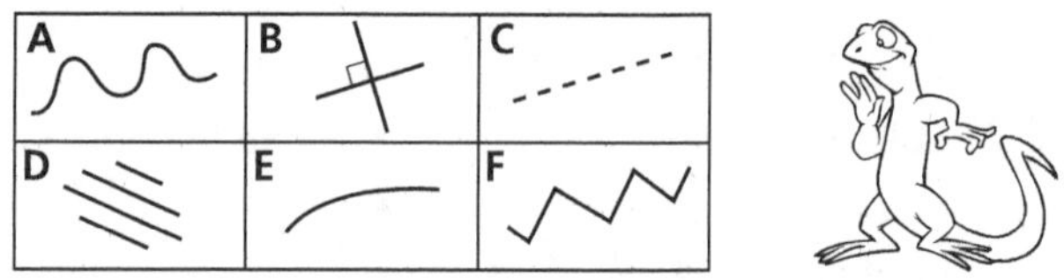

a parallel? ____ **b** perpendicular? ____
17. Write 903 in words.
    ____
    ____
18. Centimetres in one metre. ____

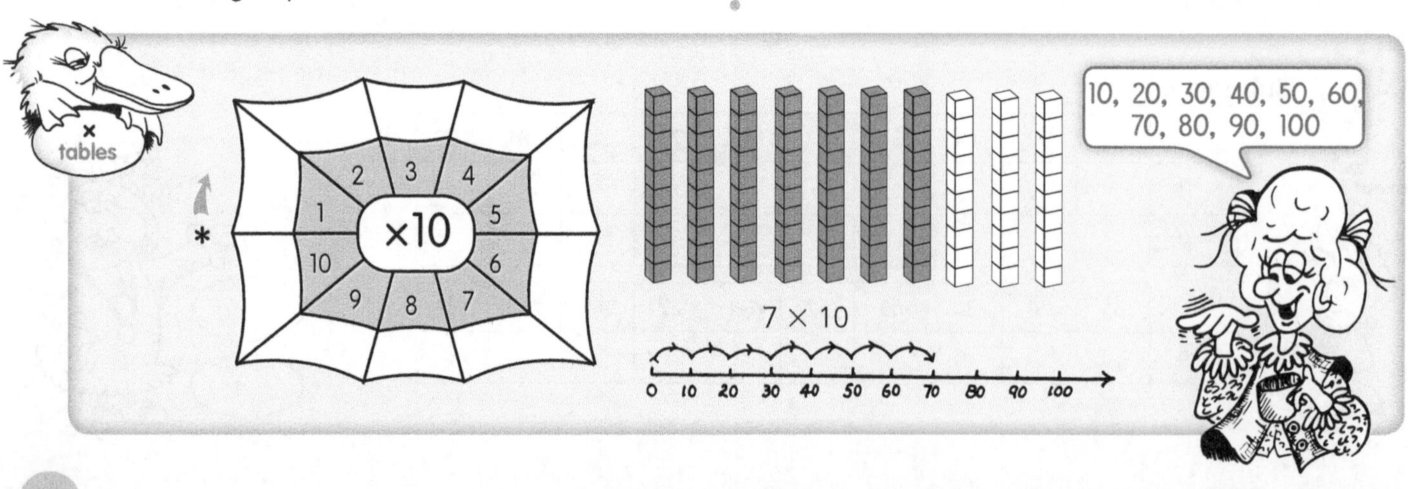

9:3 ☐ out of 12

1 18 − 6

2 19 − 5

3 20 − 4

4 4, 8, 12, 16, 20, ____, ____

5 Multiply 5 by 10. ____

6 Use this picture to fill in the boxes.

a ☐ − 6 = ☐

b ☐ − 9 = ☐

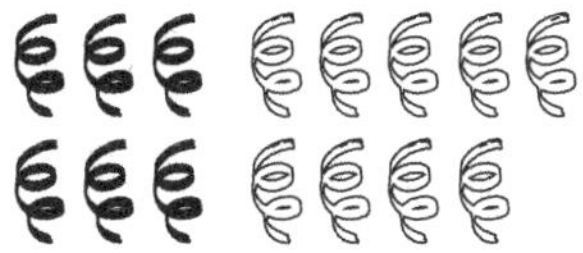

7 Write four hundred and seventy-six as a numeral. ____

8

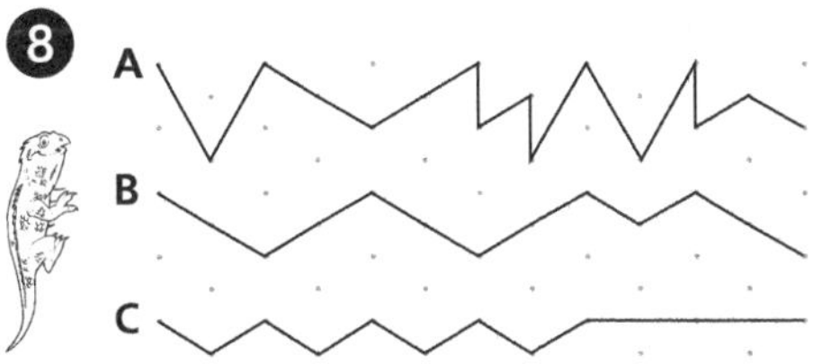

a Which is the longest path? ____

b Which is the shortest path? ____

9 Are you taller than 1 metre? ____

10 Round off 66 to the nearest 10. ____

11 Is 22 an even number? ____

12 Use this picture to complete the graph.

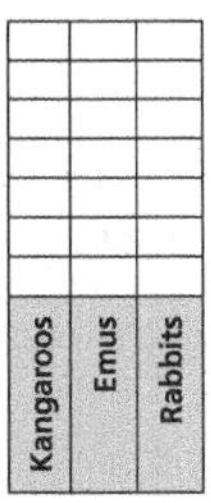

9:4 Extension ☐ out of 10

1 Write 753 in words. ____

2 Is 497 less than 794? ____

3 Do "ten-thirty", "half past 10" and "30 past 10" mean the same? ____

4 The month after March. ____

5 Is winter the coldest season? ____

6 50c + 50c + 20c + $1 ____

7 Colour the coins that are equal in value to twenty-two 10 cent coins.

8 What is the total value of three $2.00 coins and three 50c coins? ____

9 The product of 10 and 5. ____

10 100 years = 1 c____

Challenge

Write as many number sentences as you can linking 4, 9 and 13.

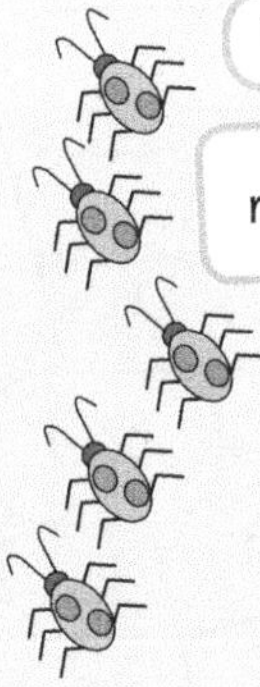

Two 5s can be traded for one 10.

rows of 5

groups of 5

lots of 5

	2	4	6	8	10
× 5					

	1	2	3	4	5
× 10					

4 fives would make 2 tens.

10:1 ☐ out of 22

1. 2 + 5 ____
2. 7 − 4 ____
3. 8 − 5 ____
4. 4 + 2 ____
5. $\begin{array}{r} 9 \\ -\ 5 \\ \hline \end{array}$
6. 1st, 2nd, ____, ____
7. 2, 4, 6, ☐, ☐ = ____
8. 20c + 20c ____
9. 10 minus 7. ____
10. $\begin{array}{r} 8 \\ +\ 1 \\ \hline \end{array}$
11. Is the height of a door greater than 1 m? ____
12. Colour the even numbers red and the odd ones blue.

11	12	13
14	15	16
17	18	19

13. 83, 82, 81, ____, ____
14. One less than 100. ____
15. 2:30 means ____ minutes past ____
16. Minutes in 1 hour. ____
17. Is March in winter? ____
18. Has each got a fair share? ____

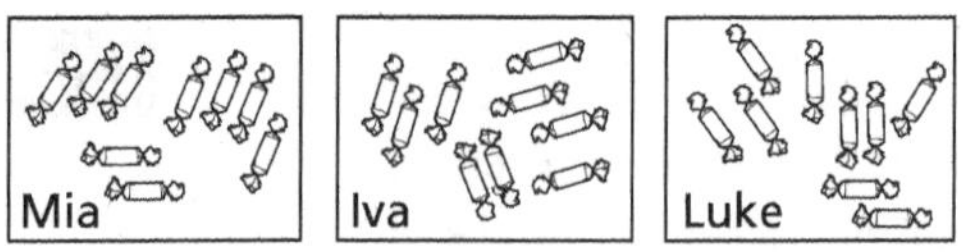

19. How many blocks are used in this model? ____

20. Months in one year. ____
21. Write 513 in words. ____
22. The abbreviation for "metres". ____

10:2 ☐ out of 17

1. 11 + 6 ____
2. 14 − 5 ____
3. 0 × 5 ____
4. 3 × 2 ____
5. $\begin{array}{r} 10 \\ \times\ 2 \\ \hline \end{array}$
6. \$4 + \$4 + \$4 ____
7. 10 tens ____
8. 500 + 600 ____
9. 15 + 7 + 5 ____
10. $\begin{array}{r} 5 \\ \times\ 2 \\ \hline \end{array}$ This means "5 times 2".
11. This digital time:
    a is read as ____
    b means ____ minutes past ____

12. 404, 406, 408, ____, ____
13. Double 6, plus double 2. ____
14. What line is on the:
    a top right? ____
    b bottom left? ____

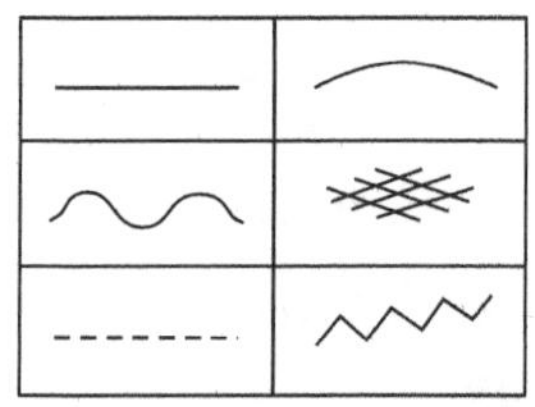

15. Draw two parallel lines.

16. Write nine hundred and five as a numeral. ____
17. Write 749 in words. ____

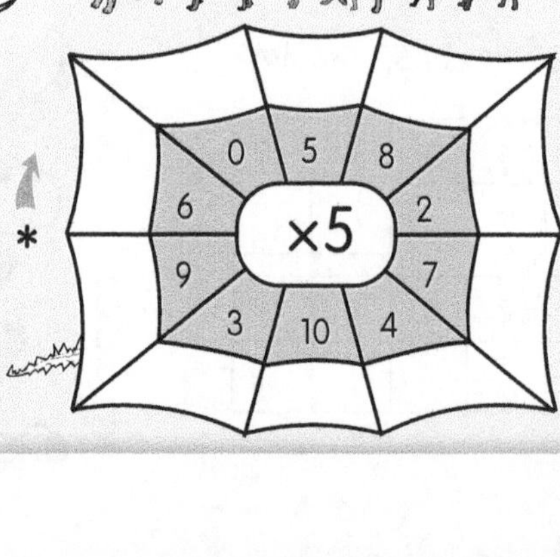

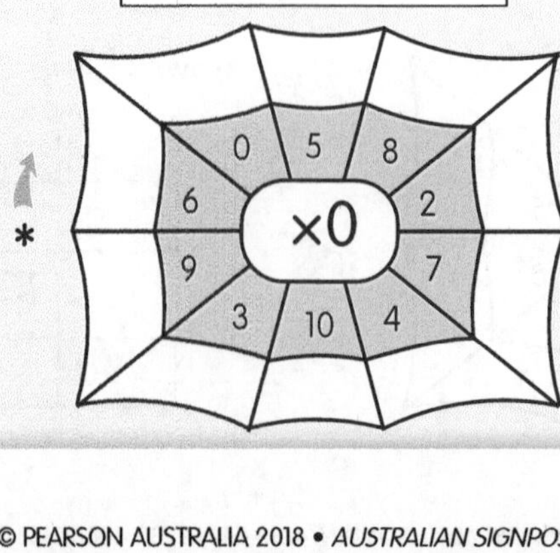

out of 14

1. 13 + 4 = ____
2. 12 + 3 = ____
3. 14 + 5 = ____
4. 635, 640, 645, ________, ________
5. Is the width of an elephant about 2 metres? ________
6. 18 metres minus 9 metres. ________
7. Use the jump strategy to find 26 + 35. ________
8. Join the dots.

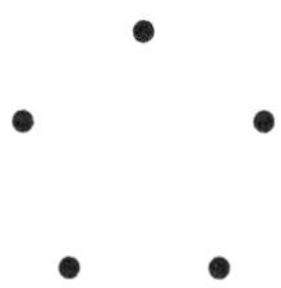

This is a regular ________.

9. Write the numeral for: ________

10. Write 839 in words. ________________________________
11. The next even number after 16. ________
12. Round off 54 to the nearest 10. ________
13. The months of winter. ________________________________
14. Complete the pattern.

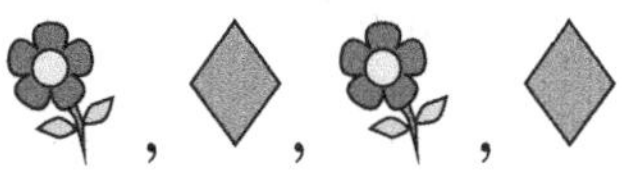

, ________, ________

Extension

out of 6

1. 69, 89, 109, ________, ________
2. Which is larger, 3 × 5 or 8 + 8? ________
3. 40c + 40c + 50c ________
4. I came 1st in a race out of 8. How many came:
   a in front of me? ________
   b behind me? ________
5. I will give Li two of these toys. How many different groups of 2 could I give? ________

6. Estimate the number of stars, group them in tens, then count.

Estimate = ________ Number = ________

Challenge

42 + 35 = ________

Explain how you found your answer.

____

____

____

Turn to ID Card B on page 7.

Give the answers for these numbers.

(15) ________ (16) ________ shapes

(17) ________ shapes (21) ________ of a cube

(22) ________ (23) ________

(28) ________ (29) ________

	Faces	Edges	Corners
Number			

11:1 ☐ out of 22

1. 10 + 1 ______
2. 13 − 3 ______
3. 5 × 2 ______
4. 7 + 7 ______
5. $\begin{array}{r} 16 \\ +\ 4 \\ \hline \end{array}$
6. 18 − 10 ______
7. 2 × 2 ______
8. Double 3. ______
9. 5 less than 7. ______
10. $\begin{array}{r} 15 \\ -\ 5 \\ \hline \end{array}$
11. The number between 45 and 47. ______
12. How many sides are on 2 squares? ______
13. Show 28 on this numeral expander.

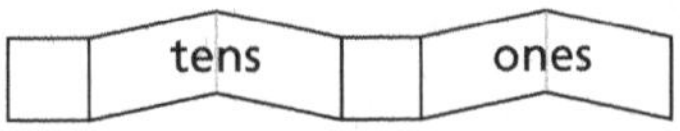

14. The word for 18. ______
15. Order from smallest to largest.

    17, 30, 5, 26 ______
16. What time is shown?

    ______
17. 20c + 10c + 50c ______
18. Months in 1 year. ______
19. This is a ______ line.

20. Is it impossible to grow a tail and long ears if I eat carrots? ______
21. Is 93 an odd number? ______
22. 10, 12, 14, 16, ______, ______

11:2 ☐ out of 17

1. 15 + 4 ______
2. 15 − 4 ______
3. 5 × 10 ______
4. 3 × 2 ______
5. $\begin{array}{r} 10 \\ \times\ 4 \\ \hline \end{array}$
6. 12 shared by 2. ______
7. 8 × 1 ______
8. Double 12. ______
9. Sum of 10 and 11. ______
10. $\begin{array}{r} 2 \\ \times\ 5 \\ \hline \end{array}$
11. **a** Write the digital time shown in words.

    ______

    b It is ______ past ______.
12. Is the height of your teacher less than 1 m? ______
13. Make the largest number possible using 1, 7 and 3. ______
14. Use the jump strategy to find 51 – 23. ______
15. Write < (less than) or > (greater than).

    a 35 ____ 21 **b** 37 ____ 59
16. Is there an even chance of spinning a **B**? ______

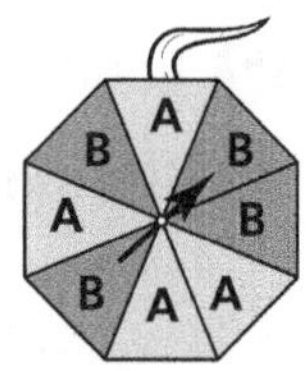

17. Write the numeral for six hundred and ninety-two. ______

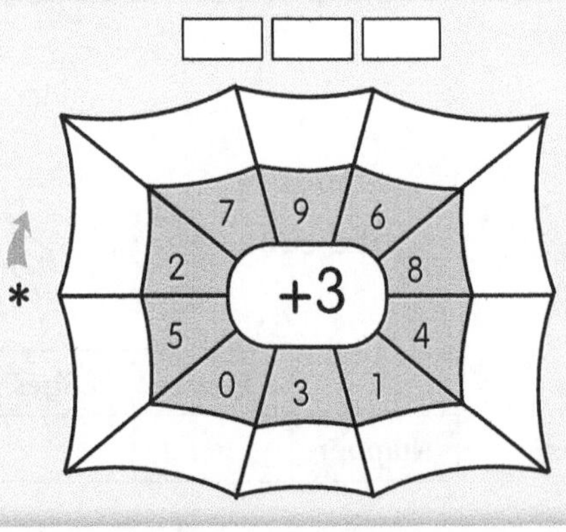

11:3 ☐ out of 10

1. 35 + 6

2. 26 + 8

3. 44 + 7

4. The digital time:
   a is read as ______
   b means ______ minutes past ______

5. Use the jump strategy to find 43 + 19. ______

6. Join the dots.
   This is a regular ______.

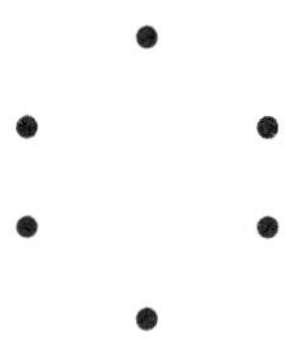

7. Write 340 in words. ______

8. Where does the ant stop if he goes:
   2 up, 3 left, 1 down,
   5 right and then 3 up? ______

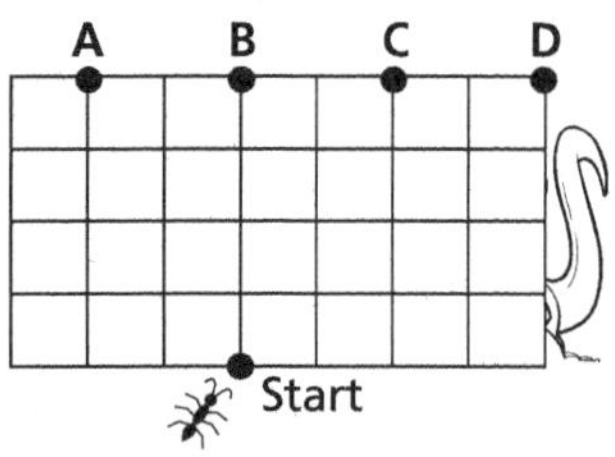

9. Certain, impossible, likely or unlikely?
   "The next person I meet will be able to hold their breath for 1 hour." ______

10. Approximately, how wide is your classroom? ______ metres.

11:4 ☐ out of 6

Extension

1. If "<" means "is less than", write true (T) or false (F) for:
   a 99 < 100 ______   b 6 × 7 < 40 ______

2. a Half of 12. ______
   b A quarter of 12. ______

3. If this pattern were repeated, what would the 8th shape be? ______

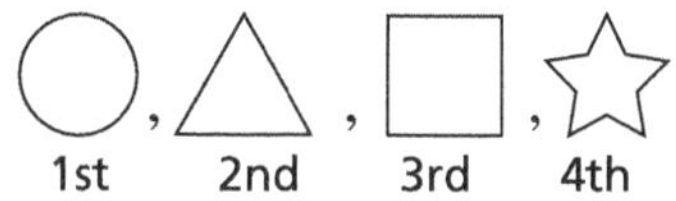

4. How many different arrangements can you make? ______

5. Ten pens fill one box.
   How many boxes can be filled with:
   a 30 pens? ______   b 70 pens? ______

6. 40 + 6 + 4 + 8 + 2 + 1 + 9 ______

Challenge

39 + 7 = ☐

Explain how you found your answer.

a How many **lots of 5** coins? ______

b How many **groups of 6** cones? ______

c How many **groups of 4** fish? ______

d How many **groups of 3** stars? ______

12:1 ☐ out of 19

1. 12 − 2 ______
2. 10 + 5 ______
3. 3 × 2 ______
4. 14 − 10 ______
5. $\begin{array}{r} 17 \\ -\ 7 \\ \hline \end{array}$
6. 3 + 8 ______
7. 0 × 2 ______
8. 20c + 10c ______
9. Take 3 from 10. ______
10. $\begin{array}{r} 12 \\ +\ 6 \\ \hline \end{array}$
11. | 9 | tens | 2 | ones | = ______
12. Months in 1 year. ______
13. What colour is a 50c coin? ______
14. The number three more than seventeen. ______
15. Round 44 to the nearest 10. ______
16. The even numbers between 43 and 48. ______
17. Write in words:
    a 40 ______ b 14 ______
18. Colour half of the tree.

19. 

______ rows of ______ = ______

12:2 ☐ out of 17

1. 19 + 6 ______
2. 21 + 12 ______
3. 21 − 6 ______
4. 32 − 4 ______
5. $\begin{array}{r} 2 \\ \times\ 10 \\ \hline \end{array}$
6. 8 × 2 ______
7. 2 × 5 ______
8. 4, 6, ☐, 10. ☐ = ______
9. 9 × 5 ______
10. $\begin{array}{r} 10 \\ \times\ 5 \\ \hline \end{array}$
11. Write 27 in words. ______
12. Use the jump strategy to find 61 − 23. ______
13. a Write the smallest 3-digit number possible using 0, 9 and 7. ______
    b Write the largest number possible using 0, 9 and 7. ______
14. Write the numeral for eight hundred and seven. ______
15. What part is shaded?

______ out of ______

16. Which line is:
    a 2 cm long? ______
    b 3 cm long? ______

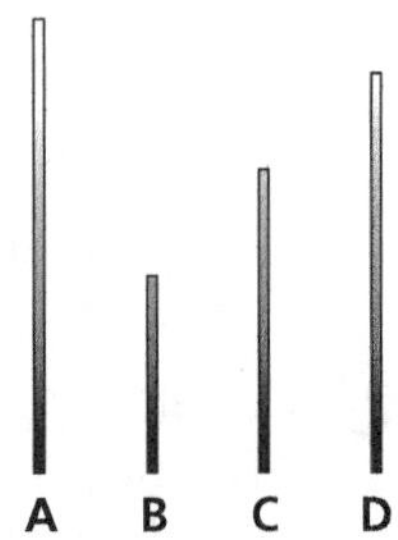

17. How many legs would there be on 6 dogs? ______

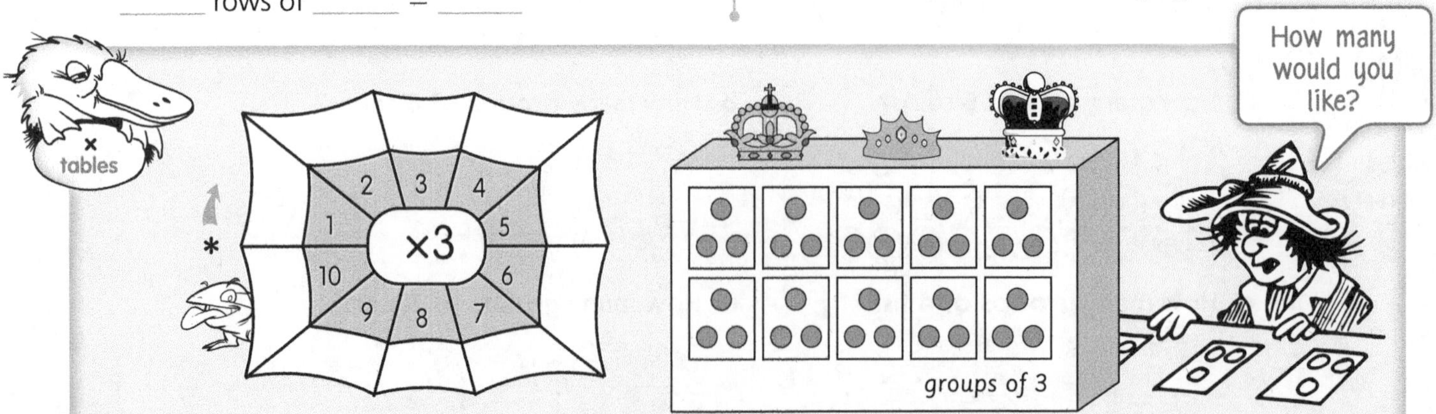

 • *AUSTRALIAN SIGNPOST MATHS 3 MENTALS* • ISBN 978 1 4886 2183 3

12:3 ☐ out of 12

1. 200 + 500 = ____
2. 600 + 300 = ____
3. 100 + 800 = ____
4. Write three hundred and twenty as a numeral. ____
5. Colour 7 tenths.

6. Write the number 128 in words. ____

____

7. < (less than) or > (greater than)?

   a 12 ____ 41 **b** 73 ____ 88

8. Going up from **A**, where do I finish if I turn 2nd on the left, then 1st right, then right then keep going?

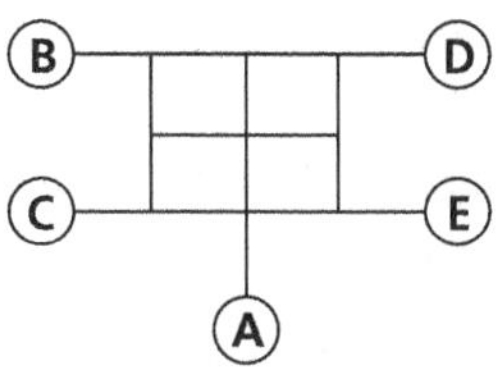

____

9. Is there an even chance of landing on **A**?

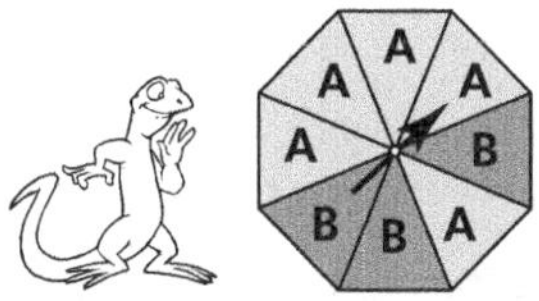

____

10. Are two of the faces of a cylinder the same?

____

11. Measure the width of this page correct to the nearest centimetre. ____
12. I have 3 bunches of 3 flowers. How many flowers altogether? ____

12:4 Extension ☐ out of 6

1. How many halves in 2 oranges? ____
2. What shape would you get if you fold the shape along the dotted line?

   a

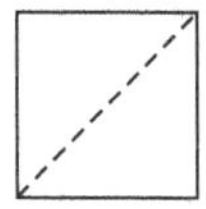

____

   b

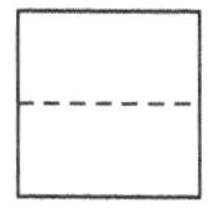

____

3. Colour one quarter of this group.

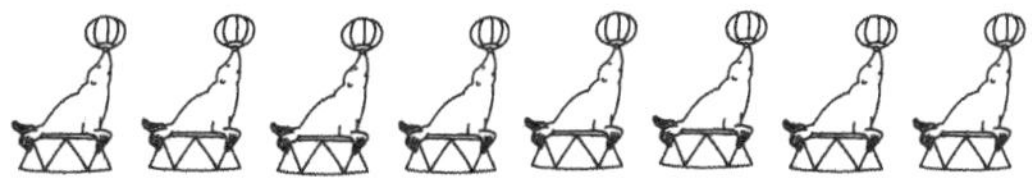

   Each quarter is ____ out of ____ equal parts.

4. Which is larger, 382, 372 or 375? ____
5. How many tens make 360? ____
6. Show this number as tens and ones.

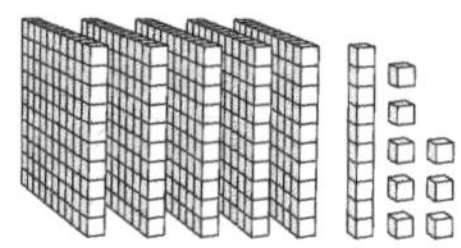

		tens		ones

Challenge

200 + 600 = ☐

Explain how you found your answer.

____

____

____

____

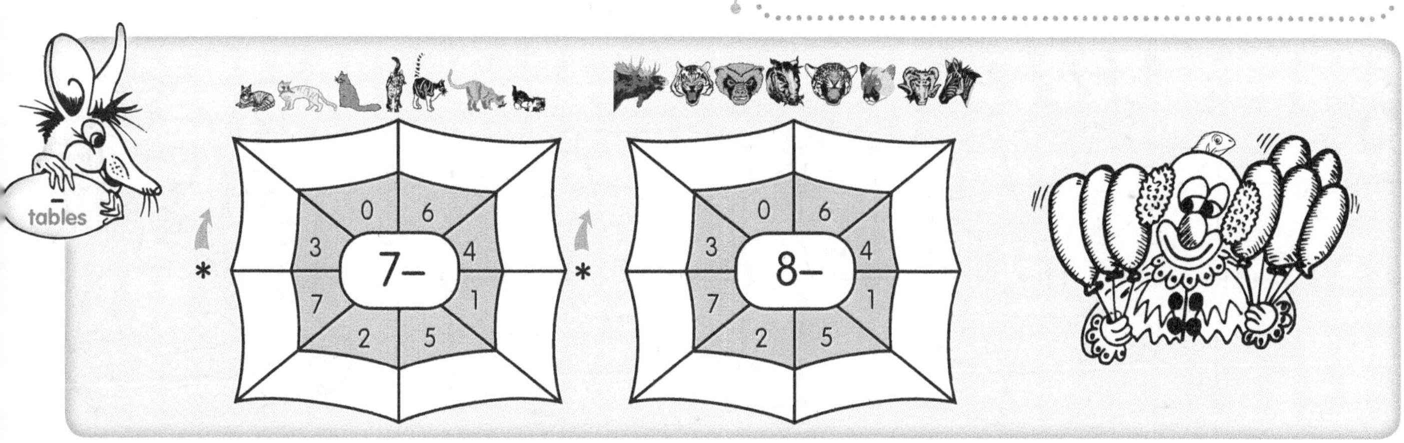

13:1   ☐ out of 17

1. 6 + 6 ______
2. 4 + 10 ______
3. 1 × 2 ______
4. 4 × 2 ______
5. $\begin{array}{r} 10 \\ +\ 9 \\ \hline \end{array}$
6. 16 − 8 ______
7. 13 − 3 ______
8. To 6 add 2. ______
9. Half of 10. ______
10. $\begin{array}{r} 18 \\ -\ 6 \\ \hline \end{array}$

11. How many points has this star? ______

12. Each half is: ▭▭
    ______ out of ______ equal parts.
13. Which is larger, 55 or 53? ______
14. Colour the shape with the larger area.

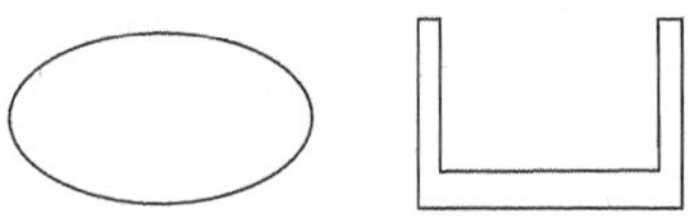

15. This picture shows ______ rows of ______ .

16. Measure each line in centimetres.
    A ________________ ______
    B ____________ ______
    C ____________________ ______
17. This shows ______ groups of ______ .

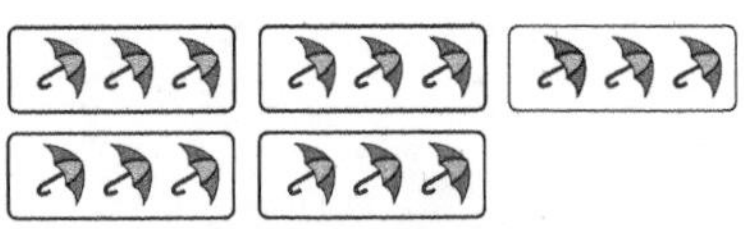

13:2   ☐ out of 19

1. 13 + 20 ______
2. 30 − 5 ______
3. 7 × 2 ______
4. 2 × 6 ______
5. $\begin{array}{r} 1 \\ \times\ 8 \\ \hline \end{array}$
6. 30 + 43 ______
7. 8 + 3 + 2 + 7 ______
8. Five times two. ______
9. Double 13. ______
10. $\begin{array}{r} 2 \\ \times\ 5 \\ \hline \end{array}$

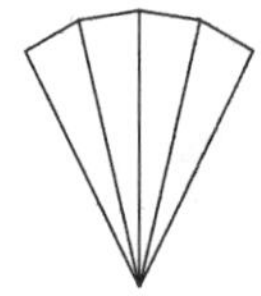

11. **a** Colour half of this shape.
    b How many quarters in one half? ______
12. How many 5 cent coins make 50c? ______
13. Write 90 in words. ______
14. Fingers on two hands. ______
15. The month after April. ______
16. Follow the directions and colour the path of the counter.

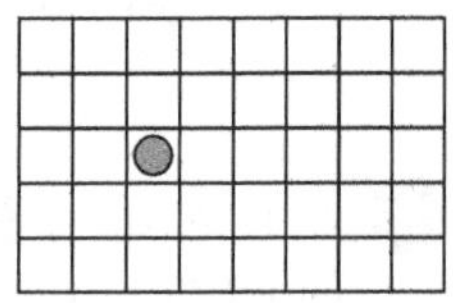

    Move 2 down, then 4 right, then 3 up.
17. Write 463 in words. ______
    ______
18. Colour the smallest area red.

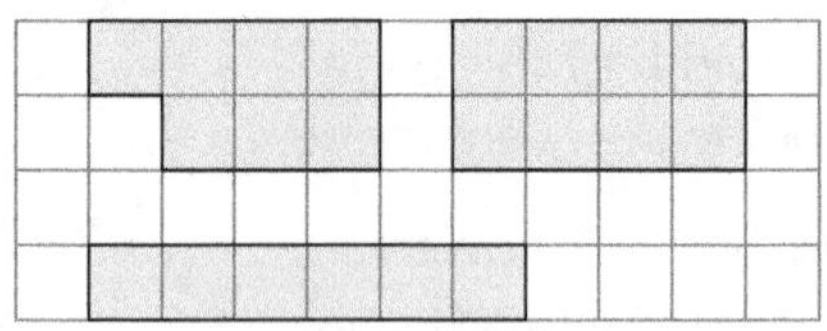

19. Amy spent $2 each day for one week. How much did she spend? ______

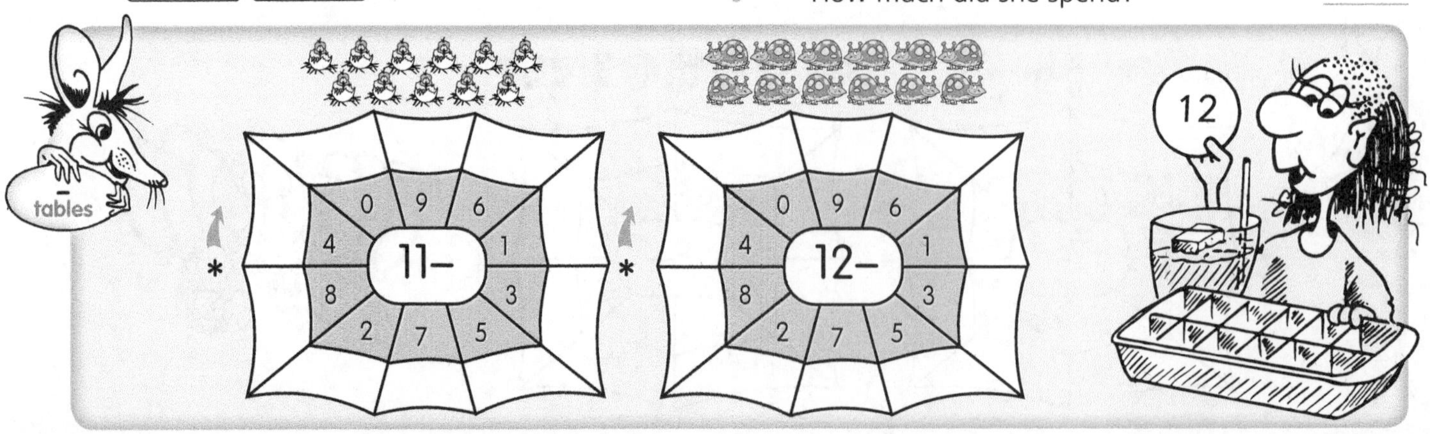

 ISBN 978 1 4886 2183 3

13:3 out of 12

1.

Tens	Ones
2	2
+1	1

2.

Tens	Ones
2	4
+2	3

3. Is the length of this about 1 cm, 3 cm or 5 cm? ______

4. 800 plus 500. ______
5. How many fingers are on three hands? ______
6. What is 15 less than 40? ______
7. What is larger, $\frac{1}{2}$ or $\frac{1}{4}$? ______
8. Which is larger, 2 099 or 2 103? ______
9. Write 3 072 in words. ______

______

10. Make the biggest number you can using 2, 4 and 7. ______
11. Write the correct sign (< or >).
    a 92 ____ 87   b 107 ____ 131
12. a 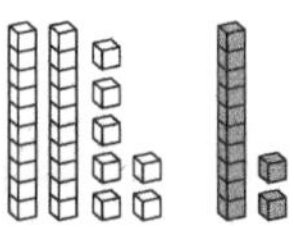
    27 + 12 = ______
    b 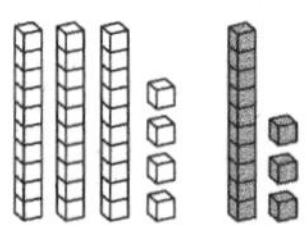
    34 + 13 = ______

13:4 out of 8

Extension

1. 12 + 8 + 5 + 5 + 15 + 5 ______
2. 50 − 10 − 10 − 10 − 10 − 10 ______
3. 3 groups of 6. ______

4. In a race I am 7th out of 10. How many:
   a are in front of me? ______
   b are behind me? ______
5. How many cakes will be in the 16th row of this pattern?

______

6. Which coin is worth more than 20 cents but less than $1? ______
7. Quarters in 6 apples. ______
8. Digits in 6 030. ______

Challenge

67 − 31 = ☐

Explain how you found your answer.

______

______

______

______

______

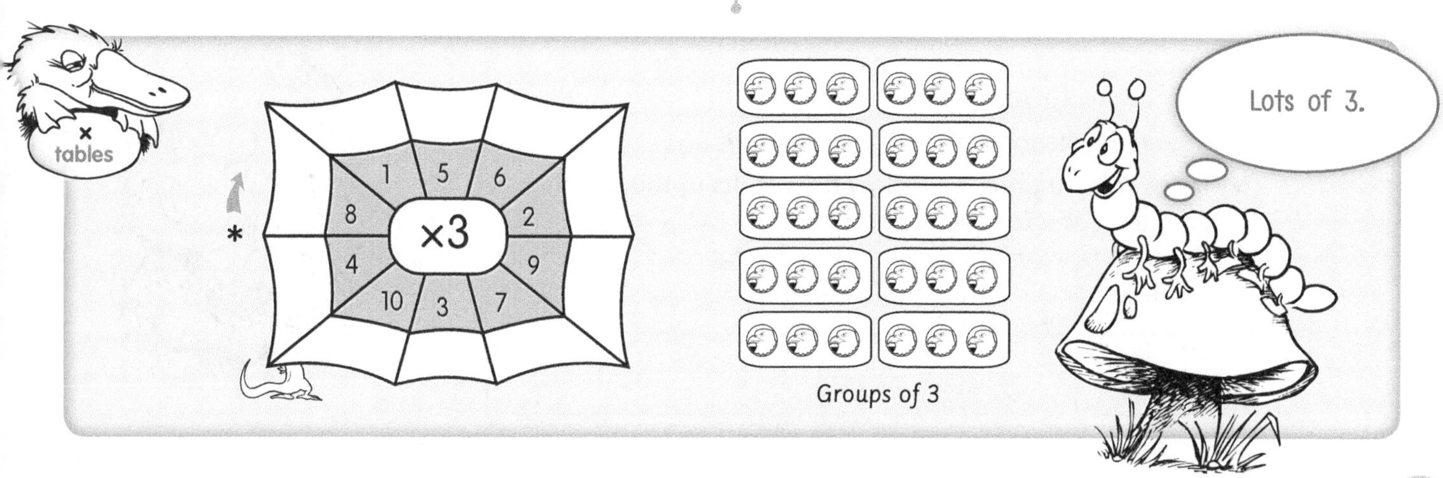

14:1   ☐ out of 17

1. 1×4 ______
2. $7 - 7$ ______
3. $10 + 2$ ______
4. 3×10 ______
5. $\begin{array}{r} 17 \\ -\ 4 \\ \hline \end{array}$
6. $18 - 10$ ______
7. $9 + 9$ ______
8. Total of 4 and 3. ______
9. 4 less than 17. ______
10. $\begin{array}{r} 18 \\ +\ 1 \\ \hline \end{array}$
11. 63 = ☐ tens ☐ ones
12. What part is shaded?

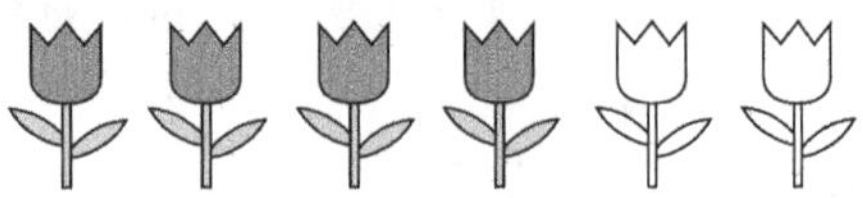

______ out of ______

13. *Impossible*, *unlikely*, *likely*, *certain*

    Which of these describes the chance of throwing a 6 on a dice? ______
14. Which is heavier, a car or a table? ______
15. What do you add to 17 to get 20? ______
16. What number is shown here? ______

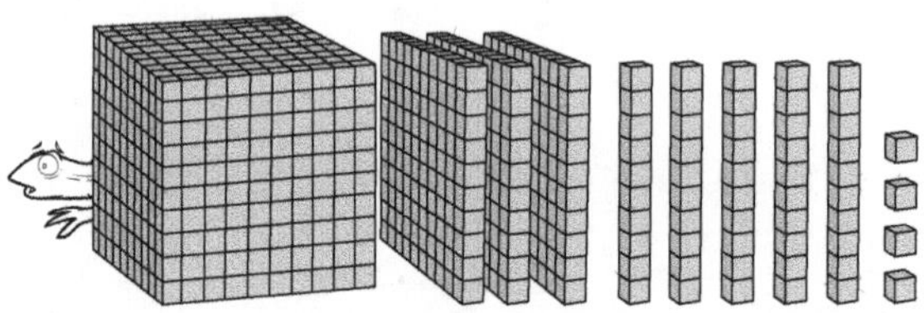

17. Colour the shape with the smaller area.

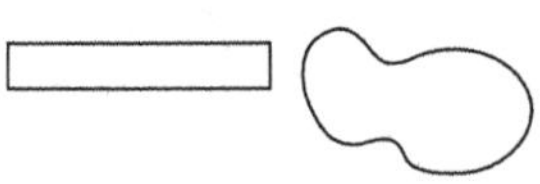

14:2   ☐ out of 17

1. $23 + 7$ ______
2. $34 - 8$ ______
3. 10×2 ______
4. 10×5 ______
5. $\begin{array}{r} 10 \\ \times\ 2 \\ \hline \end{array}$
6. 23 plus 11. ______
7. 34 take away 5. ______
8. 15, 20, ____, 30
9. \$5 + \$5 + \$5 ______
10. $\begin{array}{r} 5 \\ \times\ 3 \\ \hline \end{array}$

11. The height of this page correct to the nearest centimetre. ______
12. I have 3 trays of cookies. There are 10 cookies on each tray. How many cookies altogether? ______
13. Write the smallest number using 3, 4, 8 and 1. ______
14. Follow the directions and colour the path of the counter.

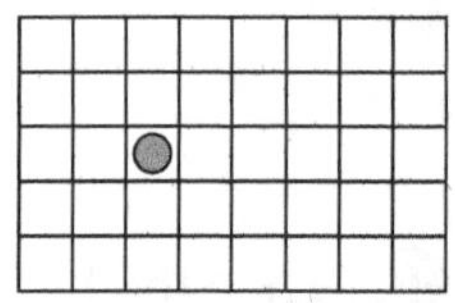

    Move 2 up, then 2 left, then 4 down, then 5 right, then 3 up.
15. Show the number 7 524 on this abacus.

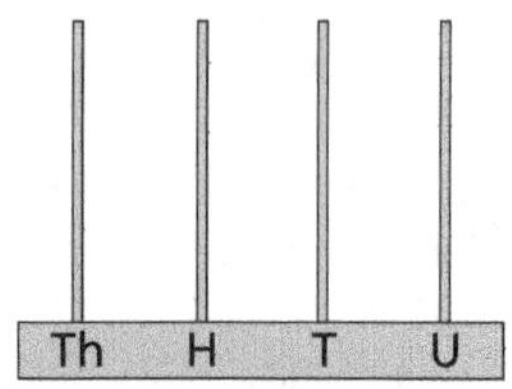

16. 3 000 + 600 + 20 + 9 ______
17. Write 2 010 in expanded notation.

______

A coin is to be tossed 10 times.

a How many *heads* would be most likely? ______

b Toss a coin 10 times and show the results in this graph. Colour a circle for each toss.

Heads	○	○	○	○	○	○	○	○
Tails	○	○	○	○	○	○	○	○

14:3 — out of 11

1.

Tens	Ones
8	1
+1	3

2.

Tens	Ones
$4	3
+ $3	4

3. Draw a shape with a smaller area than this pentagon.

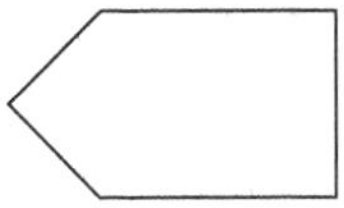

4. The number before 21. ______

5. Is 36 closer to 30 or 40? ______

6. 24, 28, 32, ______, ______, ______, ______

7. a Are these numbers equally likely to be spun? ______

   b How many 2s are most likely in 12 spins? ______

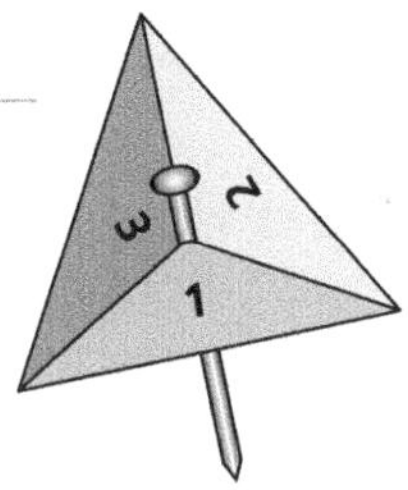

8. Which is bigger, one quarter or one half? ______

9. I have 6 rows of 3 trees. How many trees altogether? ______

10. Write the numeral six thousand and thirty-one. ______

11. a 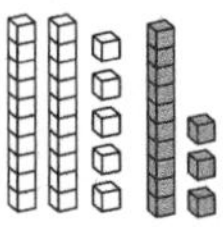

   25 + 13 = ______

   b 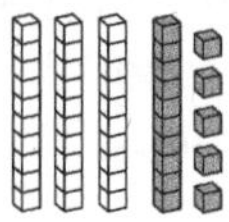

   30 + 15 = ______

14:4 — Extension — out of 6

1. 4 + 4 + 4 = ☐ × 4   ☐ = ______

2. Is the length of a ruler closer to one quarter or one half of a metre? ______

3. 

   What fraction is shaded?

   A $\frac{4}{20}$ B $\frac{5}{10}$ C $\frac{1}{4}$ ______

4. Quarters in 5 pears. ______

5. If "<" means "is less than", write true or false for:

   a 39 < 41 ______

   b 80 < (2 × 40) ______

6. Write in words: 9, 19, 90. ______

______

Challenge

Starting at the circle, colour squares to make a path that ends at the triangle.

Write the directions for the path.

See 14:2, question 14.

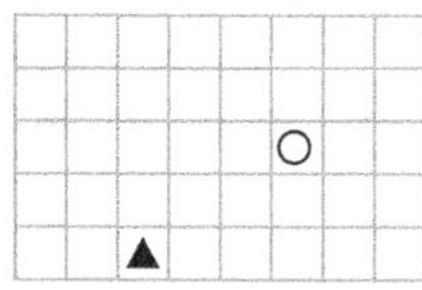

______

______

______

______

______

______

Concept

Complete these cards.

a 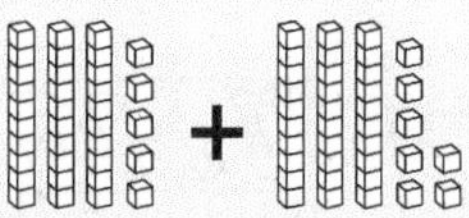

☐ + ☐ = ☐

b 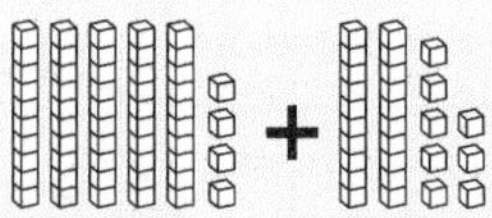

☐ + ☐ = ☐

c 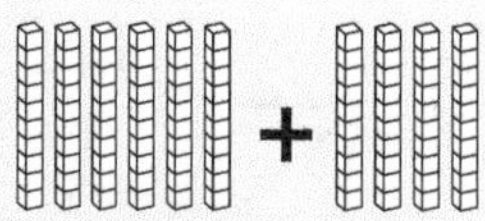

☐ + ☐ = ☐

10 ones can be traded for **1 ten**.

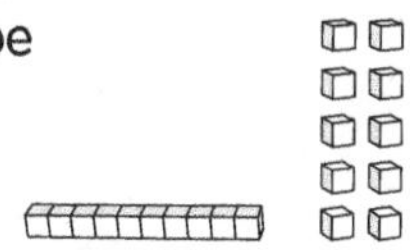

10 tens can be traded for **1 hundred**.

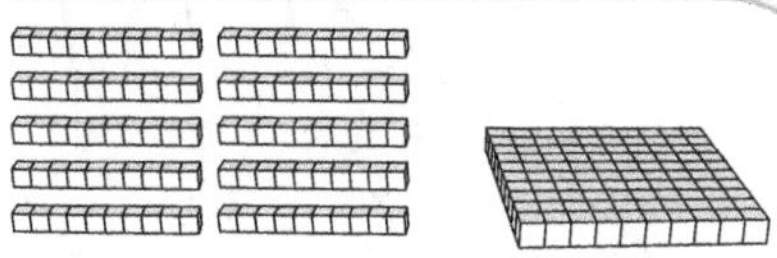

15:1 out of 16

1. 10 + 6 ______
2. 2 + 9 ______
3. 3 × 10 ______
4. 8 × 10 ______
5. 14 − 2 ______
6. 19 − 9 ______
7. 15 − 10 ______
8. To 5 add 3. ______
9. Double 7. ______
10. 13 + 4 ______

11. What part is shaded?

______ out of ______

12. Write the number shown on this abacus.

______

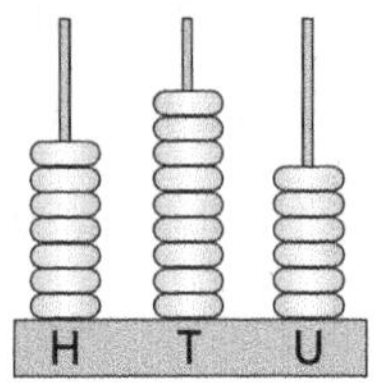

13. Which of the terms *impossible*, *unlikely*, *likely* or *certain* describes the chance of you finding $20 tomorrow?

______

14. Circle the correct number sentence for this picture.

A 2 × 5 = 10
B 2 × 7 = 14
C 12 − 2 = 10
D 7 + 5 = 12

15. 22, 33, 44, 55, ______, ______

16. What 2 shapes make this pattern?

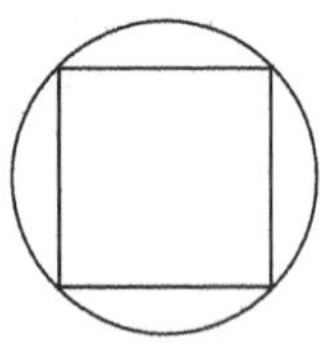

______

15:2 out of 14

1. 67 + 22 ______
2. 39 − 9 ______
3. 8 × 10 ______
4. 7 × 10 ______
5. 5 × 4 ______
6. 9 lots of 10. ______
7. 80, 90, ☐, 110. ☐ = ______
8. 12 shared among 3. ______
9. $7 + $7 + $7 ______
10. 5 × 3 ______

11. **a** The smallest area below. ______
    b The largest area below. ______

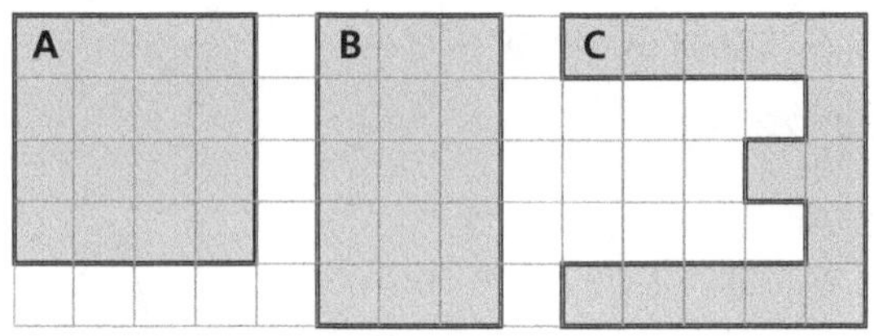

12. **a** How many 2s would you expect in 6 spins? ______
    b How many 3s would you expect in 9 spins? ______

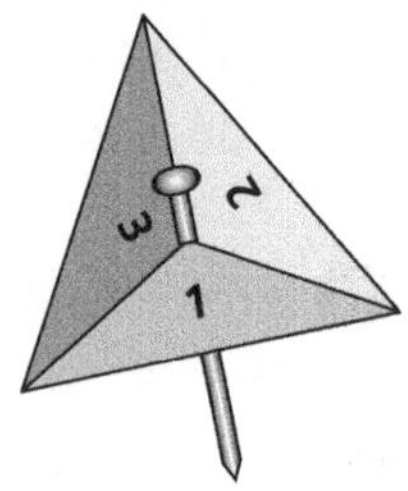

13. 

Four lots of five. ______

14. Write the numeral for the number shown on this abacus.

______

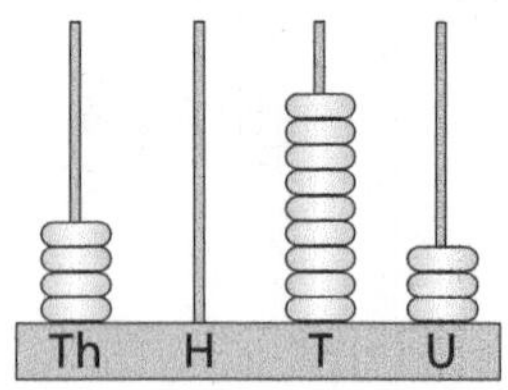

 ISBN 978 1 4886 2183 3

15:3 ☐ out of 10

1

Tens	Ones
$4	4
+ $5	3

2

Tens	Ones
$6	3
+ $2	1

3 a What part is shaded?

_____ out of _____

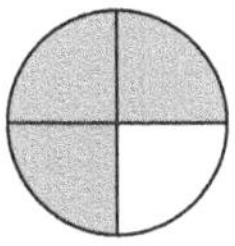

b 3 quarters plus 1 quarter. _____

4 Half past five is also: 5: _____

5 This hexagon has:

a _____ sides

b _____ corners

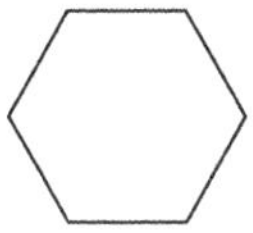

6 94 = _____ tens + _____ ones

7 I have a 50c coin, a 20c coin and a 10c coin. How much money do I have? _____

8 Digits in 1 325. _____

9 How many place-value ones do you need to cover this area? _____

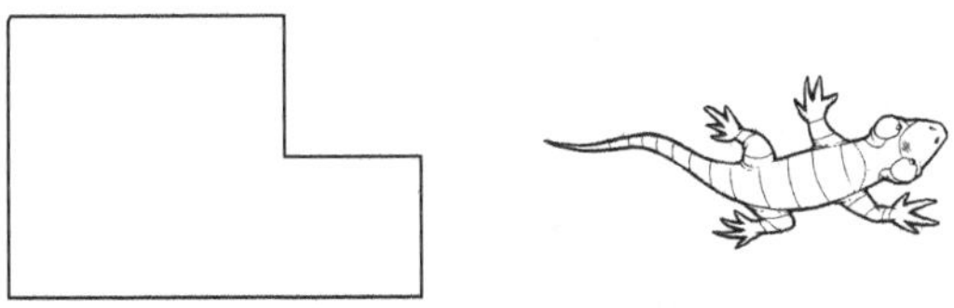

10

a 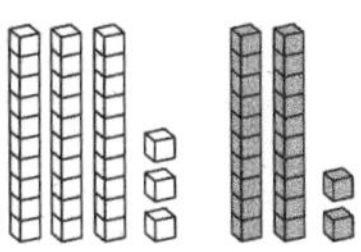

33 + 22 = _____

b 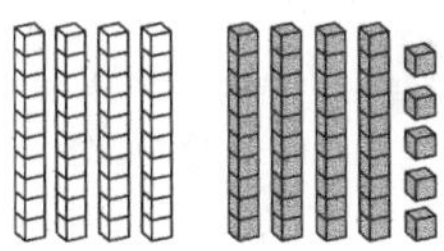

40 + 45 = _____

15:4 ☐ out of 5

Extension

1 

1st, 2nd, 3rd, 4th

If this pattern were repeated, what would be the 13th shape? _____

2 Quarters in 10 oranges. _____

3 5 pentagons have _____ sides.

4 1 4 2 4 3

Two of these cards are to be drawn from a hat and added. What is the most likely total? _____

5 Which is the largest area? _____

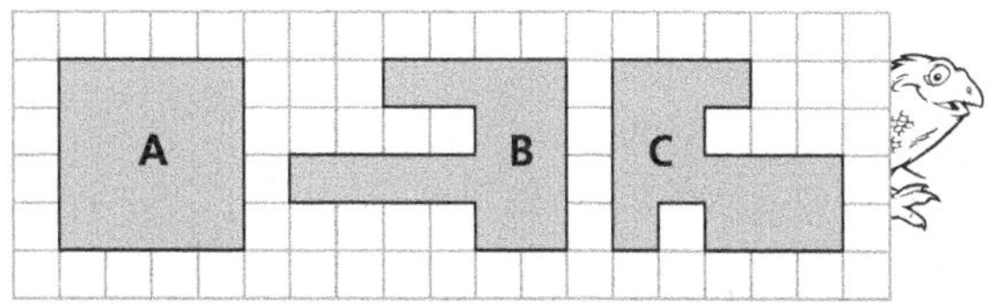

Challenge

Write chance statements about this spinner.

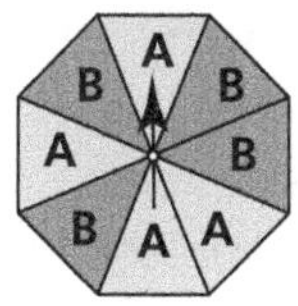

_____

_____

_____

_____

_____

_____

_____

Turn to ID Card B on page 7.

Give the answers for these numbers.

(1) _____ line (4) _____ lines

(5) _____ lines (12) _____

(13) _____ (16) _____ shapes

(17) _____ shapes (18) _____

(19) _____ (20) _____

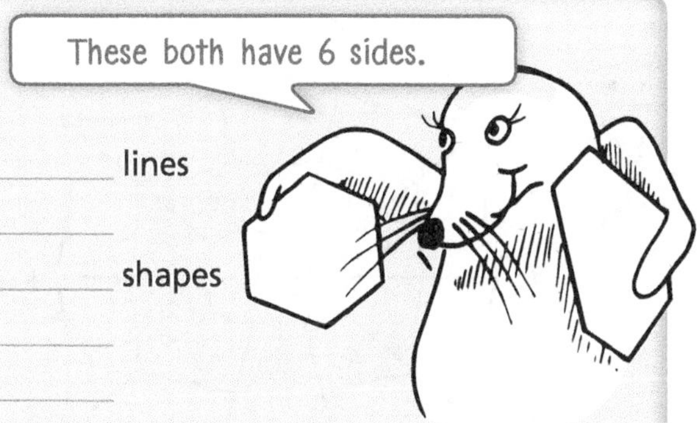

16:1 ☐ out of 17

1. 16 − 6 ______
2. 1 × 10 ______
3. 10 + 7 ______
4. 13 − 10 ______
5. 18 + 2 (written vertically: 18 over + 2)
6. 5 × 10 ______
7. 8 + 8 ______
8. 7 take away 3. ______
9. Sum of 5 and 8. ______
10. 16 − 8 (written vertically: 16 over − 8)
11. Which has the greater mass, a blown up balloon or a cricket ball? ______

12. Write the numeral for seventy. ______
13. Which coin shows a man on one side and a woman on the other? ______
14. Which Australian coins are:
    a gold? ______ b silver? ______
15. Name the shape:

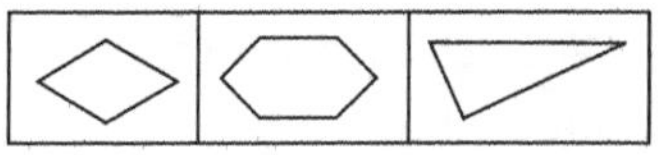

    a in the middle. ______
    b on the left. ______
16. ______ rows of ______ = ______
    ______ × ______ = ______

17. Which has the greater area? ______

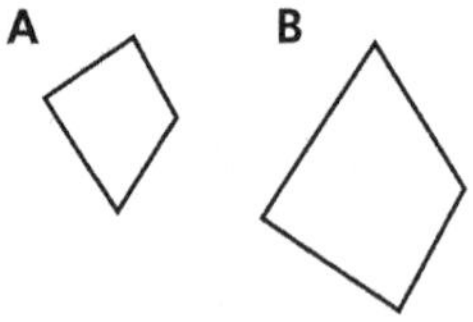

16:2 ☐ out of 17

1. 24 + 14 ______
2. 28 − 5 ______
3. 4 × 1 ______
4. 5 × 9 ______
5. 10 × 6 (written vertically: 10 over × 6)
6. Half of 18. ______
7. $80 less $20. ______
8. 3 × 10 ______
9. 6 + 6 + 6 ______
10. 10 × 3 (written vertically: 10 over × 3)

11. 5, 10, 15, ______, ______, 30
12. How many:
    a corners? ______
    b angles? ______

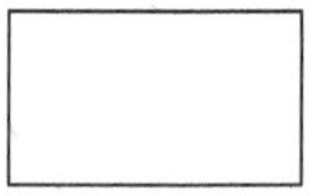

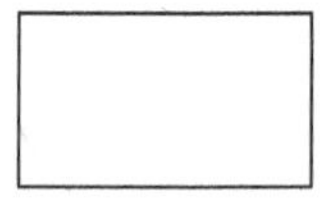

13. 5 × 3 = ______ 3 × 5 = ______
14. Colour $\frac{3}{8}$ of this shape.

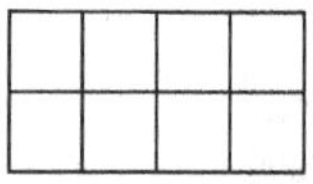

15. 2 × 3 = ______
    6 ÷ 2 = ______
    ______ × 3 = 6

16. Each person at the table used 2 plates. How many plates were used if there were:
    a 6 people at the table? ______
    b 9 people at the table? ______

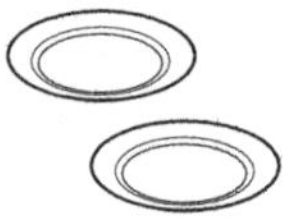

17. How many place-value ones blocks are needed to cover this area?
    Area = ______ blocks.

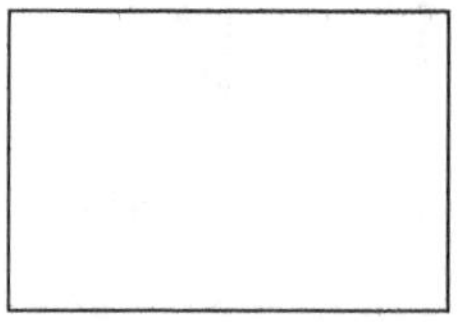

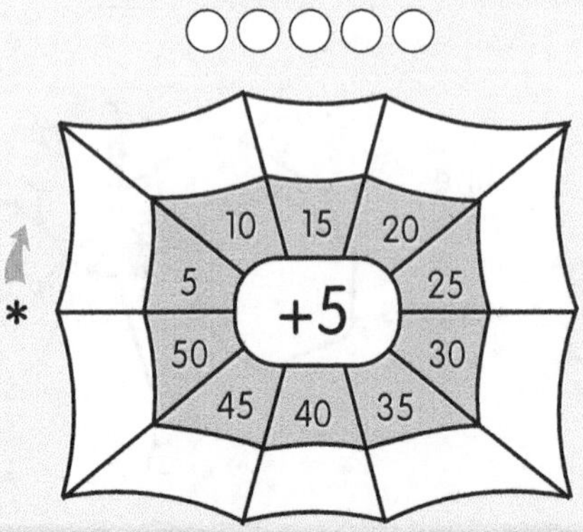

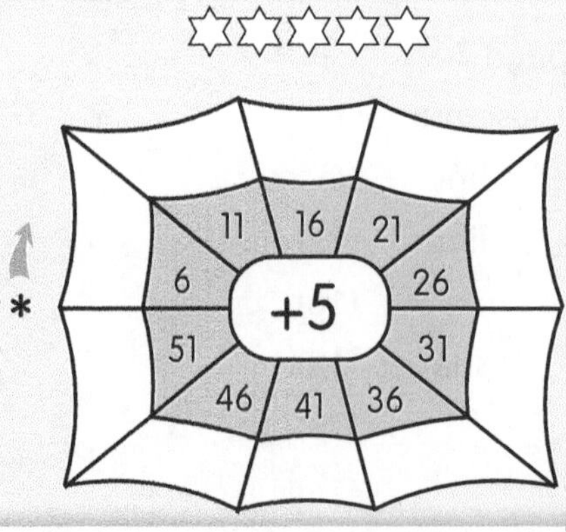

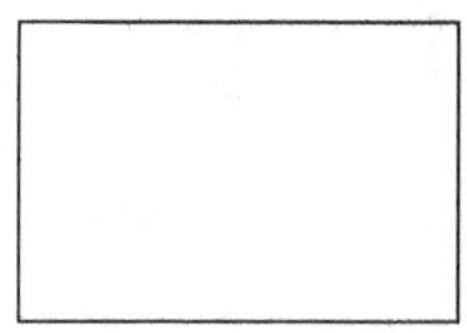

© PEARSON AUSTRALIA 2018 • *AUSTRALIAN SIGNPOST MATHS 3 MENTALS* • ISBN 978 1 4886 2183 3

16:3 ☐ out of 10

1. 37 − 4 = ____

2. 56 − 3 = ____

3. 87 − 2 = ____

4. Circle the larger fraction.

   $\frac{2}{4}$ or $\frac{3}{4}$

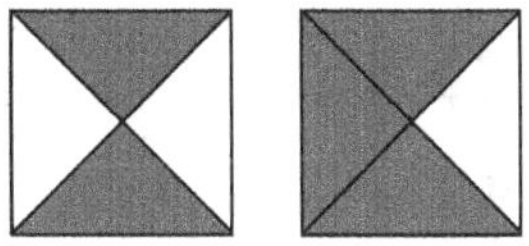

5. Is seven an odd number? ____

6. 1, 3, 5, 7, ____, ____

7. 2 × 3 = ____ 3 × 2 = ____

8. Which box shows:

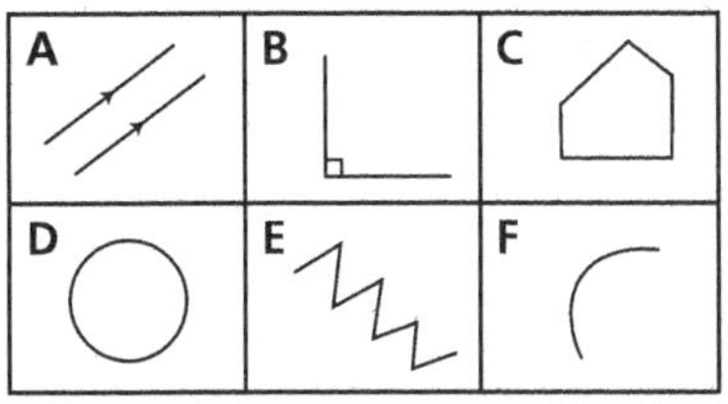

   a a zigzag line? ____

   b an irregular shape? ____

   c parallel lines? ____

   d a right angle? ____

   e a curved line? ____

9. Aziz saved his pocket money for five weeks. If he got $2 a week, how much did he save? ____

10. a 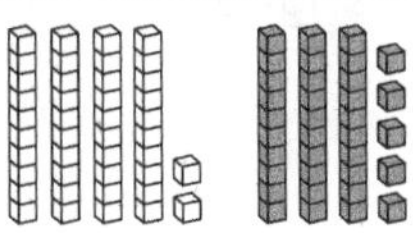

    42 + 35 = ____

    b 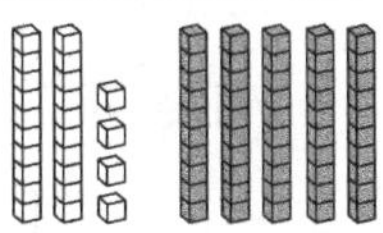

    24 + 50 = ____

16:4 Extension ☐ out of 4

1. If 2 sheets of paper cover one desk, how much paper is used to cover each group of desks?

   a 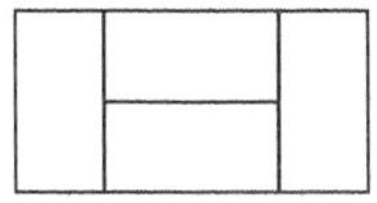 ____

   b 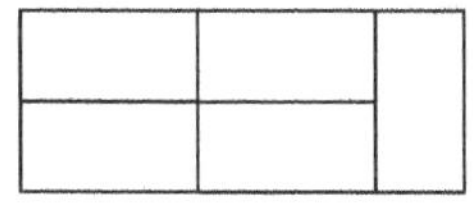 ____

2. True or false?

   a 4 × 5 = 2 × 10 ____

   b 8 × 5 = 4 × 10 ____

3. 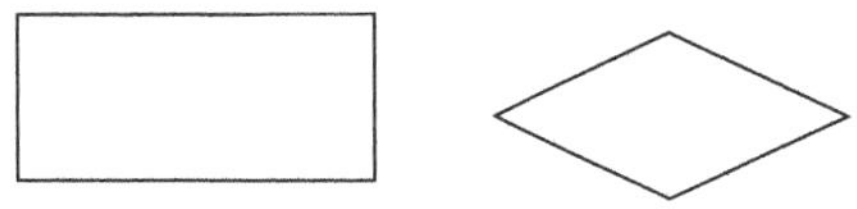

   How many sides are on 3 rectangles and 4 rhombuses? ____

4. Fourteen fish are to be put into two equal groups. How many fish in each group?

   14 ÷ 2 = ____

Challenge

84 − 29 = ☐

Explain how you found your answer.

____

____

____

____

Our Numerals **Roman Numerals**

Use these clocks to give the Roman numeral for:

a 4 ____ **b** 5 ____ **c** 9 ____

d 10 ____ **e** 11 ____ **f** 12 ____

Write our numeral for:

g IX ____ **h** XI ____ **i** VI ____

17:1 out of 13

1. 1 + 10 ______
2. 14 − 4 ______
3. 0 × 10 ______
4. 12 − 10 ______
5. $\begin{array}{r} 10 \\ +\ 8 \\ \hline \end{array}$
6. 4 + 8 ______
7. 10 × 10 ______
8. Digits in 13. ______
9. 3 × $5 ______
10. $\begin{array}{r} 14 \\ -\ 0 \\ \hline \end{array}$
11. What fraction has been coloured?

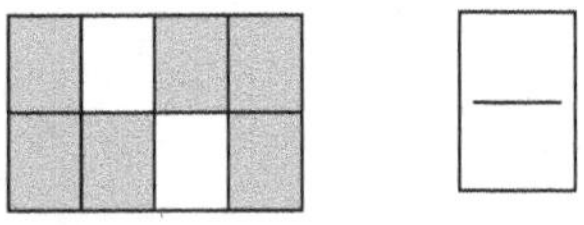

12. 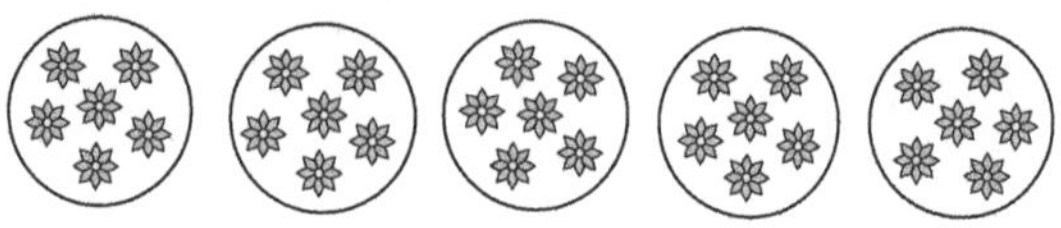

______ groups of ______ = ______

13. 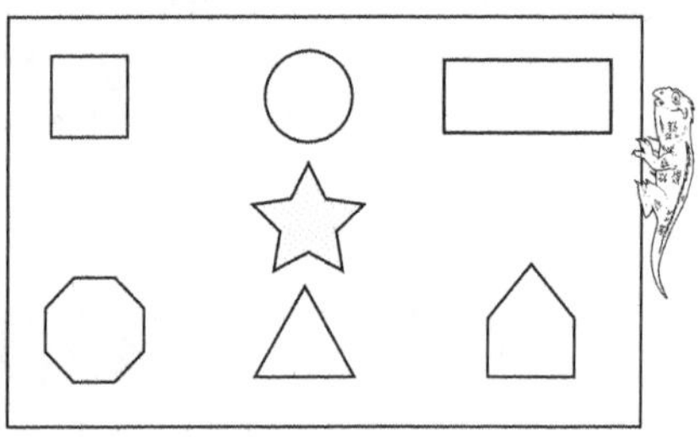

What shape is:

a in the centre? ______

b to the right of the triangle? ______

c at the top left-hand corner? ______

d under the star? ______

e above the pentagon? ______

17:2 out of 19

1. 22 + 18 ______
2. 22 + 28 ______
3. 38 − 12 ______
4. 28 − 12 ______
5. $\begin{array}{r} 2 \\ \times\ 4 \\ \hline \end{array}$
6. 3 × 10 ______
7. 32, 34, ______, 38
8. 8c + 8c + 8c ______
9. 20 minus 13. ______
10. $\begin{array}{r} 2 \\ \times\ 6 \\ \hline \end{array}$
11. 4, 6, 8, ______, ______, ______, ______
12. Which container holds about 1 litre? ______

13. Write the even numbers between 10 and 19. ______
14. How many 5c coins make 50c? ______
15. 3 × 5 = ______
15 ÷ 3 = ______
______ × 5 = 15

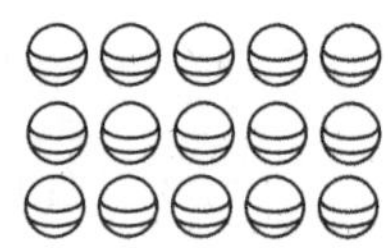

16. 3 × 1 = ______ 1 × 3 = ______
17. 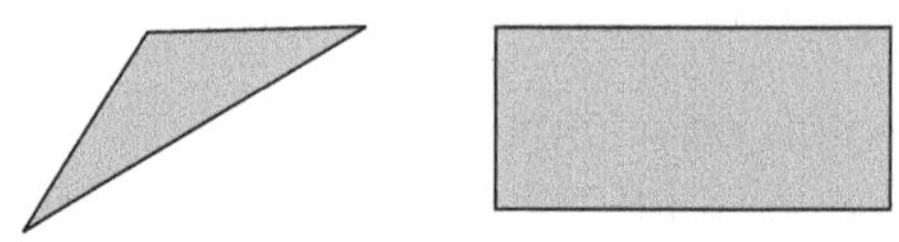

a A triangle has ______ angles.

b A rectangle has ______ angles.

18. The value of 7 in 73. ______
19. 2:30 can also be written as:

______ past ______

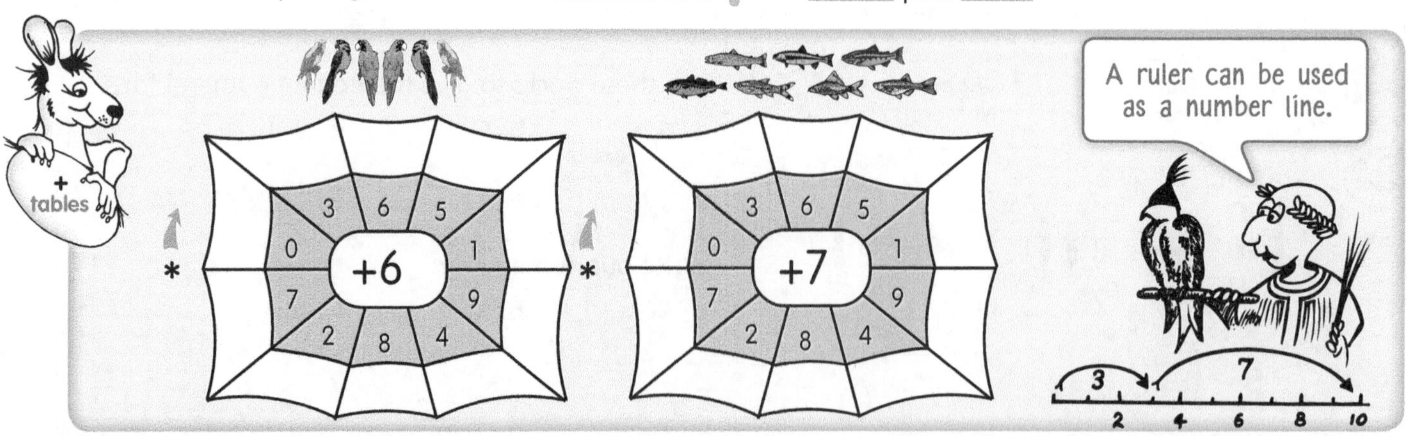

Answers

ID Card Answers

ID Card A

1 metres 2 centimetres 3 litres 4 grams 5 kilograms 6 minutes 7 counting numbers 8 even numbers 9 odd numbers 10 ordinal numbers 11 zero 12 digits 13 6 × 2 14 4 × 10 15 8 × 10 16 divide 17 divide 18 is equal to 19 number line 20 number sentence 21 numeral expander 22 abacus 23 picture graph 24 tally 25 column graph 26 table 27 digital watch 28 analogue clock 29 calendar 30 balance scales

ID Card B

1 curved line 2 angle 3 right angle 4 parallel lines 5 perpendicular lines 6 triangle 7 square 8 rectangle 9 diamond or rhombus 10 trapezium 11 parallelogram 12 pentagon 13 hexagon 14 circle 15 line of symmetry 16 regular shapes 17 irregular shapes 18 flip 19 slide 20 turn 21 corner 22 edge 23 face 24 cube 25 prism 26 pyramid 27 base 28 cylinder 29 cone 30 sphere

1:1

1 a 7 b 8 c 11 d 19 e 25 f 36 g 22 h 27 **2** 10

3 equal **4** 6, 8 **5** a 7 b number line **6** 9 **7** 2

8 9 (trucks)

1:2

1 10 **2** 10 **3** 5 **4** 3 **5** 6 **6** 3 **7** $14 **8** 13 **9** 10 **10** 5

11 8 − 4 = 4

12 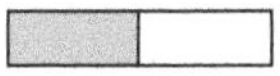 Half of the rectangle will be coloured.

13 a half past 8 (or 30 past 8) b half past 4 (or 30 past 4)

14 Four birds will be coloured.  **15** a 42 b 44

Activity

12, 20, 24, 17, 35, 55, 13, 27, 30, 41
10, 18, 22, 15, 33, 53, 11, 25, 28, 39

1:3

1 4 **2** 12 **3** 11 **4** 13 **5** 17 **6** 8 **7** 17 **8** 9 **9** nineteen

10 a 25 b 23 **11** 20 **12** 52 **13** January **14** 2nd, 3rd, 4th, 5th

15 quarters  **16** 4th **17** 48, 50

18 1 pelican will be coloured.  **19** 55c

1:4

1 6 **2** 42, 32, 22 **3** 4 **4** 30 (minutes) **5** a oval b square

Challenge

Answers will vary. Patterns could be of numbers or pictures.

Activity

Answers will vary.

2:1

1 a 44 b 38 c 59 d 53 e 32 f 24 **2** a 10 b 10 **3** 30 **4** 18

5 false **6** seven **7** no **8** 7 **9** 4

2:2

1 13 **2** 6 **3** 18 **4** 15 **5** 7 **6** 14 **7** 17 **8** $10 **9** 12

10 5c **11** a back to back b around (the tree) **12** 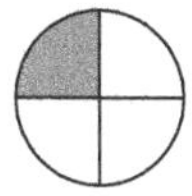

13 10 cents, 20 cents, 1 dollar **14** **A** rectangle, **B** hexagon, **C** trapezium **15** 100 dollars, 20 dollars, 5 dollars

Activity

20 cents, 50 cents, 5 cents, 10 cents, 2 dollars

2:3

1 13 **2** 16 **3** 20 **4** 17 **5** 14 **6** $15 **7** 25 **8** 18

9 seventeen **10** a 31 b 35 **11** a jug b book **12** 4

13 Answers will vary. One answer is 'I have 4 apples and John has 3.'

14 The fish will be circled.

2:4

1 a 8 b 8 **2** a 3 b 1 **3** BE KIND **4** quarter to 4 (3:45)

5 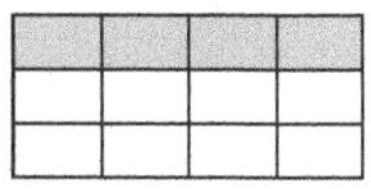 Four sections will be coloured. **6** 30

Challenge

Answers will vary. One answer is 9 + 6 = 15.

Activity

a 18 **b** 14 **c** 12 **d** 16 **e** 19 **f** 18 **g** 17 **h** 13 **i** 19 **j** 17

3:1

1 a 43 b 69 c 55 d 34 e 39 f 37 g 60 h 46

2 a 12, 15, 18, 21, 24 b 16, 20, 24, 28 c 28, 35, 42, 49

3 3rd, 4th **4** $10 **5** a 10 b 10 c 9 d 1

3:2

1 9 **2** 15 **3** 5 **4** 17 **5** 1 **6** 12 **7** 15 **8** 11 **9** 11 **10** 2

11 a 9 b 8 **12** 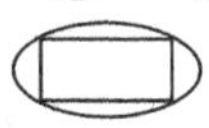 **13** 50 cents, 2 dollars, 5 cents

14 7, 15, 17 **15** 14, 14, 12

Activity

10 dollars, 50 dollars, 5 dollars, 100 dollars, 20 dollars. The notes will be coloured: blue, gold (orange or yellow), purple, green and red.

3:3

1 12 **2** 16 **3** 14 **4** a 59 b 58 **5** 3 out of 4

6 2nd, 3rd, 4th, 5th **7** fifty-two **8** 11:30 **9** $\frac{1}{2}$ **10** 7

11 $1 and $2 coins **12** a 17 b 9 c 17

3:4

❶ a 10 b 10 c 10 d 10 ❷ quarters ❸ $1.85 ❹ 85c ❺ 95c

Challenge

Answers will vary. One answer could be 20c + 20c + 10c = 50c.

Activity

66, 59, 40, 55, 73, 19, 24, 53, 76, 70
64, 57, 38, 53, 71, 17, 22, 51, 74, 68

4:1

❶ a 64 b 82 c 36 d 46 e 108 f 120 ❷ 62 ❸ a book

❹ a 11 b 15 c 17 ❺ The large pot will be circled.

❻ a 5 b 5 c 4 d 1 ❼ 12

4:2

❶ 12 ❷ 20 ❸ 24 ❹ 7 ❺ 2 ❻ 15 ❼ 9 ❽ 118

❾ 30 cm ❿ 1 ⓫ no ⓬ 8 ⓭ 12 (edges) ⓮ a 24, 30, 36, 42

b 40, 50, 60, 70 c 36, 45, 54, 63 ⓯ a Greg b Sue c 7

Activity

Sunday, Monday, Tuesday, Wednesday, Thursday, Friday, Saturday

4:3

❶ 20 ❷ 20 ❸ 19 ❹ 60, 50, 40 ❺ 653 ❻ 3 out of 8 are shaded. ❼ a 1 b 0 ❽ 19, 19 ❾ 7, 12 ❿ 8 (corners) ⓫ triangle and circle ⓬ a blue b orange c 12 d 10

4:4

❶ yes ❷ a 17 b 14 ❸ a 20 b 25 c 40 ❹ a **A** b **B** ❺ flip

Challenge

23 − 6 = 17. Explanations will vary. One answer is: 'I used the jump strategy. I subtracted 3 from 23 to get 20 then subtracted the other 3 to get 17.' (A number line could be drawn to show this.)

Activity

(Answers may vary.) **a** sometimes (S) **b** never (N) **c** never (N)
d sometimes (S) **e** always (A) **f** sometimes (S)

5:1

❶ a 85 b 120 c 111 d 121 e 49 f 46 ❷ no ❸ yes ❹ gold

❺ 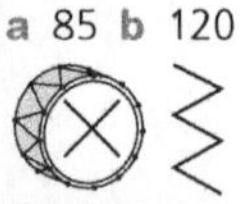 ❻ 10 ❼ 90 ❽ no ❾ 16 ❿ silver ⓫ autumn

5:2

❶ 2 ❷ 15 ❸ 0 ❹ 16 ❺ 12 ❻ 12 ❼ 28 ❽ $2 ❾ 9

❿ 18 ⓫ 391, 535, 902 ⓬ a **A** b **B** ⓭ 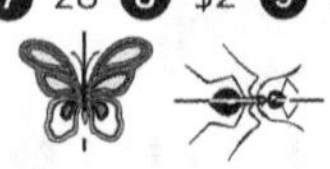

⓮ 24, 22, 20 ⓯ 36 ⓰ 5 ⓱ **A** and **D**

Activity

6, 8, 10, 12, 14
12, 16, 20, 24, 28
20, 30, 40, 50, 60, 70, 80, 90

5:3

❶ 20 ❷ 20 ❸ 20 ❹ 50c ❺ a September b 30 (days)

❻ 10 ❼ 15 ❽ cube ❾ a dog b mouse c 13 d 7

5:4

❶ 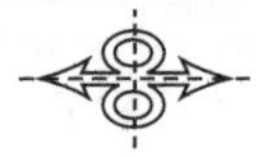 ❷ 30 ❸ 20 ❹ 32 (dots) ❺ 6 (hills)

❻ 3 ❼ 60

Challenge

Answers will vary. One answer is: 'This is a cube. It has 6 faces, 12 edges and 8 corners. A cube can stack and slide. An everyday object that is like a cube is a dice.'

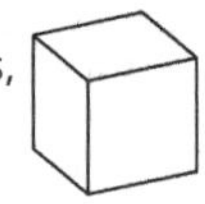

Activity

Language

(6) *triangle* (7) *square* (8) *rectangle* (9) *diamond* or *rhombus*
(13) *hexagon* (14) *circle*. A hexagon has 6 sides.

6:1

❶ 1 ❷ 5 ❸ 5 ❹ 6 ❺ 2 ❻ 8 ❼ 3 ❽ 20c ❾ 10 ❿ 5c

⓫ gold ⓬ 7 (bugs) ⓭ 12 (months) ⓮ 12, 4 and 18 will be crossed. 15 and 21 will be circled. ⓯ no ⓰ 4

⓱ a 6 b 9 ⓲ 60 ⓳ 

6:2

❶ 16 ❷ 7 ❸ 6 ❹ 18 ❺ 16 ❻ 4 ❼ 16 ❽ 60c ❾ 3

❿ 10 ⓫ Monday ⓬  ⓭ 758, 857, 875 ⓮ 359

⓯  ⓰ yes

Activity

0, 10, 16, 4, 12, 18, 8, 20, 6, 8
4, 8, 12, 16, 20
4, 8, 12, 16, 20

6:3

❶ 13 ❷ 11 ❸ 13 ❹ 4 (ninths) ❺ 10 ❻ quarter past 12

❼ December ❽ **C** ❾ a 3:00 b 11:00 ❿ 60 ⓫ 80 ⓬ forty

⓭ a 1 b 2 ⓮ 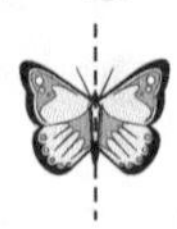

6:4

❶ a 23 b 15 ❷ | 9 | tens | 2 | ones | ❸ 30 (minutes)

❹ 52 (weeks) ❺ 6, 3 ❻ SMILE AT ME ❼ a 80 b 80

Challenge

Answers will vary. The capital letter A or an addition sign are two examples.

Activity

a C b B

7:1

1 10 **2** 5 **3** 1 **4** 8 **5** 2 **6** 8 **7** 10c **8** 50 ones **9** 6
10 6 **11** 18 **12** 9531 **13** a chair **14** **a** December, January and February **b** March, April and May
15 14 **16**

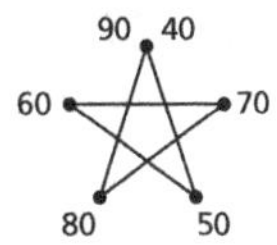

17 67 6 tens 7 ones

7:2

1 14 **2** 13 **3** 14 **4** 15 **5** 13 **6** 12 **7** 3 **8** 16
9 70 (ones) **10** 19 **11**  **12** 12 **13** 3
14 7:00 or 7 o'clock **15** three hundred and seventy-four **16** 21, 20
17 398, 541, 649 **18** 30 **19** 21st, 22nd

Activity

a 2 rows of 7 **b** 3 rows of 10 **c** 3 groups of 6

7:3

1 25 **2** 21 **3** 28 **4** 234 2 hundreds 3 tens 4 ones
5 two hundred and thirty-four **6** 119, 121, 123, 125 **7** 
8 **a** 6:00 **b** 10:00 **9** none **10** 50c coin **11** **B** and **C**

7:4

1 **a** 51 **b** 62 **2** 30 **3** 86 **4** 78 **5** 
6 three hundred and forty-two **7** 1, 2 and 4 **8** 61 **9** 8 (weeks)

Challenge

Answers will vary.

Activity

9, 12, 15, 18, 21
18, 24, 30, 36, 42
16, 24, 32, 40, 48, 56, 64, 72

8:1

1 11 **2** 5 **3** 11 **4** 7 **5** 3 **6** 9 **7** 8 **8** 15c **9** 6 **10** 8
11 8 tens and 4 ones **12** 76, 129, 212, 236, 318 **13** 1357
14 forty-four **15** 7 **16** **a** 8, 10, 12 **b** 12, 15, 18 **c** 20, 25, 30
17  **18** 18, 20

8:2

1 18 **2** 3 **3** 14 **4** 9 **5** 17 **6** 14 **7** 19 **8** 18 **9** 15
10 16 **11** 3 **12** twelve **13** **a** 13 − 5 = 8, 23 − 5 = 18, 33 − 5 = 28
b 16 − 7 = 9, 26 − 7 = 19, 36 − 7 = 29 **14** yes **15** 397 **16** **a** June
b 12 (months) **17** 738, 740 **18** 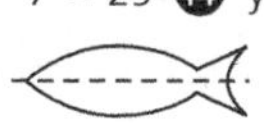 **19** 30, 35, 40 **20** 973

Activity

18, 29, 24, 17, 13, 38, 47, 62, 23, 21
21, 25, 44, 15, 37, 42, 50, 53, 28, 39

8:3

1 30 **2** 19 **3** 21 **4** A **5** 5 hundreds 5 tens 0 ones
6 September, October and November **7** 70 **8** 846
9 **a** Leah **b** Anna **c** 7 **d** 26 (lollipops)

8:4

1 3 **2** 50 **3** 8
4 3 or 5 (assuming the lines are extended until they cross)
5 60 (minutes) **6** 8th **7** 14 (days) **8** 
9 53 tens and 1 one

Challenge

5 + 6 = 11, 6 + 5 = 11, 11 − 5 = 6 and 11 − 6 = 5

Activity

	29	50	64	37	82	48	73	96	101	129
−10	19	40	54	27	72	38	63	86	91	119
−9	20	41	55	28	73	39	64	87	92	120

	31	78	80	65	52	66	27	94	113	139
−9	22	69	71	56	43	57	18	85	104	130

9:1

1 4 **2** 8 **3** 10 **4** 2 **5** 3 **6** 10 m **7** 9 **8** 5 **9** 8 **10** 8
11 16 **12**  **13** **C** will be circled.
14 7 hundreds 2 tens 5 ones
15 11, 13, 15, 17, 19 **16** fifty **17** March, April, May **18** 1 month
19 5 groups of 5 = 25

9:2

1 19 **2** 16 **3** 0 **4** 30 **5** 4 **6** 16 **7** 90 ones **8** 70 **9** 16
10 8 **11** 25, 30 **12** 2 groups of 3 **13** **a** 6:08 **b** 7:15 **14** 502, 512
15 1000 **16** **a** **D** **b** **B** **17** nine hundred and three **18** 100 (centimetres)

Activity

10, 20, 30, 40, 50, 60, 70, 80, 90, 100

9:3

1 12 **2** 14 **3** 16 **4** 24, 28 **5** 50 **6** **a** 15 − 6 = 9
b 15 − 9 = 6 **7** 476 **8** **a** **A** **b** **C** **9** yes **10** 70 **11** yes
12 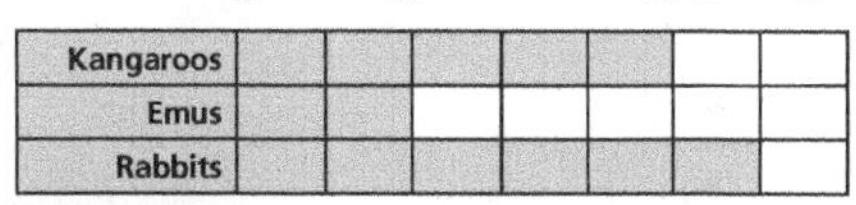

9:4

1 seven hundred and fifty-three **2** yes **3** yes **4** April **5** yes
6 $2.20 **7** The $2 and 20 cent coins will be coloured. **8** $7.50
9 50 **10** 1 century

Challenge

4 + 9 = 13, 9 + 4 = 13, 13 − 9 = 4, 13 − 4 = 9

Activity

5, 10, 15, 20, 25, 30, 35, 40, 45, 50

	2	4	6	8	10
× 5	10	20	30	40	50

	1	2	3	4	5
× 10	10	20	30	40	50

10:1

1 7 **2** 3 **3** 3 **4** 6 **5** 4 **6** 3rd, 4th **7** 8 **8** 40c **9** 3

10 9 **11** yes **12** The even numbers 12, 14, 16 and 18 will be coloured red. The odd numbers 11, 13, 15, 17 and 19 will be coloured blue.

13 80, 79 **14** 99 **15** 30 minutes past 2 **16** 60 (minutes) **17** no

18 yes **19** 6 (blocks) **20** 12 (months)

21 five hundred and thirteen **22** m

10:2

1 17 **2** 9 **3** 0 **4** 6 **5** 20 **6** $12 **7** 100 **8** 1 100 **9** 27

10 10 **11** a one twenty-seven b 27 minutes past 1 **12** 410, 412

13 16 **14** a curved line b broken line

15 Two parallel lines will be drawn.  **16** 905

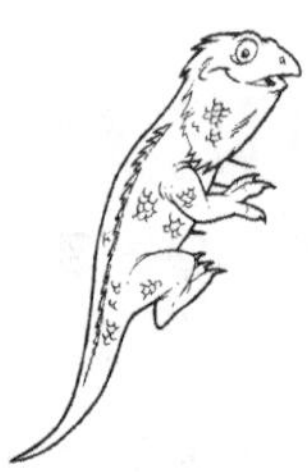

17 seven hundred and forty-nine

Activity

30, 0, 25, 40, 10, 35, 20, 50, 15, 45
0, 0, 0, 0, 0, 0, 0, 0, 0, 0

10:3

1 17 **2** 15 **3** 19 **4** 650, 655 **5** yes **6** 9 metres **7** 61

8 The dots will be joined to make a pentagon. This is a regular pentagon.

9 518 **10** eight hundred and thirty-nine **11** 18 **12** 50 **13** June, July, August **14** 

10:4

1 129, 149 **2** 8 + 8 **3** $1.30 **4** a 0 b 7 **5** 3

6 Estimates will vary. The stars will be grouped into 5 groups of 10 with 2 left over. Number = 52

Challenge

77. One explanation could be: 'I used the split strategy. I added the tens first. 4 and 3 makes 7. Then I added the ones. 2 and 5 makes 7. 7 tens and 7 ones makes 77.'

Activity

(15) *line of symmetry* (16) *regular* shapes (17) *irregular* shapes
(21) *corner* of a cube (22) *edge* (23) *face* (28) *cylinder* (29) *cone*

	Faces	Edges	Corners
Number	6	12	8

11:1

1 11 **2** 10 **3** 10 **4** 14 **5** 20 **6** 8 **7** 4 **8** 6 **9** 2 **10** 10

11 46 **12** 8 (sides) **13** 2 tens 8 ones **14** eighteen

15 5, 17, 26, 30 **16** half past 9 (or nine thirty) **17** 80c

18 12 (months) **19** curved **20** yes **21** yes **22** 18, 20

11:2

1 19 **2** 11 **3** 50 **4** 6 **5** 80 **6** 6 **7** 8 **8** 24 **9** 21

10 10 **11** a ten seventeen b seventeen past ten **12** no **13** 731

14 28 **15** a > b < **16** yes **17** 692

Activity

5, 10, 12, 9, 11, 7, 4, 6, 3, 8
12, 8, 7, 9, 6, 8, 13, 11, 10, 5

11:3

1 41 **2** 34 **3** 51 **4** a six forty-two b 42 minutes past 6 **5** 62

6 The dots will be joined to make a hexagon. This is a regular hexagon.

7 three hundred and forty **8** C **9** impossible **10** Answers will vary.

11:4

1 a T b F **2** a 6 b 3 **3** star **4** 4 **5** a 3 b 7 **6** 70

Challenge

46. One explanation could be: 'I used the jump strategy. I added 1 to 39 to make 40, then I added 6 to 40 to make 46.'

Activity

a 6 **b** 4 **c** 6 **d** 9

12:1

1 10 **2** 15 **3** 6 **4** 4 **5** 10 **6** 11 **7** 0 **8** 30c **9** 7

10 18 **11** 92 **12** 12 (months) **13** silver **14** 20 **15** 40 **16** 44 and 46 **17** a forty b fourteen **18**  **19** 2 rows of 5 = 10

12:2

1 25 **2** 33 **3** 15 **4** 28 **5** 20 **6** 16 **7** 10 **8** 8 **9** 45

10 50 **11** twenty-seven **12** 38 **13** a 709 b 970 **14** 807

15 5 out of 10 **16** a C b A **17** 24

Activity

3, 6, 9, 12, 15, 18, 21, 24, 27, 30

12:3

1 700 **2** 900 **3** 900 **4** 320 **5** 

6 one hundred and twenty-eight **7** a < b < **8** D **9** no

10 yes **11** 21 cm **12** 9

12:4

1 4 halves **2** a triangle b rectangle

3  2 out of 8

4 382 **5** 36 **6** 51 tens 8 ones

Challenge

800. One explanation could be: 'I used patterns to find the answer. I know that 2 + 6 = 8, so 200 + 600 = 800.'

Activity
4, 7, 1, 3, 6, 2, 5, 0
5, 8, 2, 4, 7, 3, 6, 1

13:1

1 12 **2** 14 **3** 2 **4** 8 **5** 19 **6** 8 **7** 10 **8** 8 **9** 5
10 12 **11** 6 **12** 1 out of 2 equal parts **13** 55 **14** The oval will be coloured. **15** 2 rows of 5 **16** **A** is 4 cm **B** is 3 cm **C** is 5 cm
17 5 groups of 3

13:2

1 33 **2** 25 **3** 14 **4** 12 **5** 8 **6** 73 **7** 20 **8** 10 **9** 26
10 10 **11** a 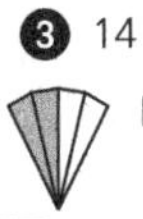 b 2 **12** 10 **13** ninety **14** 10 (fingers) **15** May
16 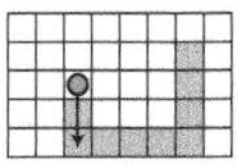 **17** four hundred and sixty-three
18  **19** $14

Activity
7, 11, 2, 5, 10, 8, 6, 4, 9, 3
8, 12, 3, 6, 11, 9, 7, 5, 10, 4

13:3

1 33 **2** 47 **3** 5 cm **4** 1300 **5** 15 (fingers) **6** 25 **7** $\frac{1}{2}$
8 2103 **9** three thousand and seventy-two **10** 742 **11** a > b <
12 a 39 b 47

13:4

1 50 **2** 0 **3** 18 **4** a 6 b 3 **5** 32 (cakes) **6** 50c coin
7 24 **8** 4 (digits)

Challenge
36. Answers will vary.

Activity
24, 3, 15, 18, 6, 27, 21, 9, 30, 12

14:1

1 4 **2** 0 **3** 12 **4** 30 **5** 13 **6** 8 **7** 18 **8** 7 **9** 13 **10** 19
11 6 tens 3 ones **12** 4 out of 6 **13** unlikely **14** a car **15** 3
16 1354 **17** The shape on the left will be coloured.

14:2

1 30 **2** 26 **3** 20 **4** 50 **5** 20 **6** 34 **7** 29 **8** 25 **9** $15
10 15 **11** 28 cm **12** 30 (cookies) **13** 1348 **14** 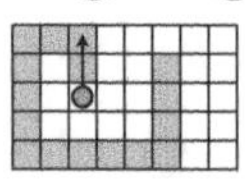
15 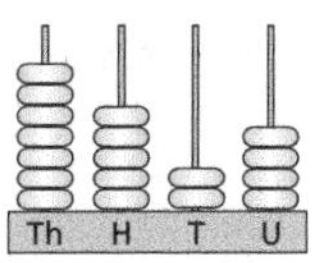

16 3629 **17** 2000 + 10

Activity
a 5 is most likely. **b** Answers will vary.

14:3

1 94 **2** $77 **3** A smaller shape will be drawn. **4** 20
5 40 **6** 36, 40, 44, 48 **7** a yes b 4 **8** one half
9 18 (trees) **10** 6031 **11** a 38 b 45

14:4

1 3 **2** one quarter of a metre **3** C **4** 20 **5** a true b false
6 nine, nineteen, ninety

Challenge
Answers will vary.

Activity
a 35 + 37 = 72 **b** 54 + 28 = 82 **c** 60 + 40 = 100

15:1

1 16 **2** 11 **3** 30 **4** 80 **5** 12 **6** 10 **7** 5 **8** 8 **9** 14
10 17 **11** 3 out of 7 **12** 796 **13** unlikely **14** **D** **15** 66, 77
16 square and circle

15:2

1 89 **2** 30 **3** 80 **4** 70 **5** 20 **6** 90 **7** 100 **8** 4 **9** $21
10 15 **11** a **C** b **A** **12** a 2 b 3 **13** 20 **14** 4093

Activity
0, 3, 5, 7, 10, 8, 2, 6, 4, 9
0, 30, 50, 70, 100, 80, 20, 60, 40, 90

15:3

1 $97 **2** $84 **3** a 3 out of 4 b 1 **4** 5:30 **5** a 6 b 6
6 9 tens + 4 ones **7** 80c **8** 4 **9** 5 **10** a 55 b 85

15:4

1 a circle **2** 40 **3** 25 (sides) **4** 5 **5** **A**

Challenge
Answers will vary. Some answers could be: 'There is an even chance that it will land on A. You are just as likely to spin an A as a B. There are 4 chances out of 8 that an A will be spun.'

Activity
(1) *curved* line (4) *parallel* lines (5) *perpendicular* lines (12) *pentagon* (13) *hexagon* (16) *regular* shapes (17) *irregular* shapes (18) *flip* (19) *slide* (20) *turn*

16:1

1 10 **2** 10 **3** 17 **4** 3 **5** 20 **6** 50 **7** 16 **8** 4 **9** 13
10 8 **11** cricket ball **12** 70 **13** $2 coin **14** a $1 and $2 coins b 5c, 10c, 20c, 50c **15** a hexagon b rhombus
16 4 rows of 6 = 24, 4 × 6 = 24 **17** **B**

16:2

1 38 **2** 23 **3** 4 **4** 45 **5** 60 **6** 9 **7** $60 **8** 30 **9** 18
10 30 **11** 20, 25 **12** a 4 b 4 **13** 15, 15 **14** 3 squares will be coloured. **15** 6, 3, 2 **16** a 12 (plates) b 18 (plates) **17** 6 (blocks)

Activity

10, 15, 20, 25, 30, 35, 40, 45, 50, 55
11, 16, 21, 26, 31, 36, 41, 46, 51, 56

16:3

1 33 **2** 53 **3** 85 **4** $\frac{3}{4}$ will be circled. **5** yes **6** 9, 11 **7** 6, 6
8 a E b C c A d B e F **9** $10 **10** a 77 b 74

16:4

1 a 8 b 10 **2** a true b true **3** 28 (sides) **4** 7, 7

Challenge

55. One explanation could be: 'I used the jump strategy. I subtracted 20 from 84 to make 64. Then I subtracted 4 to make 60. Then I subtracted 5 to make 55.'

Activity

a IV **b** V **c** IX **d** X **e** XI **f** XII **g** 9 **h** 11 **i** 6

17:1

1 11 **2** 10 **3** 0 **4** 2 **5** 18 **6** 12 **7** 100 **8** 2 **9** $15
10 14 **11** $\frac{6}{8}$ **12** 5 groups of 6 = 30
13 a star b pentagon c square d triangle e rectangle

17:2

1 40 **2** 50 **3** 26 **4** 16 **5** 8 **6** 30 **7** 36 **8** 24c **9** 7
10 12 **11** 10, 12, 14, 16 **12** B **13** 12, 14, 16, 18 **14** 10 **15** 15, 5, 3 **16** 3, 3 **17** a 3 b 4 **18** 70 **19** half past 2 (or thirty past 2)

Activity

6, 9, 12, 11, 7, 15, 10, 14, 8, 13
7, 10, 13, 12, 8, 16, 11, 15, 9, 14

17:3

1 33 **2** 51 **3** 77 **4** $\frac{5}{8}$ will be circled. **5** 15 **6** 3 **7** 30, 30
8 a rhombus b hexagon c 3 d 7

17:4

1 yes **2** a 60 b 30 **3** a 7 b 33 **4** 16, 32, 64
5 a 30 b 150c or $1.50 **6** 85c

Challenge

Answers will vary. Containers could include a large tin of paint, a 5 L ice-cream container, a bath, a large jug, a kitchen sink or a bucket.

Activity

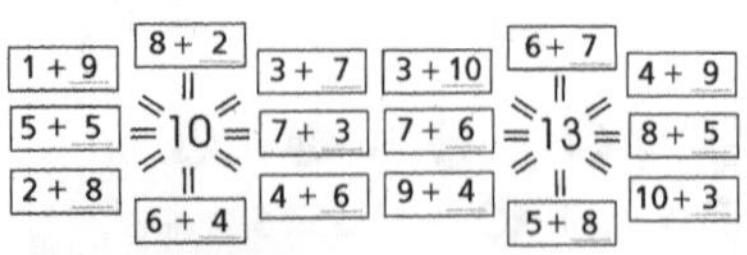

18:1

1 12 **2** 12 **3** 9 **4** 4 **5** 10 **6** 20 **7** 10 **8** 8 **9** 8 **10** 18
11 25, 30, 35, 40 **12** 60c **13** a 1 litre bottle **14** kg **15** 80c
16 a C b A **17** an eggcup **18** 9 (blocks)

18:2

1 88 **2** 13 **3** 36 **4** 90 **5** 15 **6** 46 **7** 27c **8** 24 **9** 66
10 30 **11** $\frac{3}{8}$ **12** 18, 20, 22 **13** 18 (blocks) **14** 64 **15** 15
16 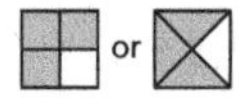 **17** 21, 24 **18** a less b more

Activity

a no **b** even chance or 2 out of 4
c less (unless the new prize added is a pen)

18:3

1 38 **2** 48 **3** 68 **4** winter **5** 70, 80, 90 **6** 50c coin
7 10 **8** 14 **9** 27 **10** 64 **11** 3 out of 4 **12** $3.70 **13** 66, 77
14 equal to

18:4

1 B **2** $1\frac{1}{4}$ **3** 24 (bolts) **4** 7, 8 and 9 **5** 11

Challenge

Answers will vary. Containers may include a cup, a bowl, a spoon, an eggcup, a can of soup, a bottle of perfume or a small drink bottle.

Activity

12, 11, 10, 9, 8, 7, 6, 5, 4, 3
13, 12, 11, 10, 9, 8, 7, 6, 5, 4

19:1

1 10 **2** 8 **3** 11 **4** 14 **5** 19 **6** 5 **7** 16 **8** 3 **9** 12
10 14 **11** 10c coin **12** no **13** fourteen, forty, forty-four **14** no
15 8 (blocks) **16** yes **17** 4th **18** A **19** half past twelve (30 past 12)

19:2

1 26 **2** 37 **3** 13 **4** 27 **5** 50 **6** 18 **7** 19 **8** 83 **9** 12
10 30 **11** Estimates will vary, 14 **12** + **13** C, A, B **14** 20c coin
15 a 7, 9, 11 b 16, 18, 20 c 33, 22, 11 **16** 6296

Activity

Answers will vary. **a** unlikely **b** certain **c** unlikely (or perhaps likely)
d impossible **e** fifty/fifty

19:3

1 44 **2** $3 **3** 26, 29, 32 **4** yes **5** The angles will be copied.

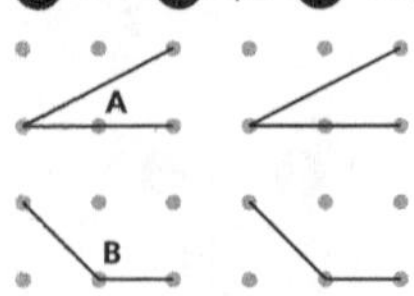

6 1537 **7** 20 − 14 = 6 so 14 + 6 = 20. The difference is 6.
8 A, C, B, D **9** B **10** 3

19:4

1 a 60c b 280c or $2.80 **2** 61 (days) **3** 3 (pairs) **4** 28 (wings)
5 30 **6** 36 (eggs) **7** 73

 ISBN 978 1 4886 2183 3

Challenge

Answers will vary. They could include a mouse, a CD, a pair of shoes, a hat.

Activity

14, 17, 11, 19, 12, 15, 18, 20, 10, 16
30, 60, 41, 54, 62, 85, 44, 67, 73, 96

20:1

❶ 11 ❷ 50 ❸ 8 ❹ 10 ❺ 15 ❻ 11 ❼ 7 ❽ 10 ❾ $8
❿ 17 ⓫ 5c, 10c, 20c and 50c ⓬ C ⓭ 4 (digits) ⓮ 16 kg
⓯ parallel ⓰ 7 ⓱ Mary

20:2

❶ 26 ❷ 34 ❸ 12 ❹ 100 ❺ 30 ❻ 5 ❼ 8 ❽ 39 ❾ 21
❿ 6 ⓫ 2 859 ⓬ seventy ⓭ 5 tens and 8 ones ⓮ 310, 372, 390
⓯ 6 000 ⓰ 7 148 ⓱ a 7 483 b 8 (tens) ⓲ 6 ⓳ 81

Activity

a 7 **b** Answers will vary.

20:3

❶ 77 ❷ 31 ❸ 23 − 17 = 6 so 17 + 6 = 23. The difference is 6.
❹ a 6, 6 b 3, 3 ❺ 0 ❻ 5 310 ❼ true ❽ 5 kg
❾ 1 place-value ten ❿ The angle will be copied.

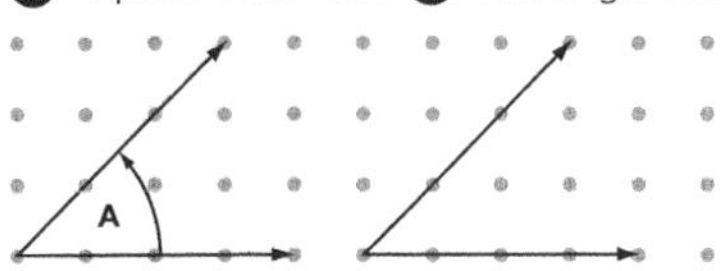

20:4

❶ a $3 b 85c ❷ a false b true ❸ a 5 balls b 4 balls
❹ a 30c b $1.05

Challenge

Answers will vary.

Activity

(7) *counting* numbers (8) *even* numbers (9) *odd* numbers
(10) *ordinal* numbers (18) is *equal* to (27) *digital* watch
(28) *analogue* clock (29) *calendar*

21:1

❶ 18 ❷ 7 ❸ 12 ❹ 9 ❺ 11 ❻ 9 ❼ 70 ❽ $14 ❾ 11 ❿ 9
⓫ 1 ⓬ 87 ⓭ 3 (digits) ⓮ hexagon and square ⓯ 1:40, forty past 1 or 20 to 2 ⓰ a carnations b tulips c 4 (daffodils) d 4 e 15

21:2

❶ 80 ❷ 35 ❸ 24 ❹ 16 ❺ 9 ❻ 81 ❼ 45 ❽ 2 (digits)
❾ 27 ❿ 10 ⓫ 6 309 ⓬ 470, 451, 439 ⓭ a 6, 6 b 4, 4
⓮ regular ⓯ 400 ⓰ 9 ⓱ 2 810

Activity

8, 4, 10, 6, 9, 5, 7, 11, 3, 1
9, 5, 14, 7, 10, 6, 8, 12, 4, 2

21:3

❶ $32 ❷ 88 ❸ a F b B and D ❹ 300 ❺ 30 (minutes)
❻ a 10:50 b 10:25 ❼ 7 (pairs) ❽ a 2, 4, 6, 8 or 0
b 1, 3, 5, 7 or 9 ❾ February ❿ 179, 181, 182 ⓫

21:4

❶ a 11 b 7 ❷ a 6 b 12 ❸ a false b true ❹ a 1, 9 and 7
b 3, 9 and 7

Challenge

Answers will vary. Answers could include 3, 6 and 9 stars.

Activity

a 60 (minutes) **b** 30 (minutes) **c** 15 (minutes) **d** 45 (minutes)
e 50 (minutes) **f** 10 (minutes)

22:1

❶ 11 ❷ 15 ❸ 9 ❹ 19 ❺ 10 ❻ 7 ❼ 0 ❽ 16 ❾ 3 ❿ 19
⓫ 2 ⓬ C ⓭ $3.00 ⓮

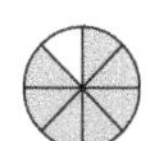

⓯ 12:41 ⓰ m ⓱ 60 (minutes)
⓲ no (Answers may vary.) ⓳ right angle ⓴ Thursday

22:2

❶ 52 ❷ 9 ❸ 9 ❹ 20 ❺ 0 ❻ 12 ❼ 50 ❽ 83 ❾ 21
❿ 12 ⓫ 500 ⓬ 10c ⓭

⓮ a Jill b Kira c 7 d 5 e 27 (baskets)

Activity

13, 8, 16, 12, 14, 9, 17, 15, 11, 18
14, 9, 17, 13, 15, 10, 18, 16, 12,19

22:3

❶ $60 ❷ $89 ❸ November and December ❹ 200 ❺ 12
❻ 15c ❼ 36 past 4 ❽

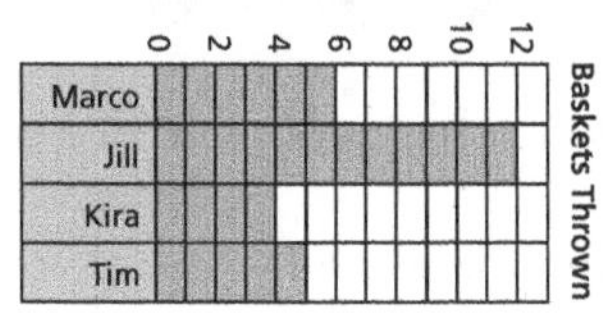

❾ parallelogram ❿ 8 m 31 cm

22:4

❶ C ❷ a 120c or $1.20 b 300c or $3 ❸ a $\frac{1}{4}$ b $\frac{1}{2}$ ❹ $110

Challenge

Answers will vary. Some answers could include:

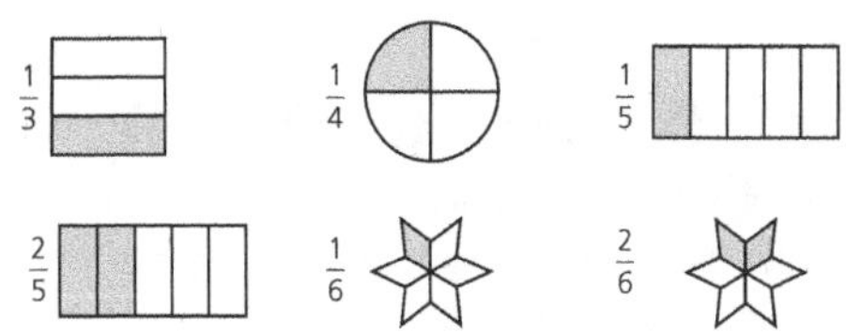

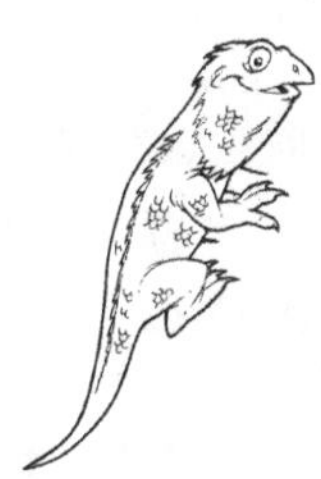

Activity

+	5	10	4	0	2	6	1	3
2	7	12	6	2	4	8	3	5
3	8	13	7	3	5	9	4	6
4	9	14	8	4	6	10	5	7
5	10	15	9	5	7	11	6	8
10	15	20	14	10	12	16	11	13

23:1

❶ 20 ❷ 8 ❸ 16 ❹ 4 ❺ 29 ❻ 10 ❼ 11 ❽ 8 ❾ 15 m
❿ 0 ⓫ 3 ⓬ a ten twenty-five b 25 minutes past 10 ⓭ no
⓮ $\frac{4}{8}$ or $\frac{1}{2}$ ⓯ yes ⓰ angle ⓱ 9 ⓲ a **A** b **C**

23:2

❶ 70 ❷ 40 ❸ 20 ❹ 18 ❺ 50 ❻ 4 ❼ 28 ❽ 90 ❾ 50
❿ 10 ⓫ 5 ⓬ 25c ⓭ true ⓮ $140 ⓯ 1 m 65 cm
⓰ yes (Some doors vary in width but the average door in a house will be about 1 m.) ⓱ 4 counters will be circled. ⓲ 3 m 92 cm
⓳ Thursday ⓴ 590, 600, 610 ㉑ no

Activity

5, 10, 15, 20, 25, 30, 35, 40, 45, 50

	2	4	6	8	10
× 5	10	20	30	40	50

	2	4	6	8	10
× 10	20	40	60	80	100

23:3

❶ 89 ❷ 99 ❸ 372 cm ❹ a car b bicycle c 4 d 16 e 48
❺ a 10:35 b 35 past 10 or 25 to 11
❻ a 30c b 65c ❼ a 50c b $1.65

23:4

❶ 99 cm ❷ a 9 b 90c ❸ $2.85
❹ a 5 squares will be coloured red. 1 square will be coloured blue. b 6 sixths ❺ 60 ❻ half ❼ $120

Challenge

Answers will vary. Angles larger than 90 degrees will be drawn.

Activity

a 14 cm **b** 12 cm **c** 22 cm

24:1

❶ 6 ❷ 16 ❸ 13 ❹ 10 ❺ 11 ❻ 8 ❼ 14 ❽ 3 (digits) ❾ 14
❿ 16 ⓫ 2 ⓬ 1 fish will be coloured. ⓭ 19, 21 ⓮ 9531
⓯ 483 ⓰ angle ⓱ June, July and August ⓲ metres ⓳ a seven thirteen b 13 minutes past 7 ⓴ +

24:2

❶ 61 ❷ 31 ❸ 0 ❹ 15 ❺ 50 ❻ 586 ❼ 4 ❽ 645 ❾ 1000
❿ 30 ⓫ 75c ⓬ $180 ⓭ 4 counters will be circled. ⓮ a nine fifty-two b 52 minutes past 9 or 8 minutes to 10 ⓯ yes ⓰ May
⓱ 22nd, 23rd ⓲ 1 2 5 tens 6 ones ⓳ 521 cm

Activity

2, 6, 10, 4, 9, 1, 7, 5, 3, 8
13, 57, 42, 18, 56, 21, 39, 25, 44, 30

24:3

❶ 63 ❷ 22 ❸ 5 m 2 cm ❹ true ❺ 10 ❻ a 21 (days) b 28 (days) ❼ 24, 30, 36 ❽ a 5 b Tuesday c Sunday ❾ 2000
❿

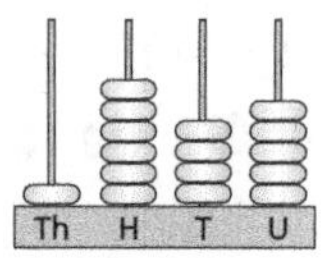

24:4

❶ a yes b yes c yes ❷ $2 ❸ 10 rectangles will be coloured.
❹ 3200 ❺ a Thursday b Tuesday ❻ 40 ❼ 60

Challenge

Answers will vary. One answer could be a square with sides of 2 cm.

Activity

a 300 **b** 700 **c** 300 **d** 800 **e** 800 **f** 500 **g** 100

25:1

❶ 6 ❷ 6 ❸ 4 ❹ 13 ❺ 17 ❻ 18 ❼ 20, 25 ❽ 7 ❾ 40, 45
❿ 13 ⓫ 7205 ⓬ 4 (digits) ⓭ 44, 48, 52, 56, 60 ⓮ 49, 54, 59, 64, 69 ⓯ 70 ⓰ 10, 5 ⓱ 52 (weeks) ⓲ July ⓳ 72 (hours)
⓴ C ㉑ yes

25:2

❶ 62 ❷ 68 ❸ 0 ❹ 18 ❺ 40 ❻ 12, 15 ❼ 30 ❽ 15 ❾ 24, 30 ❿ 10 ⓫ 2 counters will be circled. ⓬ 9000 ⓭ 24 cm
⓮ yes ⓯ false ⓰ true ⓱ a 4:35 b 35 minutes past 4

Activity

84, 61, 48, 46, 42, 59, 75, 43, 57, 40
82, 59, 36, 64, 50, 57, 83, 61, 65, 48

25:3

❶ 23 ❷ 30 ❸ 24 ❹ 9 ❺ seven thousand and twenty-eight
❻

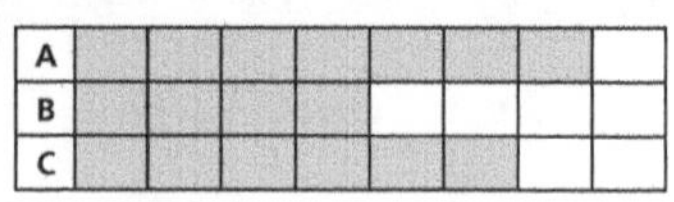

❼ a October b 5 (Tuesdays) c Friday d 31 (days)
e 7th October f 27th October

25:4

❶ 2 bells are coloured red. 4 bells are coloured blue. $\frac{6}{8}$ or $\frac{3}{4}$
❷ a $\frac{1}{5}$ b $\frac{1}{20}$ ❸ a 9:15 b 1:15 ❹ a 70 b 90

Challenge

Answers will vary. Any number from 3500 to 4499 could be written.

Activity

(6) *triangle* (7) *square* (8) *rectangle* (9) *diamond* or *rhombus*
(10) *trapezium* (11) *parallelogram* (12) *pentagon* (13) *hexagon*

26:1

1 10 **2** 16 **3** 25 **4** 5 **5** 24 **6** 3 **7** 13 **8** 13 **9** 8, 10
10 14 **11** a 12 b 3 **12** a 35 mm b 16 mm c 43 mm
13 a 50 mm b 3 c 13 (creatures) **14** 24, 28, 32
15 4 (seasons) **16** 60 (minutes) **17** November

26:2

1 64 **2** 91 **3** 10 **4** 45 **5** 40 **6** 20, 22 **7** 82, 92 **8** 52
9 11 **10** 0 **11** <u>5</u> × 5 = 25 so 25 ÷ 5 = <u>5</u> **12** 46 mm
13 a 4:02, 2 past 4 b 10:36, 36 past 10 **14** 30, 5
15 June **16** 31 (days) **17** , 9

Activity

13, 7, 10, 14, 8, 5, 12, 15, 6, 9
14, 8, 11, 15, 9, 6, 13, 16, 7, 10

26:3

1 43 **2** 62 **3** 35c **4** 25, 29, 33, 37, 41 **5** The numbers 412, 392, 351 and 406 will be circled. **6** 3 (digits) **7** July **8** May
9 13, 15, 21 **10** Add 2. **11** 6 cm **12** <u>3</u> × 5 = 15 so 15 ÷ 5 = <u>3</u>
13 a 46 b 48

26:4

1 $2\frac{1}{2}$ **2** 35 **3** a 10:00 b 12:13 **4** a 4 (books) b 3 (books)
2 sheets of paper will not be used. **5** a $1.85 b 55c

Challenge

Answers will vary. One answer could be:
a 0, 2, 4, 6, 8, 10, … **b** 20, 17, 14, 11, 8, 5, …
c 1, 2, 4, 8, 16, 32, … **d** 0, 8, 16, 24, 32, 40, …
e 10, 20, 30, 40, 50, 60, 70, 80, …

Activity

a 7 + 6 = 13, 6 + 7 = 13, 13 − 6 = 7, 13 − 7 = 6
b 8 + 5 = 13, 5 + 8 = 13, 13 − 8 = 5, 13 − 5 = 8
c 4 + 8 = 12, 8 + 4 = 12, 12 − 4 = 8, 12 − 8 = 4

27:1

1 11 **2** 30 **3** 2 **4** 14 **5** 18 **6** 10 **7** 30 **8** 12
9 2 (digits) **10** 4c **11** 16, 20 **12** 378 **13** 55 + 37 = 92
14 a 8, 8 b 6, 6 **15** 3 (months) **16** a 3rd b 5th

27:2

1 90 **2** 77 **3** 16 **4** 30 **5** 60 **6** 50 + <u>41</u> = 91 **7** 32 **8** 6
9 10 **10** 25 **11** <u>5</u> × 2 = 10 so 10 ÷ 2 = <u>5</u> **12** a 1 cm 8 mm
b 2 cm 8 mm **13** 8 **14** a 7000 b 70 **15** a behind b above
16 a eight forty-seven b 47 minutes past 8

Activity

13, 9, 6, 4, 10, 12, 8, 5, 11, 7
15, 11, 8, 6, 12, 14, 10, 7, 13, 9
odd + odd = even

27:3

1 32 **2** 24 **3** 46 **4** a 3:56, 56 past 3 b 6:53, 53 past 6
5 83 mm **6** 3000 **7** 712 **8** 6, 6 **9** 30 (minutes) **10** Saturday
11 2 (days) **12** a 61 b 52

27:4

1 a 36 b 35 **2** 4 **3** 10 **4** a yes b 3 (books)
5 179 (monkeys) **6** 24 (months) **7** 0 **8** 140 **9** 7

Challenge

Answers will vary. One answer could be: **a** 1, 11, 21, 31, 41, 51, ….
b 1, 2, 4, 8, 16, 32, … **c** 128, 64, 32, 16, 8, 4, …
d 70, 63, 56, 49, 42, 35, … **e** 5, 10, 15, 20, 25, 30, …

Activity

a 40 **b** 30 **c** 40 **d** 20 **e** 90

28:1

1 3 **2** 10 **3** 14 **4** 12 **5** 20 **6** 5 **7** 11 **8** 16 **9** 6
10 13 **11** 4734 **12** 746, 756, 766 **13** tally **14** a 300 b 30
15 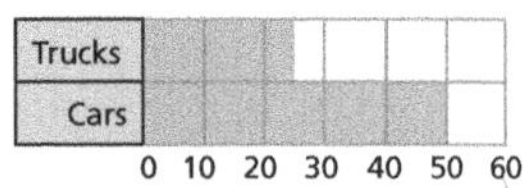

16 a circle b rectangle

28:2

1 89 **2** 77 **3** 20 **4** 56 **5** 9 **6** 708 **7** 4 **8** 9 **9** 68
10 45 **11** a [1][4] hundreds [7] tens [9] ones
b [1][4][7] tens [9] ones **12** 1062 **13** 1999
14 a 2 b 4 **15** a 90 b 104

Activity

5, 13, 9, 6, 10, 8, 12, 7, 11, 14
7, 15, 11, 8, 12, 10, 14, 9, 13, 16
even + even = even

28:3

1 60 **2** 71 **3** 4 and 5 **4** Answers will vary. One answer is 2, 4, 6, 8, 10. **5** <u>8</u> × 2 = 16 so 16 ÷ 2 = <u>8</u> **6** a < b < **7** 35 **8** 13
9 60 (minutes) **10** 2 (pairs) **11** 30 (days) **12** × **13** a 62 b 90

28:4

1 50 **2** 22 − 12 = 10 **3** 6 **4** 20 (3 people shared the lollies.)
5 

Challenge

Answers will vary.

Activity

10, 9, 8, 7 10, 9, 8 10, 9 10

29:1

1 4 **2** 15 **3** 12 **4** 3 **5** 3 **6** 6 **7** 18 **8** 16 **9** 90c **10** 14 **11** 9529 **12** 30 (children) **13** C **14** 100 **15** 203 **16** a bear b 8 c 22

29:2

1 35 **2** 33 **3** 22 **4** 5 **5** 35 **6** 6 **7** 79 **8** 90c **9** 8 **10** 27 **11**  **12** 3 and 4 **13** a 10 b 15

14 a R1 and R3 b staff room c canteen d office and library e toilets

Activity

0, 3, 5, 8, 4, 6, 2, 7, 3, 9
7, 3, 10, 2, 6, 8, 4, 9, 5, 1
even – even = odd
odd – even = odd

29:3

1 21 **2** 70 **3** 80, 75, 70 **4** 857 **5** one hundred and fifty-four **6** 400 **7** 355, 365, 375 **8** Answers will vary. One answer is 5, 10, 15, 20, 25. **9** a red b 8 c 60 **10** a 61 b 81

29:4

1 A **2** a true b false **3** a true b true **4** yes **5** 39, 50, 61, 72 **6** 40

Challenge

Answers will vary. One answer could be 4 < 9 or 2 + 5 > 11 − 8.

Activity

8, 16, 12, 9, 13, 11, 15, 17, 10, 14
10, 18, 14, 11, 15, 13, 17, 19, 16, 13
odd – even = odd

30:1

1 12 **2** 10 **3** 10 **4** 11 **5** 21 **6** 12 **7** 60 **8** 15 **9** 8 **10** 12 **11** a 20 to 4 b 3:40 **12** yes (Answers may vary.) **13** 20 (ears) **14** a false b false **15** a 70 b 40 **16** 45 + 35 = 80

30:2

1 66 **2** 300 **3** 40 **4** 30 **5** 90 **6** 6 **7** 35 **8** 8 **9** 101 m **10** 18 **11** 942, 952, 962 **12** 12 (books) **13** 30 (flowers) **14** 3, $3\frac{1}{2}$ **15** 999, 1 588, 1 692 **16** 5 198 **17** 10 (blocks)

Activity

1 **a** unlikely **b** likely **c** impossible **d** certain **2** less chance

30:3

1 53 **2** 62 **3**

First number	1	2	3	4	5	6
Second number	2	4	6	8	10	12

4 93, 91, 89 **5** 35 **6** yes **7** $1.37 **8** 283, 293, 303 **9** a 4 b 3 **10** a 63 b 64

30:4

1 6 **2** 6 boats will be coloured. **3** 95 (seals) **4** 5 (blocks) **5** square and rhombus (diamond) **6** a 6 b 11 **7** 29 (books)

Challenge

Answers will vary. One example is: 'John had 44 birds. Two escaped. How many are left?'

Activity

(11) *zero* (12) *digits* (13) 6 × 2 (14) 4 × 10 (15) 8 × 10 (16) *divide* by (17) *divide* by (21) *numeral* expander

31:1

1 18 **2** 10 **3** 10 **4** 11 **5** 61 **6** 60 g **7** 17 **8** 18 **9** 100c or $1 **10** 8 **11** yes **12** 30 g **13** yes **14** 10 (birds) **15** 19 (bottles) **16** Add 20.

31:2

1 93 **2** 74 **3** 28 **4** 60 **5** 40 **6** 5 **7** 9 **8** 90c **9** 300 g **10** 20 **11** 1324 **12** 3 599 **13** 34 **14** 6, 15, 18 **15** C

Activity

a 5 out of 8 or $\frac{5}{8}$ **b** 2 out of 5 or $\frac{2}{5}$
c 5 out of 6 or $\frac{5}{6}$ **d** 6 out of 7 or $\frac{6}{7}$

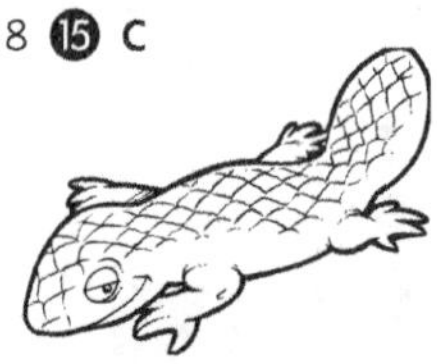

31:3

1 85 **2** 74 **3** Rule: Add 5. **4** 1790 **5** 6 000 **6** a A b B **7** 7218 **8** 7 **9** a 82 b 73

31:4

1 a 15 (bricks) b 27 (bricks) **2** 7 **3** 25, 40, 55, 70 **4** rectangle **5** 36 (books)

Challenge

Answers will vary. Some answers could be: this book, a pair of shoes, pencil case, stapler, mobile phone or box of tissues.

Activity

a 17 **b** 31 **c** 15 **d** 47 **e** 41 **f** 71 **g** 65 **h** 27 **i** 33 **j** 51

32:1

1 16 **2** 7 **3** 9 **4** 9 **5** 22 **6** 27 **7** 19 **8** 9 **9** $65 **10** 64 **11** 746 **12** 807, 629, 153 **13** The third triangle will be crossed out. **14** 4 000 **15** a 8 (angles) b 6 (faces) c prism (triangular) d **B**, **C** and **F** e **D**, **E** and **H** **16** 24 (eggs)

32:2

1 18 **2** 86 **3** 14 **4** 70 **5** 14 **6** 61 **7** $27 **8** $1 **9** 3 m **10** 80 **11** 60 kg **12** 28, 30, 32, 34 **13** no **14** 3 669 **15** 80 (pages) **16** a A b B **17** a 8 b 5

Activity

Answers will vary. A likely order would be: **C**, **E**, **B**, **A**, **F**, **D**.

32:3

1 112 **2** 102 **3** 43rd **4** Friday **5** Saturday the 9th **6** 10 g

7 20 (pages) **8** a 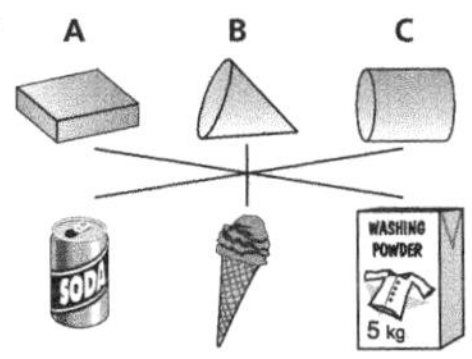 b cone c yes d yes

9 a 93 b 78

32:4

1 (1, 1 and 5), (1, 2 and 4), (1, 3 and 3), (2, 2 and 3) **2** 30

3 18 (toys) **4** 160 **5** 45 **6** 34, 51, 68 **7** 120 (players).
There are 2 teams on each court, so there are 12 people on each court.
12 × 10 = 120

Challenge

Answers will vary. One answer could be:
This is called a triangular prism. It has 6 corners,
5 faces, 9 edges and 2 triangular bases. All other
faces are rectangles. It can stack and slide.
A Toblerone chocolate bar is the shape of a triangular prism.

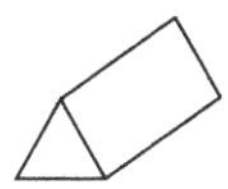

Activity

a 3, 1 **b** 4, 2 **c** 6, 3 **d** 9, 3

33:1

1 10 **2** 11 **3** 90 **4** 10 **5** 52 **6** 12 **7** 8 **8** 11 m **9** 16

10 23 **11** half past 7 (or 30 past 7) **12** 50c

13  10 (flowers)

14 52 (weeks) **15** a 4 b 3 **16** 80 (toes)

17

	3	7	4	5	2	10	6	9
× 5	15	35	20	25	10	50	30	45

18 a 20 (drinks) b $20 **19** 4 × 3

33:2

1 58 **2** 81 **3** 15 **4** 14 **5** 7 **6** 14 **7** 80 **8** 51 **9** 48

10 28 **11** prism (square or rectangular) **12** 2057 **13** three thousand seven hundred and five **14** cube **15** 6 birds will be coloured.

16 20 (monkeys) **17** B

Activity

a 14 **b** 19 **c** 59 **d** 46 **e** 27 **f** 38 **g** 49 **h** 30

33:3

1 14 **2** 52 **3** 4052 **4** 3 flying saucers will be coloured. **5** 370, 368 **6** a R b J c D d L e B **7** a 6 (edges) b 4 (faces)

33:4

1 a 12 (edges) b 14 **2** 60 (minutes) or 1 hour **3** a 8 b 13

4 26 (legs) **5** 5

Challenge

Answers will vary.

Activity

(2) *angle* (3) *right* angle (23) *face* (24) *cube* (25) *prism*
(26) *pyramid* (27) *base* (28) *cylinder* (29) *cone* (30) *sphere*

34:1

1 23 **2** 8 **3** 11 **4** 20 **5** 31 **6** 1 **7** 56 **8** 20c **9** 14

10 66 **11** 4 **12** the width of a door

13 a row 2 b fruit c soap d row 1 e lollies

34:2

1 81 **2** $63 **3** 36 **4** 13 **5** 54 **6** 12 **7** 54 **8** 10 **9** 5

10 61 **11** 3 **12** 100 (centimetres) **13** 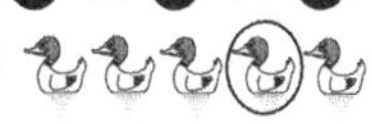

14 5 (school days) **15** 23 (pegs) **16** B **17** 231 **18** 83

Activity

a 8 **b** 20

34:3

1 722 **2** 336 **3** a  b 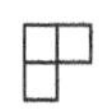 **4** 59 **5** 4 cm, 40 mm

6 43 **7** 6 moons will be shaded. **8** 11th, 12th **9** yes

10 10 **11** 90 m

34:4

1 5341 **2** a 10 b 20 **3** 6 **4** 12 (lines of symmetry) **5** 70

6 35 **7** 27 **8** 16 (dice)

Challenge

A sphere will be drawn. A sphere has no corners, edges
or flat faces. It has one curved surface. It is round
and smooth. It can roll. It cannot stack or slide.
A basketball is the shape of a sphere.

Activity

a 7, 3, 4 **b** 12, 7, 5 **c** 10, 8, 2 **d** 10, 4, 6 **e** 13, 8, 5 **f** 12, 3, 9

35:1

1 12 **2** 7 **3** 15 **4** 9 **5** 96 **6** 15 **7** 2 **8** $25 **9** 30

10 12 **11** 377 **12** 472 **13** 100 (centimetres) **14** 4 metres

15 2 cm, 20 mm **16** 4 **17** sphere **18** false **19** five thousand one hundred and ninety

35:2

1 63 **2** 83 **3** 50 **4** 8 **5** 33 **6** 40 kg **7** $3.60 **8** 60 cm

9 35 **10** 70 **11** 2002 **12** four thousand and twenty **13** 59

14 no **15** a C b cube **16** yes **17** a > b <

Activity

9, 17, 10, 14, 18, 12, 16, 11, 15, 13
odd + odd = even
even + odd = odd

35:3

1 120 **2** 571 **3** 600 **4** 43 **5** Answers will vary.
6 300 (centimetres) **7** a Brown St b Jones St c Bond St
d Smith St e Bond St, Smith St and Brown St

35:4

1 a 4 sheep will be coloured red. b 2 sheep will be coloured blue.
2 a 12 b 9 **3** a 51 b 32 **4** a 9 b 19
5

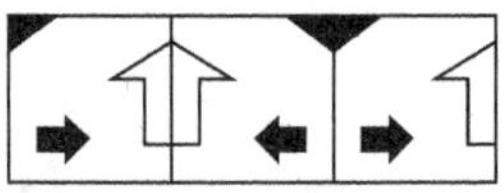

Challenge

Answers will vary.

Activity

(11) *zero* (12) *digits* (18) is *equal* to (19) *number* line (20) *number sentence* (21) *numeral* expander (22) *abacus* (30) *balance* scales

36:1

1 16 **2** 6 **3** 10 **4** 7 **5** 78 **6** 6 **7** 4 **8** 4 **9** 9 **10** 3
11 seven thousand and eight **12** a **A**, **B** and **D** b **A** and **C**
c **C** d **C** **13** slide
14 The shape will be redrawn to the right.

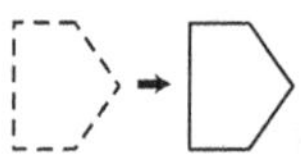

15 7 000 (mL) **16** 400 mL **17** 3 577

36:2

1 92 **2** 61 **3** 9 **4** 40 **5** 61 **6** 35 **7** 35 **8** 3 **9** 41
10 81 **11** 800 (cm) **12** a > b < **13** no **14** cube and cylinder
15 a **B** b **C** **16** $4.00 **17** 5 L

Activity

(1) *metres* (2) *centimetres* (3) *litres* (4) *grams* (5) *kilograms*
(6) *minutes* (23) *picture* graph (24) *tally* (25) *column* graph (26) *table*

36:3

1 834 **2** 622 **3** 5962 **4** a 6 b 8 **5** a **C** b **B** **6** $5.90
7 2 (L) **8** a 12 b 4 **9** $2.70 **10** $2.25 **11** 31 (days)
12 18, 21, 24 **13** 10

36:4

1 a 2 cm b 6 cm **2** 2 **3** △ **4** a 26 b 28
5 a 7:45 b 6:45 **6** 3

Challenge

Anwers will vary.
One answer is:
'This is a rectangular prism. It has 6 faces, 12 edges, and 8 corners. Its 2 bases are rectangles as are all other sides. It can stack and slide. It is shaped like a box.'

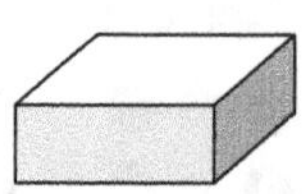

Activity

a 18 (bushes) **b** 20 (bushes)

37:1

1 8 **2** 18 **3** 18 **4** 10 **5** 14 **6** 5 **7** 11 **8** 12 **9** 6
10 10 **11** cone **12** flip **13** 24, 32, 40, 48 **14** 7 L
15 a 10:35 b 35 past 10 **16** 45 **17** **B** and **C**

37:2

1 82 **2** 12 **3** 20 **4** 2 **5** 60 **6** 40 **7** 17 **8** $12 **9** 16
10 16 **11** yes **12** a **C** b cube **13** $6.10 **14** 25 **15** 5 (litres)
16 circle and triangle **17** 400 (centimetres) **18** a $7.50 b $11.30
19 a 357 b 596

Activity

a 50 cents **b** 95 cents **c** 65c **d** 20c **e** 90c **f** 100c or $1

37:3

1 738 **2** 235 **3** $6.80 **4** 5 000 (millilitres) **5** The last small circle will be crossed out. **6** 25 (blocks) **7** 6 (eggs) **8** 62 **9** yes
10 45, 60, 75, 90 **11**

Front **Side**

12 6 (faces)

37:4

1 a 23 (points) b 30 (faces) c 24 (edges)
2

Shape A **Flip of A** **Slide of A**

3 a 28 b 41 **4** 38 (legs) **5** 1 m 50 cm

Challenge

Answers will vary. One answer could be:
a 25, 50, 75, 100, 125, 150 **b** 200, 170, 140, 110, 80, 50
c 9, 18, 27, 36, 45, 54 **d** 60, 54, 48, 42, 36, 30
e 50, 100, 150, 200, 250, 300

Activity

Answers will vary, but should increase.

17:3 ☐ out of 8

1. $\begin{array}{r} 40 \\ -\ 7 \\ \hline \end{array}$

2. $\begin{array}{r} 60 \\ -\ 9 \\ \hline \end{array}$

3. $\begin{array}{r} 80 \\ -\ 3 \\ \hline \end{array}$

4. Circle the larger fraction.

$\frac{5}{8}$ or $\frac{4}{8}$

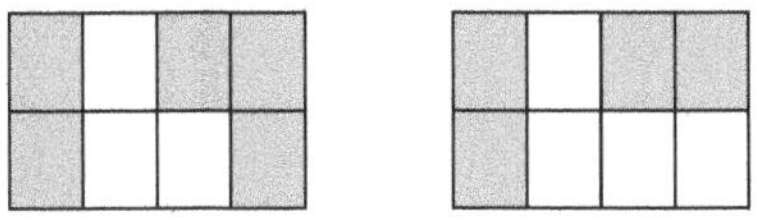

5. 3 rows of 5. ______

6. How many people can each be given 4 lollies? ______

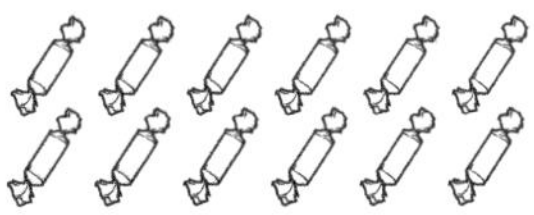

7. $10 \times 3 =$ ______ $3 \times 10 =$ ______

8. **Favourite Shape**

Pentagon	⬠ ⬠ ⬠ ⬠
Hexagon	⬡ ⬡ ⬡
Rhombus	◊ ◊ ◊ ◊ ◊ ◊

a What was the most popular shape? ______

b What was the least popular shape? ______

c How many more rhombuses than hexagons? ______

d How many hexagons and pentagons altogether? ______

17:4 ☐ out of 6

Extension

1. In a pentagon, is the number of sides equal to the number of angles? ______

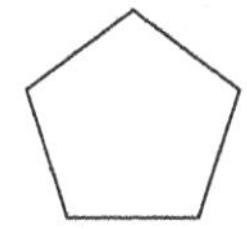

2. a $6 \times 10 =$ ______ b $3 \times 10 =$ ______

3.

Container	Estimate	Measure
Jug	8 cups	7 cups
Tub	28 cups	33 cups

How many cups does:

a the jug hold? ______

b the tub hold? ______

4. 1, 2, 4, 8, ______ , ______ , ______

5. a How many 5 cent coins? ______

b What is the total value? ______

6. 20c + 5c + 10c + 50c ______

Challenge

Draw and label containers that hold more than 1 litre.

1 + ___ = 10
5 + ___ = 10
2 + ___ = 10
8 + ___ = 10
6 + ___ = 10
3 + ___ = 10
7 + ___ = 10
4 + ___ = 10

3 + ___ = 13
7 + ___ = 13
9 + ___ = 13
6 + ___ = 13
5 + ___ = 13
4 + ___ = 13
8 + ___ = 13
10+ ___ = 13

Finish the boxes.

18:1 — ☐ out of 18

1. 6 × 2 ______
2. 9 + 3 ______
3. 19 − 10 ______
4. 1 × 4 ______
5. $\begin{array}{r} 18 \\ -\ 8 \\ \hline \end{array}$
6. 10 + 10 ______
7. 11 − 1 ______
8. 3 less than 11. ______
9. Double 4. ______
10. $\begin{array}{r} 11 \\ +\ 7 \\ \hline \end{array}$

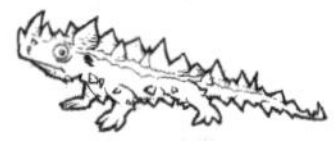

11. 10, 15, 20, ______, ______, ______, ______
12. I bought a cake for 10c and an iceblock for 50c. How much did I spend? ______
13. Which holds more, a cup or a 1 litre bottle? ______
14. The abbreviation for "kilogram". ______
15. 1 mouse costs 40c. How much for 2 mice? ______

16. Which angle is:
    a smallest? ______ **b** largest? ______

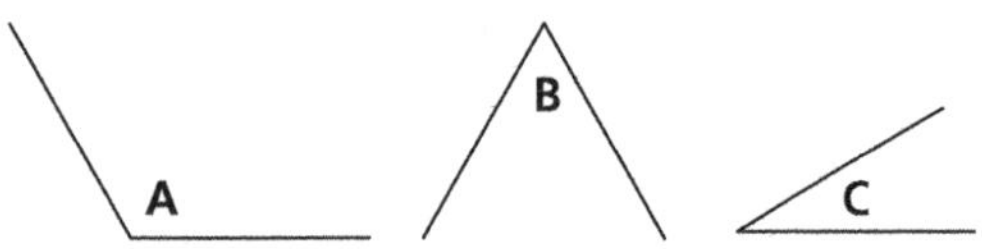

17. Which holds more, an eggcup or a teaspoon? ______
18. How many blocks have been used? ______

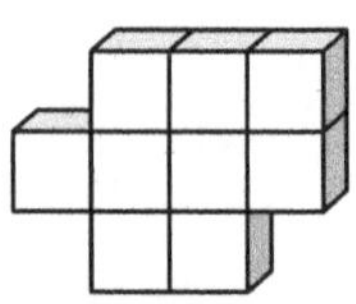

18:2 — ☐ out of 18

1. 66 + 22 ______
2. 25 − 12 ______
3. 6 × 6 ______
4. 10 × 9 ______
5. $\begin{array}{r} 5 \\ \times\ 3 \\ \hline \end{array}$
6. 4 tens and 6 ones. ______
7. 9c + 9c + 9c ______
8. 4 lots of 6. ______
9. 33, 44, 55, ☐. ☐ = ______
10. $\begin{array}{r} 5 \\ \times\ 6 \\ \hline \end{array}$
11. What fraction has been coloured?

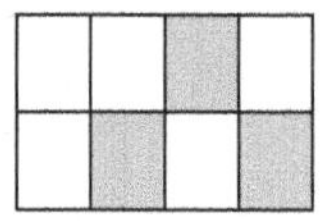

$\frac{\square}{\square}$

12. 12, 14, 16, ______, ______, ______
13. How many blocks were used to make this shape? ______

14. Add 58 and 6. ______
15. Multiply 5 by 3. ______
16. Shade $\frac{3}{4}$.

17. 12, 15, 18, ______, ______
18. More or less than a kilogram?
    a this book ______
    b your desk ______

This is a class lucky dip.

a Is Gino likely to pick the pen? ______

b What is the chance that Gino will pick something starting with 'c'? ______

c If we add another different prize to the lucky dip, will Gino have more or less chance of picking the pen? ______

 • *AUSTRALIAN SIGNPOST MATHS 3 MENTALS* • ISBN 978 1 4886 2183 3

18:3
out of 14

❶ $\begin{array}{r} 42 \\ -\ 4 \\ \hline \end{array}$ ❷ $\begin{array}{r} 51 \\ -\ 3 \\ \hline \end{array}$ ❸ $\begin{array}{r} 73 \\ -\ 5 \\ \hline \end{array}$

❹ The season after autumn. ______

❺ 40, 50, 60, ______, ______, ______

❻ Which coin has the greatest surface area? ______

❼ How many 20c coins in $2? ______

❽ Multiply 7 by 2. ______

❾ 18 + 7 + 2 ______

❿ How many animals in 32 pairs? ______

⓫ What part is shaded?

______ out of ______

⓬ $1 + $2 + $50c + 20c ______

⓭ 33, 44, 55, ______, ______

⓮ Is the volume of **A**, *less than*, *equal to* or *more than* the volume of **B**?

A **B**

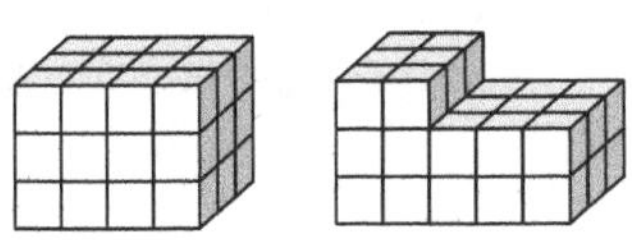

______

18:4
Extension

out of 5

❶ The bottom part is cut off. The part left would be:

A half of the volume

B more than half

C less than half

______

❷ $\frac{1}{4} + \frac{1}{4} + \frac{1}{4} + \frac{1}{4} + \frac{1}{4}$ ______

❸ Twelve bolts have the same mass as 2 shoes. How many bolts have the same mass as 4 shoes? ______

❹ Three different 1-digit numbers that add to give 24. ______

❺ How many blocks would be in the 6th level? ______

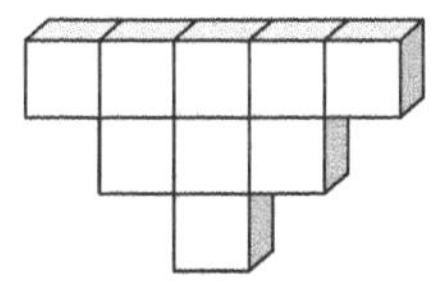

Challenge

Draw and label containers that hold less than 1 litre.

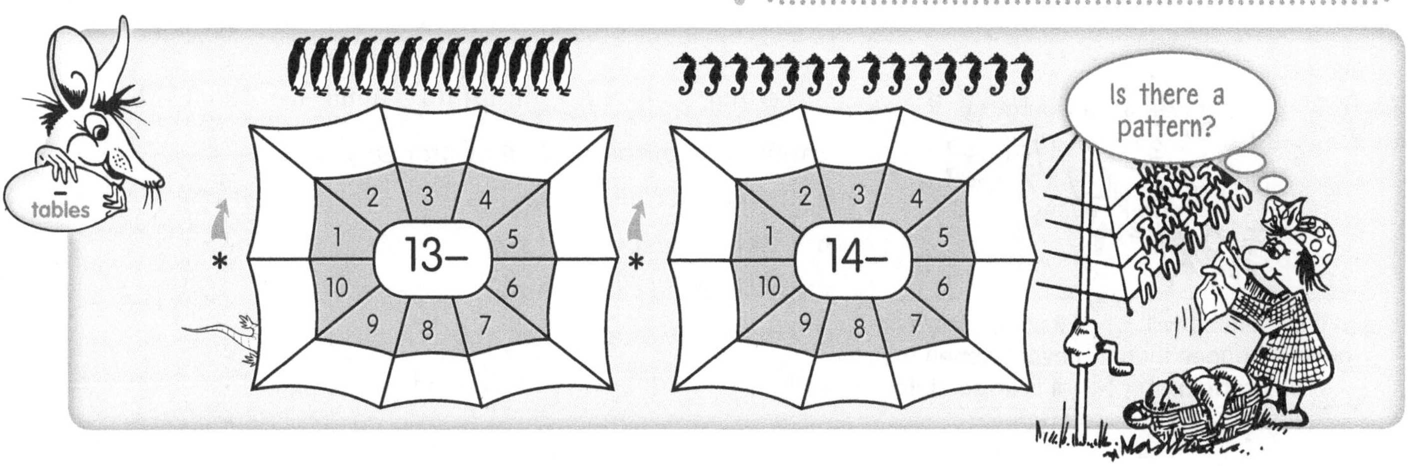

19:1 ☐ out of 19

1. 18 − 8 ____
2. 11 − 3 ____
3. 9 + 2 ____
4. 10 + 4 ____
5. $\begin{array}{r} 13 \\ +\ \ 6 \\ \hline \end{array}$
6. 1 × 5 ____
7. 16 − 2 + 2 ____
8. Take 6 from 9. ____
9. Total of 8 and 4. ____
10. $\begin{array}{r} 19 \\ -\ \ 5 \\ \hline \end{array}$

11. What coin has a lyrebird on one side and the queen on the other? ____
12. Is this book heavier than 1 kilogram? ____
13. Write in words: 14, 40, 44.
____
14. Would 3 pencils weigh the same as three of these books? ____
15. How many blocks have been used? ____

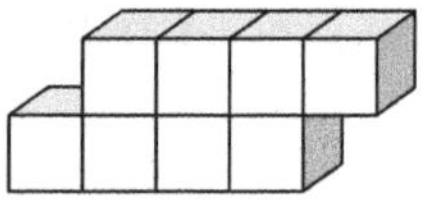

16. Does 34 plus 30 equal 64? ____
17. Wednesday is the ____ th day of the week.
18. Which has the greatest value? ____

A B C

19. 12:30 can also be written as ____

19:2 ☐ out of 16

1. 19 + 7 ____
2. 8 + 29 ____
3. 44 − 31 ____
4. 67 − 40 ____
5. $\begin{array}{r} 10 \\ \times\ \ 5 \\ \hline \end{array}$
6. 18 − 5 + 5 ____
7. 15, 17, ____, 21
8. 8 tens and 3 ones. ____
9. Half of 24. ____
10. $\begin{array}{r} 10 \\ \times\ \ 3 \\ \hline \end{array}$

11. Estimate then count the number of cubes used.

Estimate = ____

Number = ____

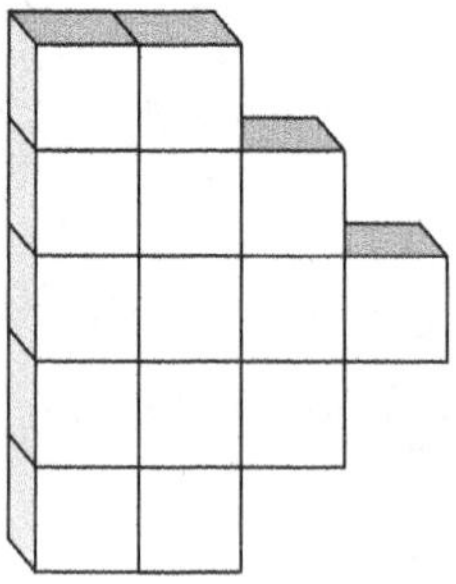

12. 12 △ 8 = 20 △ = ____
13. Write these angles in order, smallest to largest. ____

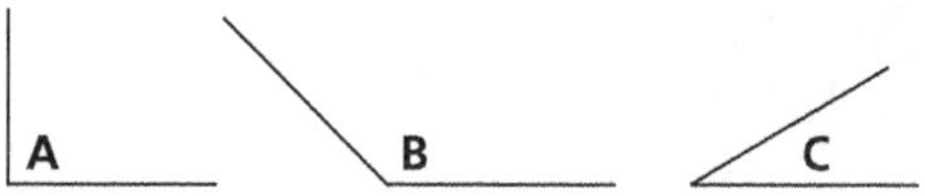

14. Which coin is worth more than 10 cents but less than 50 cents? ____
15. **a** 1, 3, 5, ____, ____, ____

b 10, 12, 14, ____, ____, ____

c 66, 55, 44, ____, ____, ____

16. Write the numeral for the number shown.

____

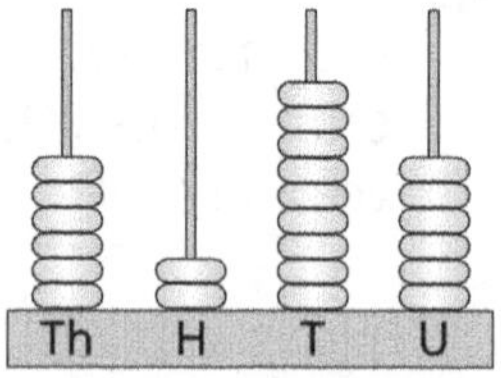

If something will **always** happen then it is **certain**.

If something will **never** happen then it is **impossible**.

certain | likely | fifty/fifty | unlikely | impossible

Choose one of the cards above for each part.

a It will rain on Saturday. ____

b I will get wet when I swim. ____

c I will fall if I climb a tree. ____

d I will grow a tail if I eat eggs. ____

e If I toss a coin, it will be a head. ____

 • *AUSTRALIAN SIGNPOST MATHS 3 MENTALS* • ISBN 978 1 4886 2183 3

19:3 out of 10

1.

Tens	Ones
8	6
− 4	2

2.

Tens	Ones
$4	9
−$4	6

3. Complete this pattern
17, 20, 23, ______, ______, ______

4. Would a chair weigh more than 1 kilogram? ______

5. Copy each angle on the dot paper.

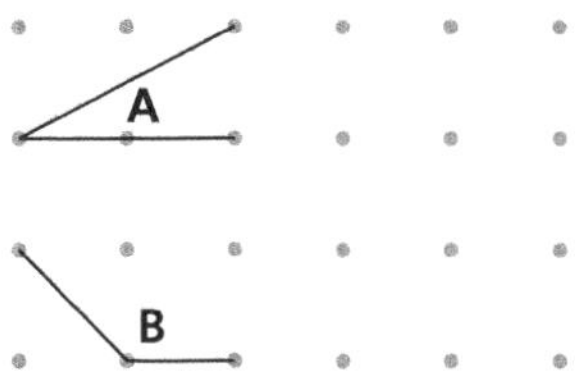

6. 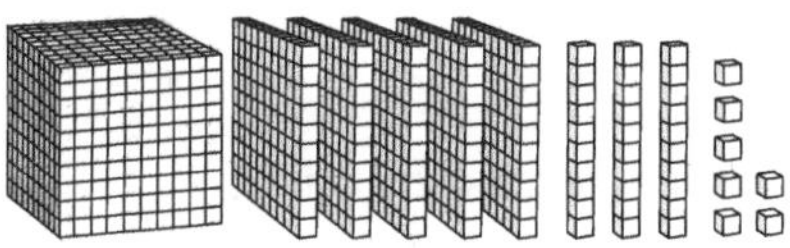

The number modelled here is ______.

7. 20 − 14 = ______ so 14 + ______ = 20

The difference between 14 and 20. ______

8. Arrange these angles in order of size, from smallest to largest.

______

9. A square corner is called a "right angle". Which angle above is a right angle? ______

10. How many 5 cent coins make 15 cents? ______

19:4 Extension out of 7

1. 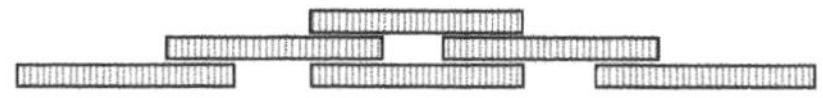

This pyramid is made of 10c coins. What is the total value if it is:

a 3 layers high? ______

b 7 layers high? ______

2. How many days altogether in August and September? ______

3. I have 3 socks. How many different pairs could I make? ______

4. Wings on 14 owls. ______

5. 60 − 10 − 5 − 5 − 10 ______

6. How many eggs in 3 dozen? ______

7. 73 was doubled and that answer was halved. What was the result? ______

Challenge

Draw and label items that weigh less than 1 kg.

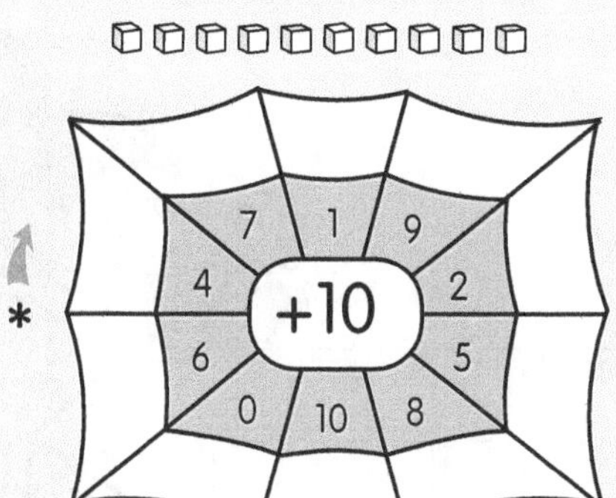

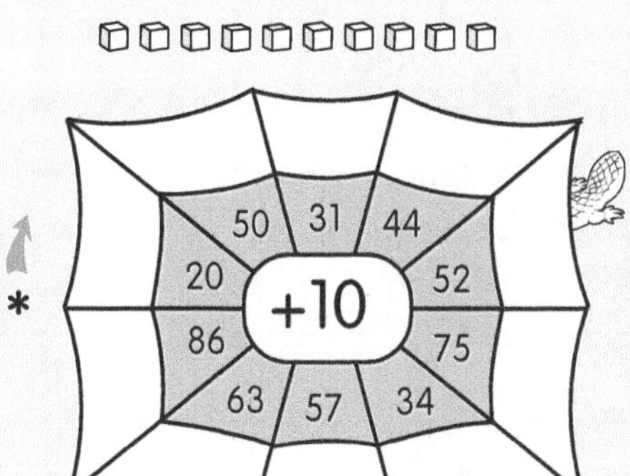

20:1 ☐ out of 17

1. 8 + 3 ______
2. 10 × 5 ______
3. 11 − 3 ______
4. 2 × 5 ______
5. $\begin{array}{r} 20 \\ -\ 5 \\ \hline \end{array}$
6. 11 − 10 + 10 ______
7. 7 + 9 − 9 ______
8. To 3, add 7. ______
9. \$5 + \$2 + \$1 ______
10. $\begin{array}{r} 14 \\ +\ 3 \\ \hline \end{array}$
11. Which Australian coins are coloured silver?

    ____
12. Which angle is the smallest? ______

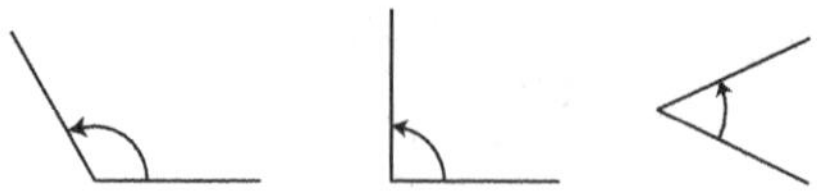

A B C

13. How many digits in 5 900? ______
14. Write the short form for sixteen kilograms. ______
15. These lines are

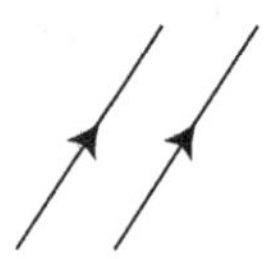

    ______________________________.
16. What is the difference between 12 and 19? ______
17. Mary has \$20, Jack has \$10 and Jill has \$5. Who has the most money? ______

20:2 ☐ out of 19

1. 18 + 8 ______
2. 46 − 12 ______
3. 6 × 2 ______
4. 10 × 10 ______
5. $\begin{array}{r} 3 \\ \times\ 10 \\ \hline \end{array}$
6. 15 shared among 3. ______
7. 16 shared among 2. ______
8. 3 tens + 9 ones. ______
9. 7 + 7 + 7 ______
10. $\begin{array}{r} 3 \\ \times\ 2 \\ \hline \end{array}$

11. 2 000 + 800 + 50 + 9 ______
12. Write the word for 70. ______
13. 58 = ______ tens and ______ ones
14. Order from smallest to largest:
    372, 310, 390 ______________
15. The number after 5 999. ______
16. Write seven thousand one hundred and forty-eight as a numeral. ______
17. **a** The number shown on the abacus.

    ____

    b How many are in the tens column?

    ____

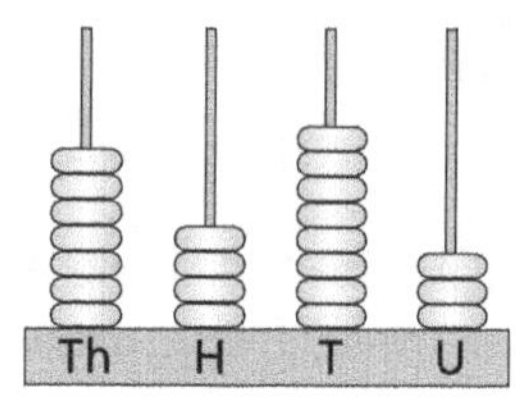

18. These are shared by four girls.

One share = ______

19. Write the numeral for eighty-one. ______

a When we throw two dice, would a total of 4 or 7 occur more often? ______

b Toss two dice 50 times. When a total of 4 or 7 is thrown, colour a square in the graph below.

Total thrown	**4**																
	7																

20:3 ☐ out of 10

1

Tens	Ones
4	5
+ 3	2

2

Tens	Ones
6	2
− 3	1

3 23 − 17 = _____ so 17 + _____ = 23

The difference between 17 and 23. _____

4

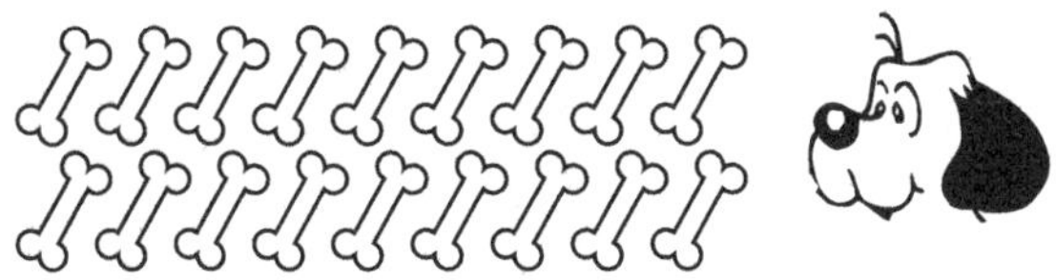

Find one share if 18 is shared by:

a 3 _____ **b** 6 _____

18 ÷ 3 = _____ 18 ÷ 6 = _____

5 4 circles have _____ corners.

6 Write the largest possible number using 3, 0, 1 and 5. _____

7 True or false? 6250 > 6241 _____

8 Write the short form for 5 kilograms. _____

9 Which is heavier, 5 place-value ones or 1 place-value ten? _____

10 Use a ruler to copy this angle. _____

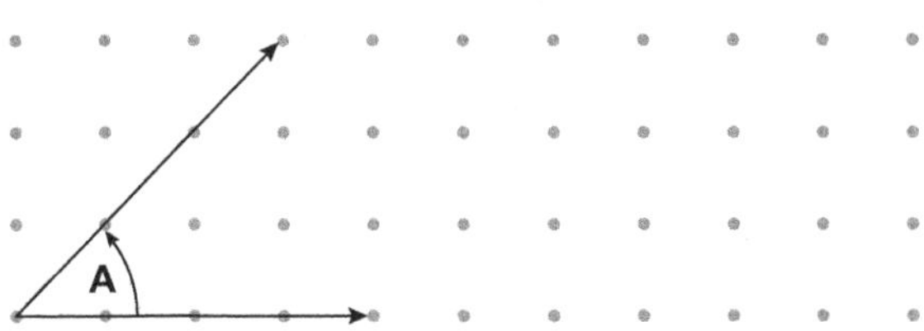

20:4 Extension ☐ out of 4

1 The total value of Australia's:

a 2 gold coins _____

b 4 silver coins _____

2 If ">" means "is greater than", write true or false for:

a 14 + 25 > 50 _____

b 100 − 70 > 20 _____

3

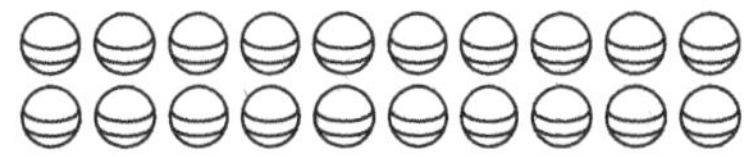

Find one share if 20 balls are shared by:

a 4 boys _____ **b** 5 girls _____

4

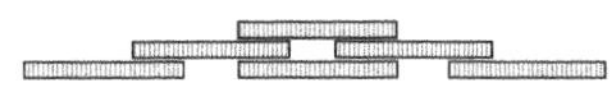

This pyramid is made of 5c coins.

What is the total value if it is:

a 3 layers high? _____

b 6 layers high? _____

Challenge

Draw a design using trapeziums and/or parallelograms.

ID Card A

Turn to ID Card A on page 6.

Give the answers for these numbers.

(7) _____ numbers (8) _____ numbers

(9) _____ numbers (10) _____ numbers

(18) is _____ to (27) _____ watch

(28) _____ clock (29) _____

21:1 ☐ out of 16

1. 9 × 2 ____
2. 14 − 7 ____
3. 8 + 4 ____
4. 11 − 2 ____
5. $\begin{array}{r} 6 \\ +\ 5 \\ \hline \end{array}$
6. 9 + 8 − 8 ____
7. 7 × 10 ____
8. $6 less than $20. ____
9. Sum of 4 and 7. ____
10. $\begin{array}{r} 15 \\ -\ 6 \\ \hline \end{array}$
11. 1 + 5 = 5 + ☐. ☐ = ____
12. 8 tens and 7 ones. ____
13. How many digits in 591? ____
14. What 2 shapes make this pattern?

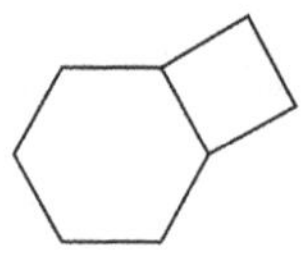

____ ____

15. This time is: ____

16.

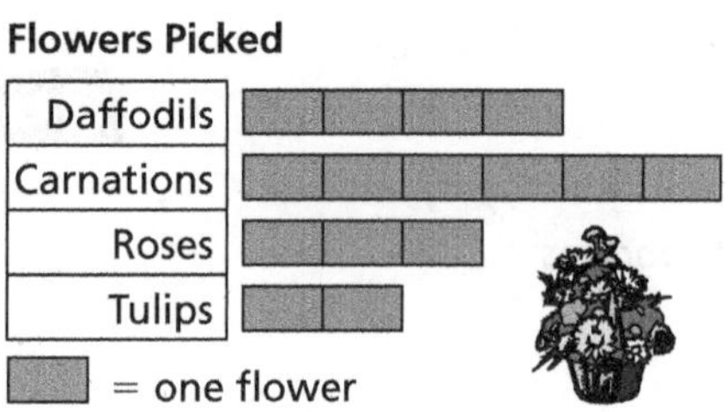

a The most popular flower. ____

b The least popular flower. ____

c How many daffodils? ____

d How many more carnations were picked than tulips? ____

e How many flowers altogether? ____

21:2 ☐ out of 17

1. 39 + 41 ____
2. 68 − 33 ____
3. 8 × 3 ____
4. 8 × 2 ____
5. $\begin{array}{r} 1 \\ \times\ 9 \\ \hline \end{array}$
6. 57 add 24. ____
7. 76 take away 31. ____
8. Digits in 19. ____
9. Total of 8, 9, 10. ____
10. $\begin{array}{r} 1 \\ \times\ 10 \\ \hline \end{array}$
11. Write six thousand three hundred and nine as a numeral. ____
12. Order from largest to smallest: 470, 439, 451 ____
13. Find one share if 24 are shared by:

a 4 ____ 24 ÷ 4 = ____

b 6 ____ 24 ÷ 6 = ____

14. These shapes are r____ shapes.

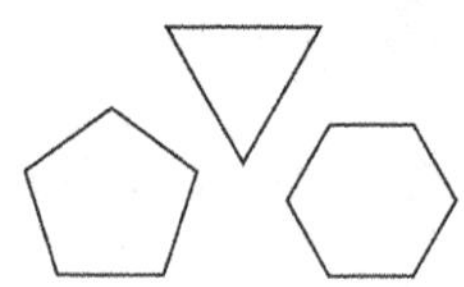

15. Is 442 closer to 400 or 500? ____
16. What is the difference between 18 and 27? ____
17. Write the numeral for 2 000 + 800 + 10. ____

*

*

© PEARSON AUSTRALIA 2018 • *AUSTRALIAN SIGNPOST MATHS 3 MENTALS* • ISBN 978 1 4886 2183 3

21:3 [ ] out of 11

1

Tens	Ones
\$6	2
−\$3	0

2

Tens	Ones
6	1
+ 2	7

3 a The line parallel to **E**. ______

b The lines parallel to **A**. ______

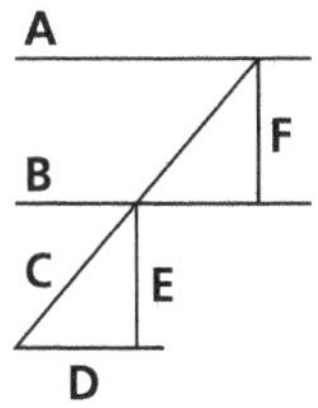

4 Round 321 to the nearest hundred. ______

5 Look at the clock in 21:1, question 15. How many more minutes until 2:10? ______

6 a 15 minutes after 10:35.

______

b 10 minutes before 10:35.

______

7 How many pairs of different counting numbers add to give 16? ______

8 a Even numbers end in:

______, ______, ______, ______ or ______

b Odd numbers end in:

______, ______, ______, ______ or ______

9 Two months before April. ______

10 178, ______, 180, ______, ______, 183

11 Show the analogue time 10 past 10 on this clock face.

21:4 Extension [ ] out of 4

1

How many boys could be given:

a 2 pens? ______ b 3 pens? ______

2 How many hexagons would be in row:

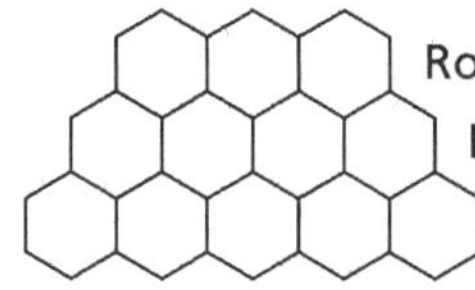

a 4? ______ b 10? ______

3 If ">" means "is greater than", write true or false for:

a $50 > 25 \times 2$ ______

b $6 \times 3 > 5 \times 3$ ______

4

1	3	9	10	12	7

Which three of these numbers add to give:

a 17? ______ b 19? ______

Challenge

There are 3 children. How many stars could you have so that each child gets a fair share? (Write at least 3 different-sized groups.)

How many minutes are in:

a one hour? ______

b half an hour? ______

c a quarter of an hour? ______

d three quarters of an hour? ______

For this clock, how many minutes is it:

e after 6 o'clock? ______

f before 7 o'clock? ______

22:1 [ ] out of 20

1. 1 + 10 ____
2. 3 × 5 ____
3. 12 − 3 ____
4. 10 + 9 ____
5. $\begin{array}{r} 17 \\ -\ \ 7 \\ \hline \end{array}$
6. 17 − 10 ____
7. 0 × 4 ____
8. Double 8. ____
9. Take 6 from 9. ____
10. $\begin{array}{r} 17 \\ +\ \ 2 \\ \hline \end{array}$

11. 2 + 1 = 1 + ☐. ☐ = ____
12. Which lines below are parallel? ____

A B C

13. $1.00 + $2.00 ____
14. Colour 7 eighths of this circle blue.

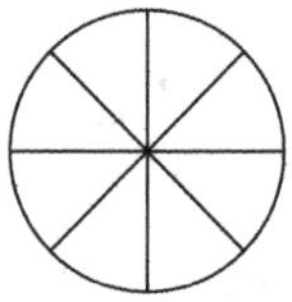

15. This time is: ____

16. The abbreviation for metres. ____
17. Minutes in 1 hour. ____
18. Is your school desk longer than 1 metre? ____
19. This is called a r________ angle.
20. The day before Friday. ____

22:2 [ ] out of 14

1. 25 + 27 ____
2. 39 − 30 ____
3. 3 × 3 ____
4. 4 × 5 ____
5. $\begin{array}{r} 0 \\ \times\ \ 5 \\ \hline \end{array}$
6. Half of 24. ____
7. Add 20 and 30. ____
8. 8 tens + 3 ones. ____
9. 7 + 7 + 7 ____
10. $\begin{array}{r} 3 \\ \times\ \ 4 \\ \hline \end{array}$

11. Is 539 closer to 500 or 600? ____
12. What is the change from $1.00 if my drink costs 90c? ____
13. Show the time 25 past 4 on the clock face.

14. **Baskets Thrown**

Marco	𝍸 I
Jill	𝍸 𝍸 II
Kira	IIII
Tim	𝍸

a Who threw the most baskets? ____
b Who threw the least baskets? ____
c How many more did Jill score than Tim? ____
d How many more did the girls score than the boys? ____
e How many baskets were thrown altogether? ____

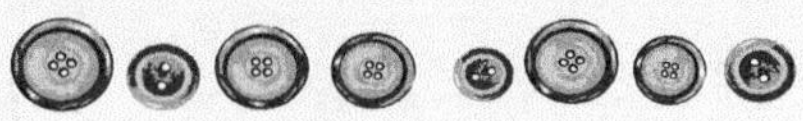

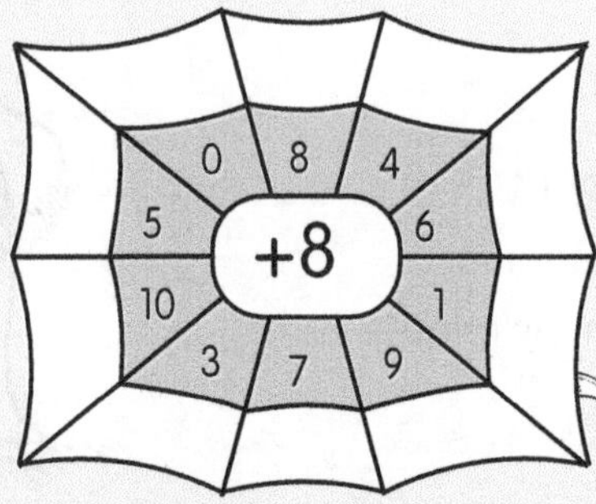

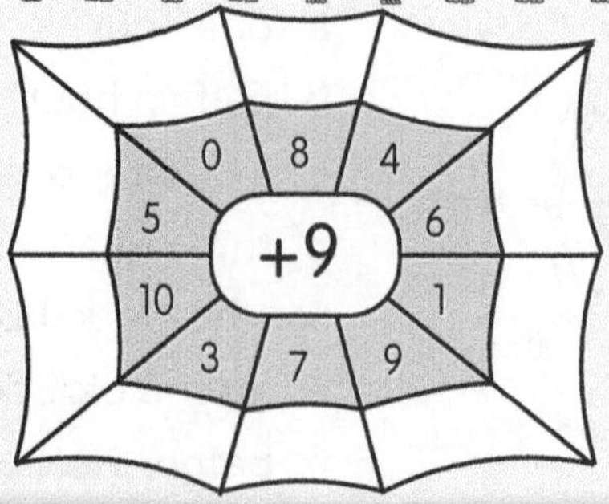

22:3 ☐ out of 10

1

Tens	Ones
$8	3
−$2	3

2

Tens	Ones
$5	4
+$3	5

3 The last two months of the year. ______

4 Round 150 to the nearest hundred. ______

5 The product of 3 and 4. ______

6 The change from $2.00 if I spend $1.85. ______

7 The time is ______ past ______.

8 Use the tally in 22:2 question 14, on the opposite page, to complete this column graph.

Baskets Thrown

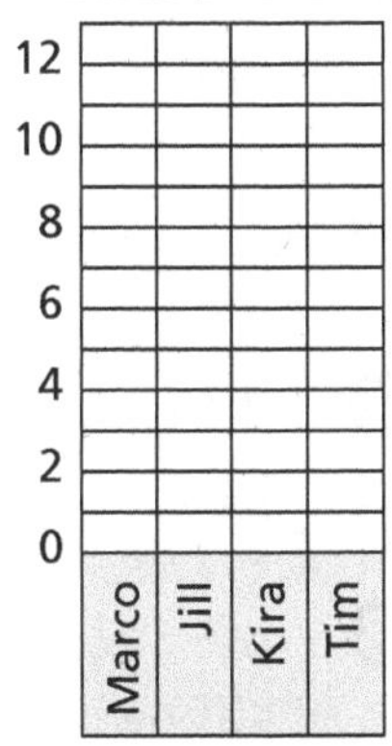

9 This shape is a ______________________.

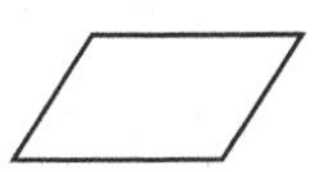

10 Write 8 metres 31 centimetres using the short form. ______

22:4 Extension ☐ out of 4

1

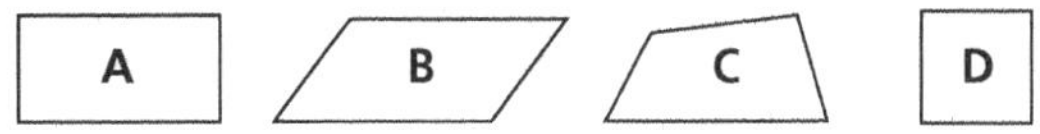

Which shape does not have opposite sides parallel? ______

2 This pyramid is made of 20 cent coins.

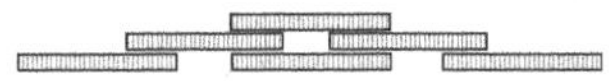

What is the total value if it is:

a 3 layers high? ______

b 5 layers high? ______

3 What fraction of an hour is

a 15 minutes? ______

b 30 minutes? ______

4 The total value of these notes.

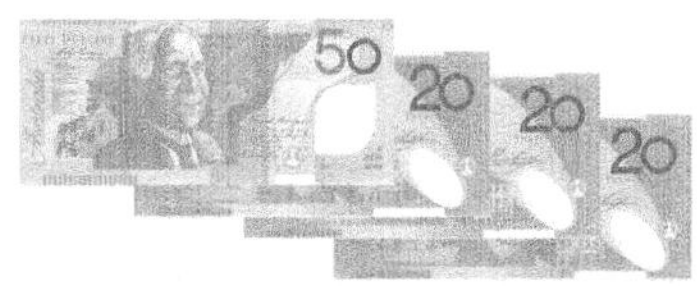

______

Challenge

Draw and label fractions that are less than one half.

+	5	10	4	0	2	6	1	3
2								
3								
4								
5								
10								

23:1 ☐ out of 18

1. 5 × 4 ______
2. 12 − 4 ______
3. 6 + 10 ______
4. 1 × 4 ______
5. 14 + 15 ______
6. 20 − 10 ______
7. 5 + 6 ______
8. 3 less than 11. ______
9. 6 m + 9 m ______
10. 7 − 7 ______
11. 3 + 2 = 2 + ☐   ☐ = ______
12. This digital time:

   a is read as ______
   b means ______ minutes past ______
13. Is 55 an even number? ______
14. What fraction is shaded? ______

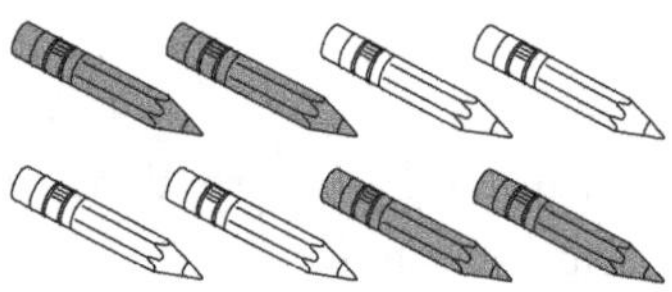

15. Is a horse taller than 1 metre? ______
16. This is called an ______.

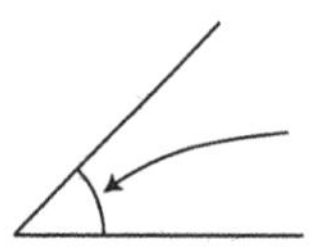

17. What number can be added to itself to equal 18? ______
18.

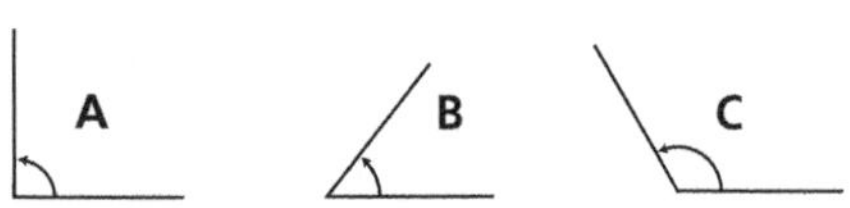

   a Which is a right angle? ______
   b Which is the largest angle? ______

23:2 ☐ out of 21

1. 33 + 37 ______
2. 80 − 40 ______
3. 5 × 4 ______
4. 3 × 6 ______
5. 5 × 10 ______
6. 12 shared by 3. ______
7. 35 subtract 7. ______
8. 10 groups of 9. ______
9. Double 25. ______
10. 5 × 2 ______
11. A pentagon has ______ sides.
12. The change from \$2 if I spend \$1.75. ______
13. True or false? $\frac{1}{4}$ is more than $\frac{1}{8}$. ______
14. The total value of these notes. ______

15. Write 1 metre 65 centimetres using the short form. ______
16. Is the width of a door about 1 metre? ______
17. Circle $\frac{1}{4}$.

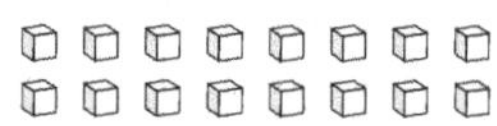

18. Write 392 cm in metres and centimetres. ______
19. 9 days after Tuesday. ______
20. 550, 560, 570, 580, ______, ______, ______
21. Is the height of your teacher less than 1 metre? ______

rows of 5

groups of 5

	2	4	6	8	10
× 5					

lots of 5

	2	4	6	8	10
× 10					

 • *AUSTRALIAN SIGNPOST MATHS 3 MENTALS* • ISBN 978 1 4886 2183 3

23:3

[ ] out of 7

1

Tens	Ones
5	6
+ 3	3

2

Tens	Ones
4	1
+ 5	8

3 Write 3 m 72 cm in centimetres. ______

4

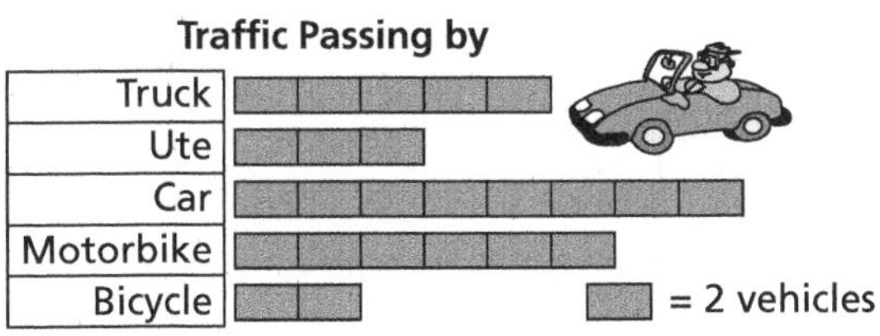

a Which was the most popular? ______

b Which was the least popular? ______

c How many more cars were there than motorbikes? ______

d How many trucks and utes were there altogether? ______

e How many vehicles altogether? ______

5 **a** The digital time is ______ : ______ .

b The analogue time is ______ past ______ .

6 The change from $1 if I spend:

a 70c ______ **b** 35c ______

7 The change from $2 if I spend

a $1.50 ______ **b** 35 cents ______

23:4

Extension

[ ] out of 7

1 1 metre − 1 centimetre = ______

2 Jenna had 36 ten cent coins. 27 were lost.

a How many coins were left? ______

b How much money was left? ______

3 Find the difference between the 2 smallest-value coins and the 2 biggest-value coins. ______

4 **a** Colour 5 sixths red and 1 sixth blue.

b 5 sixths + 1 sixth ______

5 17 + 13 + 18 + 12 ______

6 50 cm is ______ of a metre.

7 I have twelve 10 dollar notes.

How much money do I have? ______

Challenge

Draw angles that are larger than a right angle.

Find the distance around each shape.

a 5 × 2: Distance = ______ cm

b 4 × 2: Distance = ______ cm

c 10 × 1: Distance = ______ cm

 • • ISBN 978 1 4886 2183 3

24:1 ☐ out of 20

1. 16 − 10 ______
2. 4 × 4 ______
3. 10 + 3 ______
4. 15 − 5 ______
5. $\begin{array}{r} 17 \\ -\ \ 6 \\ \hline \end{array}$
6. 2 × 4 ______
7. 6 + 8 ______
8. Digits in 287. ______
9. Add 6 and 8. ______
10. $\begin{array}{r} 14 \\ +\ \ 2 \\ \hline \end{array}$
11. 2 + 4 = 4 + ☐ ☐ = ______
12. Colour one sixth of the fish.

13. 13, 15, 17, ______, ______, 23
14. Write the number on the abacus. ______

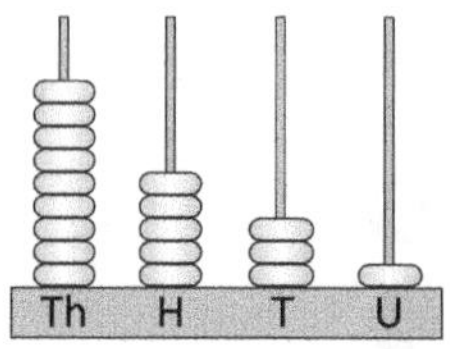

15. 400 + 80 + 3 ______
16. This is called an ______________ .

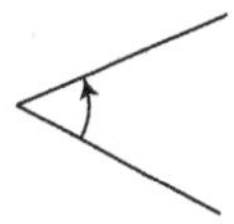

17. The months in winter.

____

____

18. Do we measure the height of objects in metres, litres or grams? ______
19. This digital time:

   a is read as

   ____

   b means ____ minutes past ____

20. 6 △ 8 = 14 △ = ______

24:2 ☐ out of 19

1. 37 + 24 ______
2. 38 − 7 ______
3. 3 × 0 ______
4. 5 × 3 ______
5. $\begin{array}{r} 10 \\ \times\ \ 5 \\ \hline \end{array}$
6. 556, 566, 576, ______
7. Digits in 3851. ______
8. 635, 640, ______, 650
9. 300 add 700. ______
10. $\begin{array}{r} 5 \\ \times\ \ 6 \\ \hline \end{array}$

11. The change from \$2.00 if I spend \$1.25. ______
12. The total value of these notes. ______

13. Circle $\frac{1}{3}$.

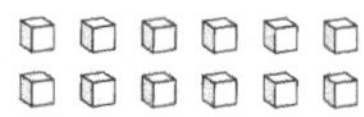

14. The digital time:

   a is read as

   ____

   b means

   ____

15. Is 3 × 5 half of 3 × 10? ______
16. The month before June. ______
17. 20th, 21st, ______, ______, 24th
18. 1 256 = ☐ ☐ ☐ tens ☐ ones
19. Write 5 m 21 cm in centimetres. ______

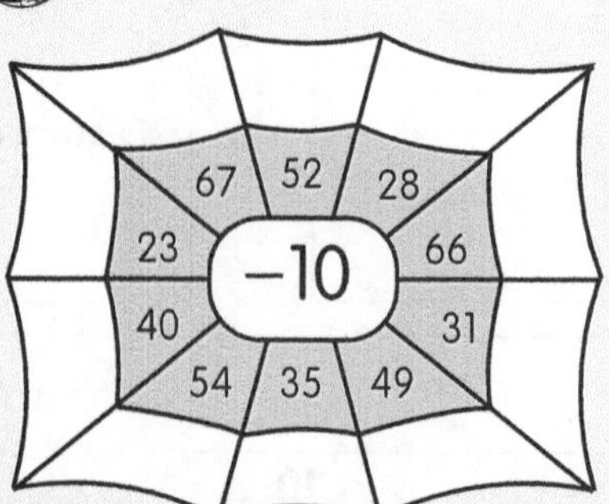

 ISBN 978 1 4886 2183 3

24:3   out of 10

1

Tens	Ones
9	7
− 3	4

2

Tens	Ones
8	2
− 6	0

3 Write 502 cm in metres and centimetres. ______

4 True or false? Two quarter turns are the same as a half turn. ______

5 How many hundreds in one thousand? ______

6 a Days in three weeks. ______

b Days in four weeks. ______

7 0, 6, 12, 18, ______, ______, ______

8 a How many Mondays? ______

b The last day is a ______.

c What day is it 3 days after the 4th of June? ______

June

S	M	T	W	T	F	S
	1	2	3	4	5	6
7	8	9	10	11	12	13
14	15	16	17	18	19	20
21	22	23	24	25	26	27
28	29	30				

Note: The calendar for June changes each year.

9 Round 2 493 to the nearest thousand. ______

10 Show the number 1 645 on this abacus.

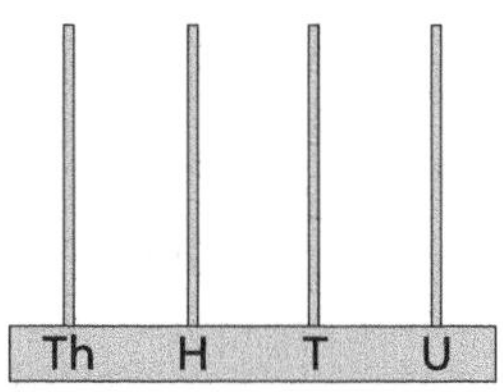

24:4   out of 7

Extension

1 Does: a $4 + 4 + 4 = 3 \times 4$? ______

b $10 \times 2 = 2 \times 10$? ______

c $78 + 34 = 34 + 78$? ______

2 One banana costs 50 cents. How much do four cost? ______

3 Colour 1 quarter of this rectangle.

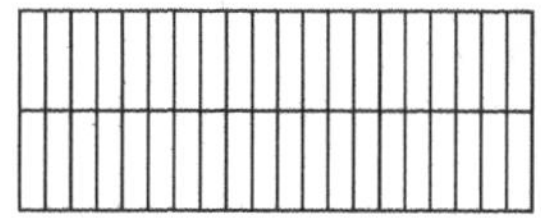

4 Round off 3 239 to the nearest hundred. ______

5 Today is Monday. What day will it be:

a in three days time? ______

b a week from tomorrow? ______

6 $100 - 20 - 20 - 20$ ______

7 $12 + 8 + 3 + 17 + 15 + 5$ ______

Challenge

Draw and label shapes that have a boundary length (perimeter) of 8 cm.

Rounding to the Nearest Hundred

Look at the tens digit to see if you should round up or down.

Round up if the tens digit is 5, 6, 7, 8 or 9.

Round down if the digit is 1, 2, 3 or 4.

a Is 340 closer to 300 or 400? ______

b Is 653 closer to 600 or 700? ______

Round each of these to the nearest 100.

c 339 ______ d 814 ______ e 751 ______ f 490 ______ g 119 ______

25:1 ☐ out of 21

1. 3×2 ____
2. $12 - 6$ ____
3. $13 - 9$ ____
4. $3 + 10$ ____
5. $\begin{array}{r} 7 \\ +\ 10 \\ \hline \end{array}$
6. $10 + 8$ ____
7. 5, 10, 15, ____, ____
8. Half of 14. ____
9. 25, 30, 35, ____, ____
10. $\begin{array}{r} 23 \\ -\ 10 \\ \hline \end{array}$
11. The numeral for seven thousand two hundred and five. ____
12. How many digits in 3018? ____
13. Start at 40. Count by 4s.
    40, ____, ____, ____, ____, ____
14. Start at 44. Count by 5s.
    44, ____, ____, ____, ____, ____
15. Round 69 to the nearest 10. ____
16. $5 \times 2 =$ ____ $10 \div 2 =$ ____
17. Weeks in 1 year. ____
18. Two months after May. ____
19. Hour in three days. ____
20. Which angle is larger than a right angle? ____

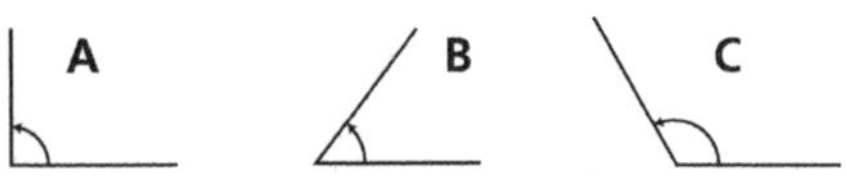

21. Is the width of your finger about 1 cm? ____

25:2 ☐ out of 17

1. $37 + 25$ ____
2. $88 - 20$ ____
3. 10×0 ____
4. 6×3 ____
5. $\begin{array}{r} 10 \\ \times\ \ 4 \\ \hline \end{array}$
6. 3, 6, 9, ____, ____
7. Half of 60. ____
8. 5 groups of 3. ____
9. 6, 12, 18, ____, ____
10. $\begin{array}{r} 2 \\ \times\ \ 5 \\ \hline \end{array}$

11. Circle $\frac{1}{8}$.

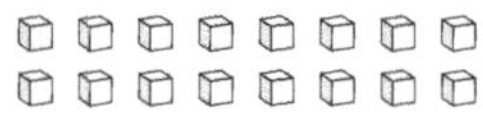

12. Round 8731 to the nearest thousand. ____
13. Find the distance around the shape. ____

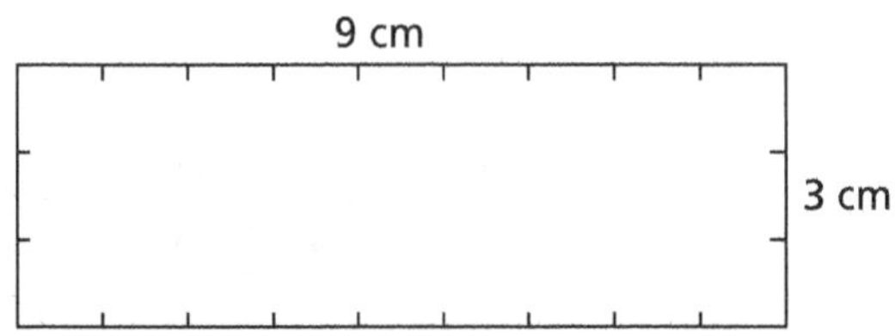

14. Is 4×10 twice 2×10? ____
15. True or false? A three-quarter turn is the same as a half turn. ____
16. True or false? $\frac{6}{6}$ equals 1.
17. a Write the digital time.

____

b The time is

____ minutes past ____.

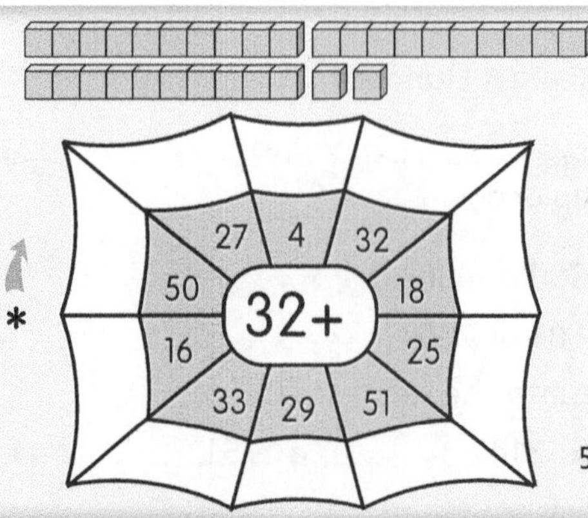

 • *AUSTRALIAN SIGNPOST MATHS 3 MENTALS* • ISBN 978 1 4886 2183 3

1.
```
   3
   2
   7
   1
   8
+  2
```

2.
```
   9
   2
   8
   7
   1
+  3
```

3.
```
   0
   1
   4
   8
   9
+  2
```

4. If the clock's hand turns a three-quarter turn, what does it point to? ______

5. Write 7028 in words.

______

______

6. Draw a column graph for this tally.

A	卌 II
B	IIII
C	卌 I

A								
B								
C								

7. a What month is this?

______

b How many Tuesdays?

______

c What day is the 12th?

______

October

S	M	T	W	T	F	S
	1	2	3	4	5	6
7	8	9	10	11	12	13
14	15	16	17	18	19	20
21	22	23	24	25	26	27
28	29	30	31			

Note: The calendar for October changes each year.

d How many days in this month? ______

e What is the date of the first Sunday? ______

f What is the date of the last Saturday? ______

1. 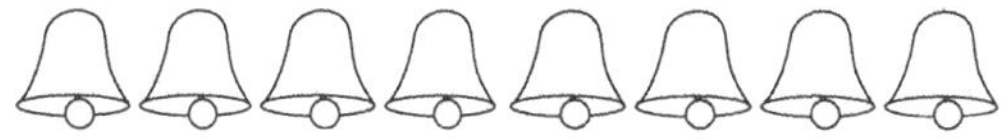

Colour one quarter of the bells red and one half of them blue. What fraction have you coloured? ______

2. What fraction of $1 is:

a 20 cents? ______ b 5 cents? ______

3. a 2 hours before 11:15.

______

b 2 hours after 11:15.

______

4.

a	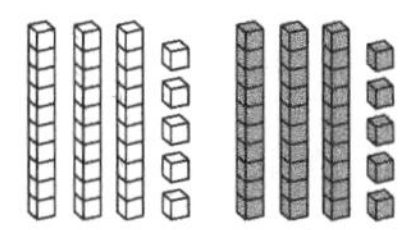 35 + 35 = ______	b	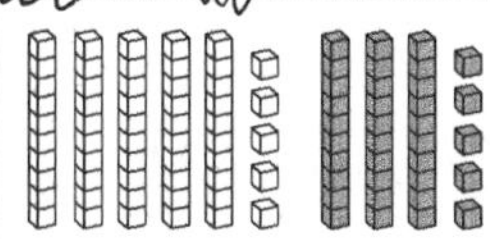 55 + 35 = ______

Challenge

Write numbers that would round to 4000.

______

______

______

______

______

______

______

Turn to ID Card B on page 7.

Give the answers for these numbers.

(6) ______ (7) ______

(8) ______ (9) ______

(10) ______ (11) ______

(12) ______ (13) ______

Make up a study card for any mistakes.

Study card
Put questions on one side and answers on the other.

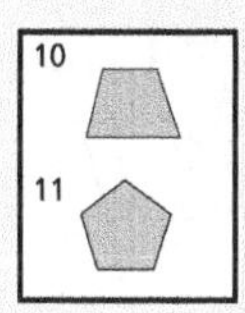

10 trapezium

11 pentagon

26:1 ☐ out of 17

1. 6 + 4 ____
2. 8 × 2 ____
3. 5 × 5 ____
4. 8 − 3 ____
5. 14 + 10 ____
6. 9 − 6 ____
7. 5 + 8 ____
8. 17 subtract 4. ____
9. 2, 4, 6, ____, ____
10. 19 − 5 ____
11. a 4 × 3 = ____ b 12 ÷ 4 = ____
12. Measure the lines in millimetres.
    a ________________ ____
    b ______ ____
    c ____________________ ____
13. a How wide is the graph below? ____

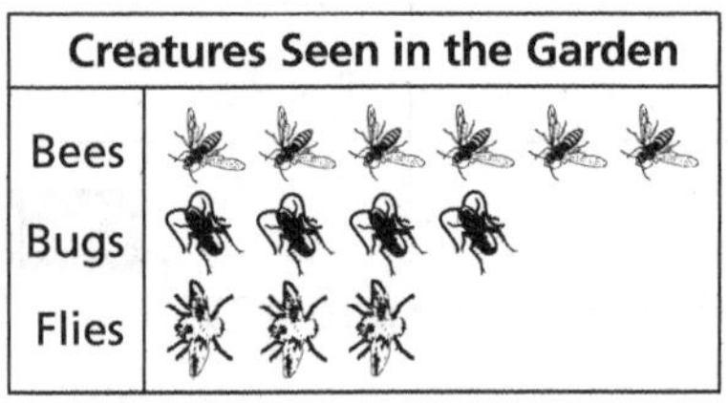

    b How many more bees than flies were seen? ____
    c How many creatures were seen altogether? ____
14. 4, 8, 12, 16, 20, ____, ____, ____
15. How many seasons in a year? ____
16. Minutes in 1 hour. ____
17. What month comes before December? ____

26:2 ☐ out of 17

1. 84 − 20 ____
2. 64 + 27 ____
3. 5 × 2 ____
4. 9 × 5 ____
5. 5 × 8 ____
6. 14, 16, 18, ____, ____
7. 52, 62, 72, ____, ____
8. Double 26. ____
9. 14 + ____ = 25
10. 0 × 8 ____
11. ____ × 5 = 25 so 25 ÷ 5 = ____
12. Write 4 cm 6 mm in millimetres. ____
13. Complete the labels.

a

4: ☐☐
☐ past 4

b

10: ☐☐
☐ past 10

14. 6 × 5 = ____ 30 ÷ 6 = ____
15. The month two months after April. ____
16. Days in October. ____
17. Draw a quarter turn anticlockwise.

What number is the hand pointing to now? ____

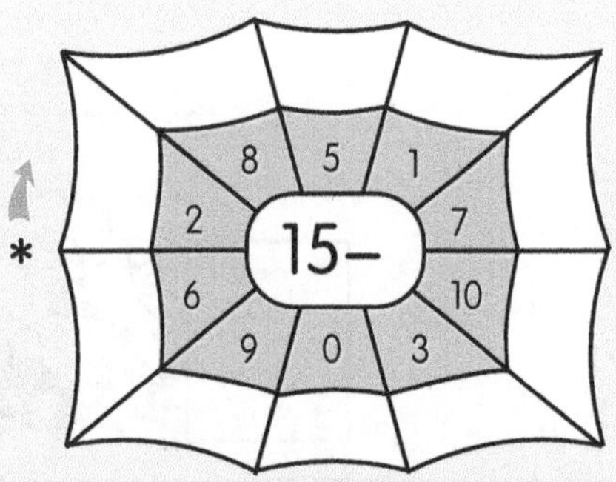

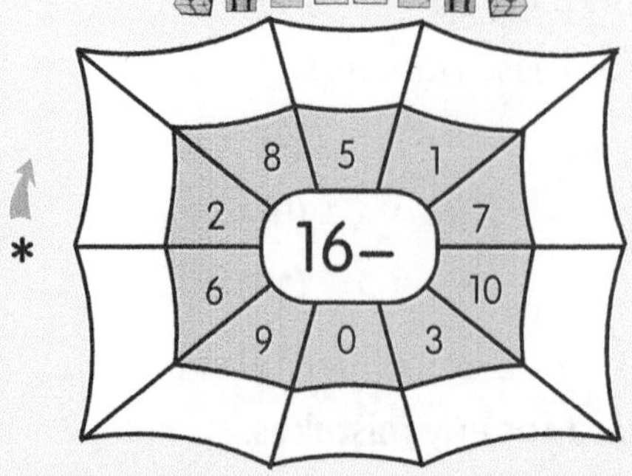

© PEARSON AUSTRALIA 2018 • *AUSTRALIAN SIGNPOST MATHS 3 MENTALS* • ISBN 978 1 4886 2183 3

26:3 ☐ out of 13

1

Tens	Ones
3	8
+	5

2

Tens	Ones
5	7
+	5

3 Michelle has a 20c coin, a 5c coin and a 10c coin. How much money does she have? ______

4 Add 4 each time.

21, ______, ______, ______, ______, ______

5 Circle the numbers that round off to 400.

321		412		392		351	
	456		333		406		349

6 How many digits in 932? ______

7 The month 2 months before September. ______

8 The fifth month of the year. ______

9 7, 9, 11, ______, ______, 17, 19, ______

10 The rule for question 9 is ______.

11 ————————————————

This line is ______ cm long.

12 ______ × 5 = 15 so 15 ÷ 5 = ______

13

a 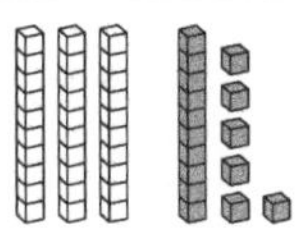

30 + 16 = ____

b 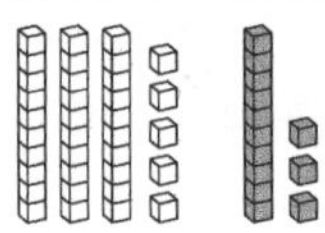

35 + 13 = ____

26:4 Extension ☐ out of 5

1 $\frac{1}{2} + \frac{1}{2} + \frac{1}{2} + \frac{1}{2} + \frac{1}{2}$ ______

2 60 − 5 − 5 − 5 − 5 − 5 ______

3 **a** 3 hours before 1:00.

______

b 47 minutes before 1:00.

______

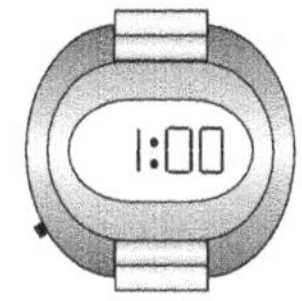

4 5 sheets of paper can make a book.

How many books can I make if I have:

a 20 sheets? ______ **b** 17 sheets? ______

5 

a The total value of the coins in **A** and **B**. ______

b The difference in value of the coins in **A** and **B**. ______

Challenge

Write a pattern with the rule:

a *Add 2.* ______

b *Subtract 3.* ______

c *Multiply by 2.* ______

d *Add 8.* ______

e *Write a pattern using only multiples of 10.*

______

☆☆☆ ★★ ☆☆☆ ★★	6 + 4 = [10], 4 + 6 = [10], 10 − 6 = [4], 10 − 4 = [6]

Complete four number sentences for each picture.

a	○○○○ ●●● ○○○ ●●●	7 + 6 = ☐, __ + __ = ☐, 13 − __ = ☐, 13 − __ = ☐
b	◇◇◇◇ ◆◆◆ ◇◇◇◇ ◆◆	__ + __ = ☐, __ + __ = ☐, __ − __ = ☐, __ − __ = ☐
c	♤♤ ♠♠♠♠ ♤♤ ♠♠♠♠	__ + __ = ☐, __ + __ = ☐, __ − __ = ☐, __ − __ = ☐

27:1   ____ out of 16

1. 6 + 5 ____
2. 10 × 3 ____
3. 11 − 9 ____
4. 7 + 7 ____
5. $\begin{array}{r} 15 \\ +\ \ 3 \\ \hline \end{array}$
6. 17 − 7 ____
7. 3 × 10 ____
8. 3 + 2 + 7 ____
9. Digits in 74. ____
10. $\begin{array}{r} 10c \\ -\ \ 6c \\ \hline \end{array}$

11. 4, 8, 12, ____, ____, 24

12. Make the smallest number, using 8, 7 and 3. ____
13. 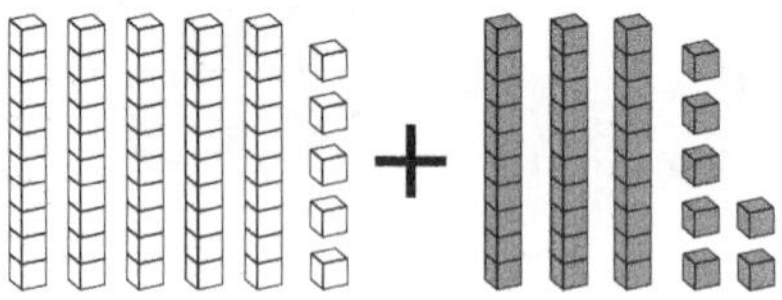

____ + ____ = ____

14. How many groups of:

a 3 hooks? ____

24 ÷ 3 = ____

b 4 hooks? ____

24 ÷ 4 = ____

15. How many months in winter? ____
16. What is the position of the:

a lion? ____   b cow? ____

27:2   ____ out of 16

1. 55 + 35 ____
2. 87 − 10 ____
3. 2 × 8 ____
4. 6 × 5 ____
5. $\begin{array}{r} 10 \\ \times\ \ 6 \\ \hline \end{array}$
6. 50 + ____ = 91
7. 20, 26, ____, 38
8. 24 shared by 4. ____
9. 5 groups of 2. ____
10. $\begin{array}{r} 5 \\ \times\ \ 5 \\ \hline \end{array}$

11. ____ × 2 = 10   so   10 ÷ 2 = ____
12. Measure the length of:

a ▬▬▬▬ ____ cm ____ mm

b ▬▬▬▬▬▬▬ ____ cm ____ mm

13. Find the smallest number that is a multiple of 4 and 8. ____
14. Write the value of 7 in:

a 7320 ____

b 2072 ____

15. Where is:

a the emu?

____ the tree

b the bird?

____ the horse.

16. 

a This time is read as ____.

b It means ____ minutes past ____.

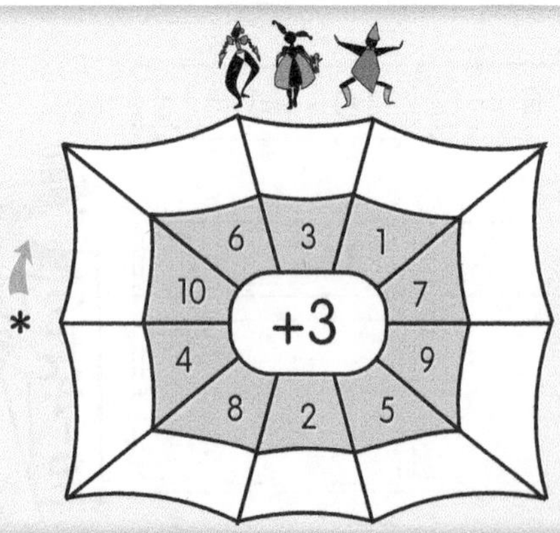

 ISBN 978 1 4886 2183 3

27:3 ☐ out of 12

1

Tens	Ones
2	9
+	3

2

Tens	Ones
1	9
+	5

3 27 + 19 ______

4 Complete the labels.

a

3: ☐

☐ past 3

b

6: ☐

☐ past 6

5 Write 8 cm 3 mm in millimetres. ______

6 The value of the 3 in 3612. ______

7 Which number is larger: 396 or 712? ______

8 How many groups of 5 in 30? ______

30 ÷ 5 = ______

9 Minutes in half an hour. ______

10 The day 3 days after Wednesday. ______

11 Days in 48 hours. ______

12

a

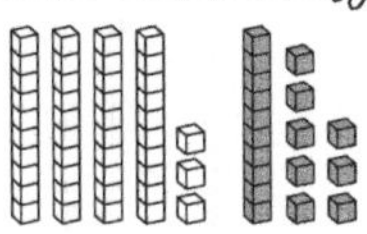

43 + 18 = ____

b

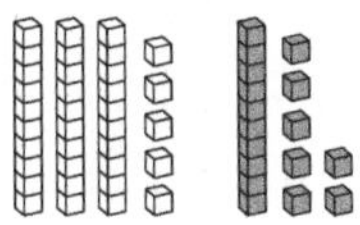

35 + 17 = ____

27:4 Extension ☐ out of 9

1 **a** 16 + 8 + 12 ______

b 14 + 5 + 16 ______

2 How many 50c coins make $2? ______

3 How many 20c coins make $2? ______

4 A bottle balanced 12 bolts.

A book balanced 4 bolts.

a Does the bottle have the same mass as 12 bolts? ______

b How many books would balance the bottle? ______

5 Our zoo has 82 monkeys. Their zoo has 15 more than ours. How many monkeys in both zoos? ______

6 Months in 2 years. ______

7 30 − 6 − 6 − 6 − 6 − 6 ______

8 20 + 30 + 40 + 50 ______

9 I had 18 lollies. I ate some and had 11 left. How many did I eat? ______

Challenge

Write a pattern with the rule:

a *Add 10.* ______

b *Double.* ______

c *Halve.* ______

d *Subtract 7.* ______

Write a pattern using only multiples of 5.

______

Rounding a Number to the Nearest Ten

If it ends in 5, 6, 7, 8 or 9, round up.

If it ends in 1, 2, 3 or 4, round down.

a Is 36 closer to 30 or 40?

b is 33 closer to 30 or 40?

Round each of these to the nearest ten.

c 44 ______ **d** 17 ______ **e** 85 ______

The answer must end in zero.

25, 26, 27, 28, 29,	35, 36, 37, 38, 39
30, 31, 32, 33, 34,	40, 41, 42, 43, 44

28:1 out of 16

1. 1 × 3 ____
2. 19 − 9 ____
3. 4 + 10 ____
4. 4 × 3 ____
5. 10 + 10 ____
6. 11 − 6 ____
7. 10 + 1 ____
8. 8 is half of: ____
9. Take 3 from 9. ____
10. 19 − 6 ____
11. 4000 + 700 + 30 + 4 ____
12. 716, 726, 736, ____, ____, ____
13. These are called t ____ marks.

14. Write the value of 3 in:
    a 8304 ____ b 2139 ____
15. On this column graph show 25 trucks and 50 cars.

Trucks						
Cars						
0	10	20	30	40	50	60

16. 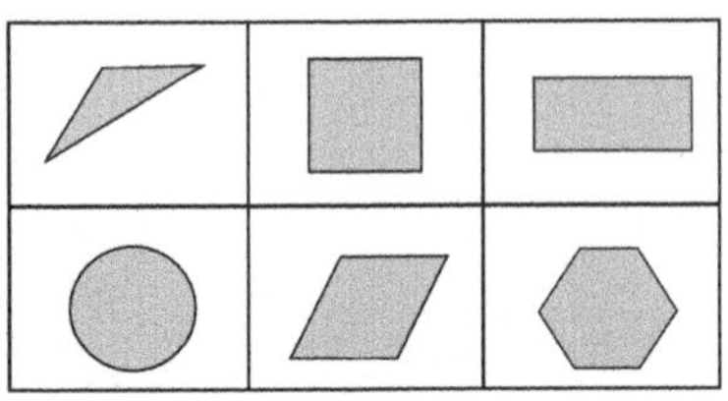

What shape is at the:
a bottom left? ____
b top right? ____

28:2 out of 15

1. 44 + 45 ____
2. 87 − 10 ____
3. 4 × 5 ____
4. 7 × 8 ____
5. 3 × 3 ____
6. 702, 704, 706, ____
7. 20 shared by 5. ____
8. 31 less than 40. ____
9. Double 34. ____
10. 5 × 9 ____
11. Fill these in for 1 479.
    a | | | hundreds | | tens | | ones |
    b | | | | tens | | ones |
12. Write the numeral for one thousand and sixty-two. ____
13. The year before 2 000. ____
14. 

    I am 3rd out of 7. How many are:
    a in front of me? ____
    b behind me? ____
15. a 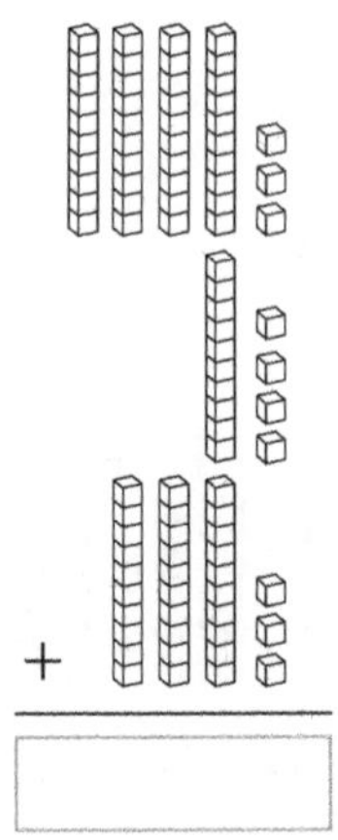 b 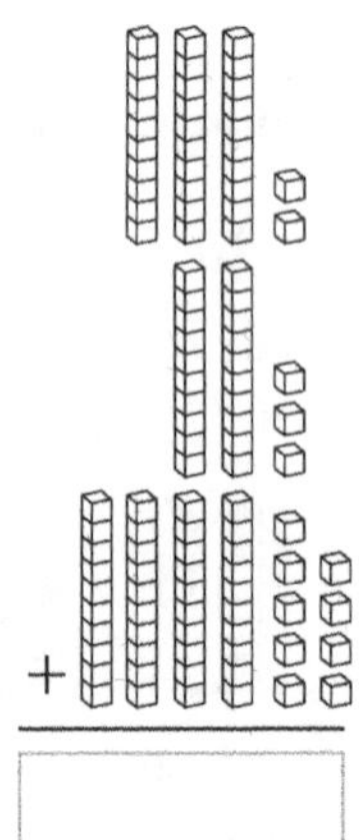

 • ISBN 978 1 4886 2183 3

28:3 — out of 13

1.

Tens	Ones
2	9
+ 3	1

2.

Tens	Ones
5	9
+ 1	2

3. If 4 × 5 = 20, then 20 is a multiple of _____ and _____.
4. Write 5 multiples of 2.

____

5. _____ × 2 = 16 so 16 ÷ 2 = _____
6. Write < or > for:

   a 2654 __________ 2664

   b 1929 __________ 1981

7. 6 + 7 + 3 + 8 + 8 + 2 + 1 __________
8. What does the tally stand for?  __________
9. How many minutes in 1 hour? __________
10. How many pairs of parallel sides has a rectangle? __________
11. Days in November. __________
12. 7 △ 3 = 21 △ = __________
13. 

    a 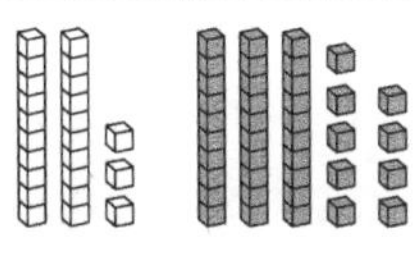

    23 + 39 = _____

    b 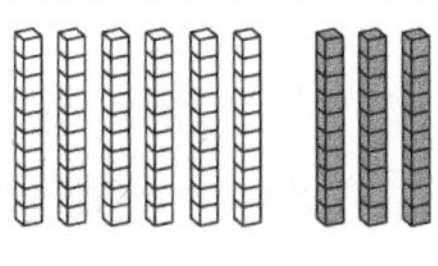

    60 + 30 = _____

28:4 — out of 5

Extension

1. 16 + 14 + 15 + 5 __________
2. Complete the number sentence if each bundle has 10 sticks. __________

   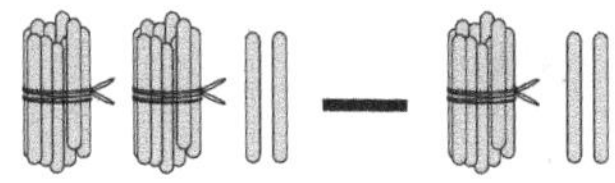

   _______ − _______ = _______

3. Mum grew 30 roses and cut 24. How many were *not* cut? __________

4. Lachlan shared 60 Smarties with 2 of his friends. How many did each child get? __________
5. 

   1st 2nd 3rd 4th 5th 6th

   If this pattern continues, what will the 26th triangle look like? __________

Challenge

Draw a path on the grid from the counter to the triangle. Describe the path.

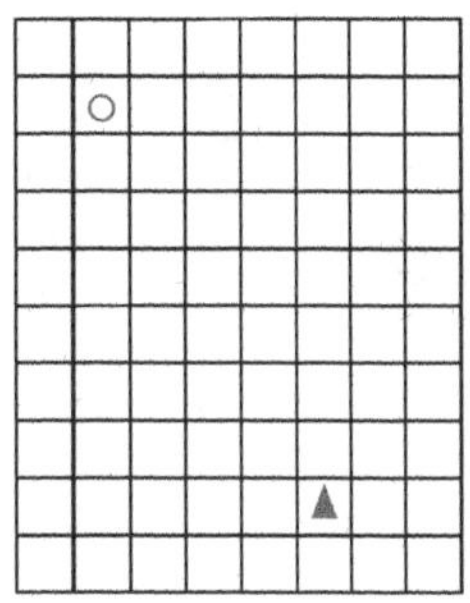

____

____

____

____

____

Using Number Lines

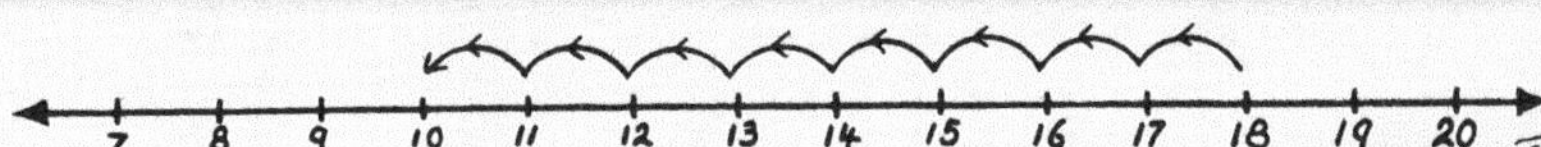

18 − 8

Start at 18 and move 8 jumps to the left.

17 − 7	
17 − 8	
17 − 9	
17 − 10	

18 − 8	
18 − 9	
18 − 10	

19 − 9	
19 − 10	

20 − 10	

29:1 ☐ out of 16

1. 14 − 10 ____
2. 5 × 3 ____
3. 6 + 6 ____
4. 13 − 10 ____
5. $\begin{array}{r} 7 \\ -\ 4 \\ \hline \end{array}$
6. 2 × 3 ____
7. 8 + 10 ____
8. 1 + 6 + 9 ____
9. 60c + 30c ____
10. $\begin{array}{r} 16 \\ -\ 2 \\ \hline \end{array}$
11. 9000 + 500 + 20 + 9 ____
12. Six teams of 5 children. How many children altogether? ____
13. Which shape covers the most area? ____

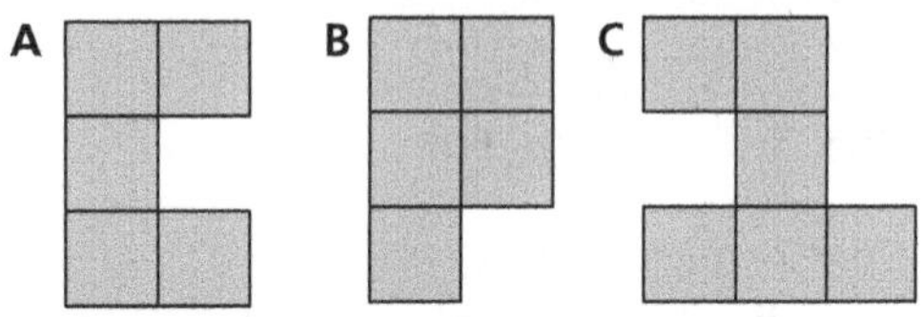

14. Round off 143 to the nearest hundred. ____
15. Which number is larger: 203 or 198? ____

16.

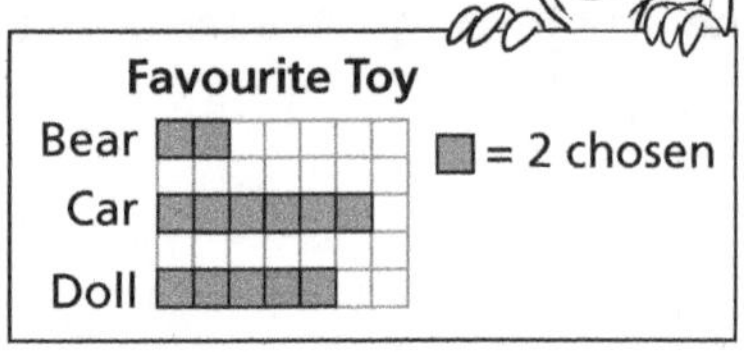

a Which toy was chosen least? ____
b How many more cars were chosen than bears? ____
c How many cars and dolls were chosen altogether? ____

29:2 ☐ out of 14

1. 50 − 15 ____
2. 43 − 10 ____
3. 32 − 10 ____
4. 25 ÷ 5 ____
5. $\begin{array}{r} 5 \\ \times\ 7 \\ \hline \end{array}$
6. 18 − 6 − 6 ____
7. 7 tens + 9 ones ____
8. 30c + 30c + 30c ____
9. 40 shared by 5. ____
10. $\begin{array}{r} 3 \\ \times\ 9 \\ \hline \end{array}$
11. Show the time 3:34 on the clock face.

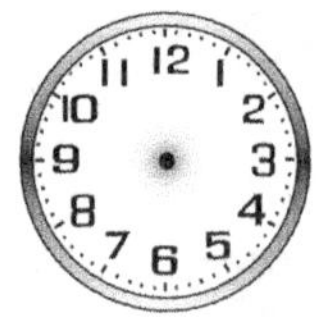

12. If 3 × 4 = 12 then 12 is a multiple of ____ and ____.
13. Write the number shown by:
    a 卌 卌 ____
    b 卌 卌 卌 ____
14.

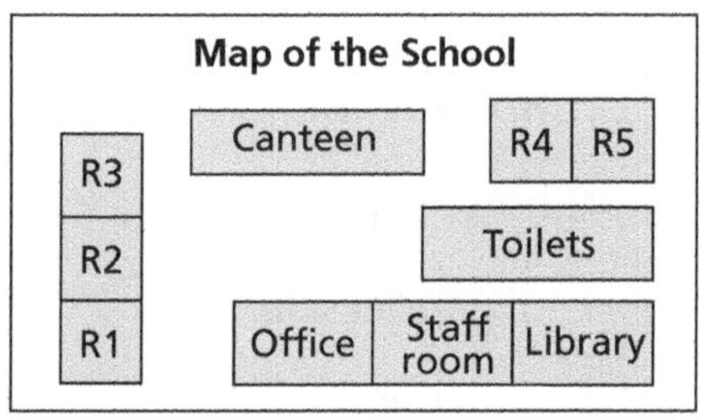

a What rooms are next to R2? ____
b What room is next to the office? ____
c What is between R3 and R4? ____
d What rooms are next to the staff room? ____
e What is between R5 and the library? ____

even − even = ____
odd − even = ____

© PEARSON AUSTRALIA 2018 • *AUSTRALIAN SIGNPOST MATHS 3 MENTALS* • ISBN 978 1 4886 2183 3

29:3 ☐ out of 10

1.
Tens	Ones
	4
+ 1	7

2.
Tens	Ones
6	4
+	6

3. 95, 90, 85, ____, ____, ____
4. The numeral for 800 + 50 + 7. ____
5. Write 154 in words. ____
6. Round off 356 to the nearest hundred. ____
7. 325, 335, 345, ____, ____, ____
8. Write 5 multiples of 5. ____
9.

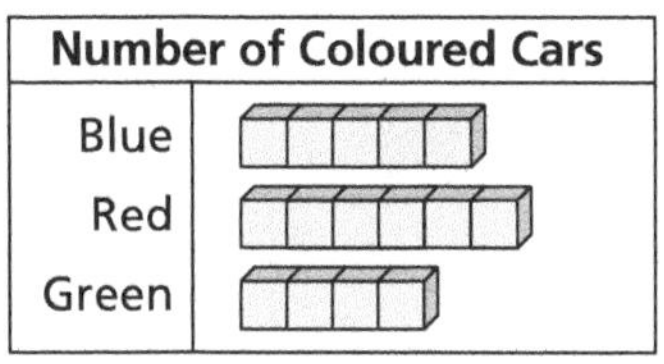

 stands for 4 cars

a What coloured car has the greatest number? ____

b How many more red cars than green cars? ____

c How many cars altogether? ____

10.

a 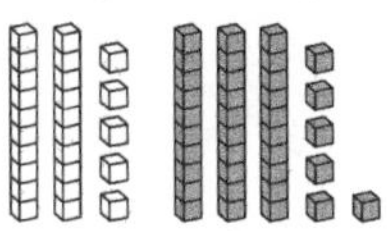

25 + 36 = ____

b 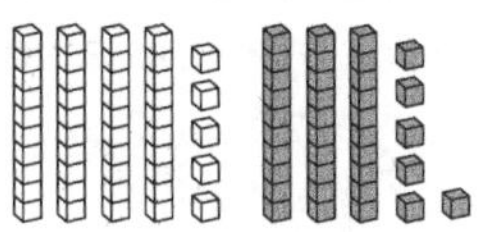

45 + 36 = ____

29:4 ☐ out of 6

Extension

1. Which has the greatest area? ____

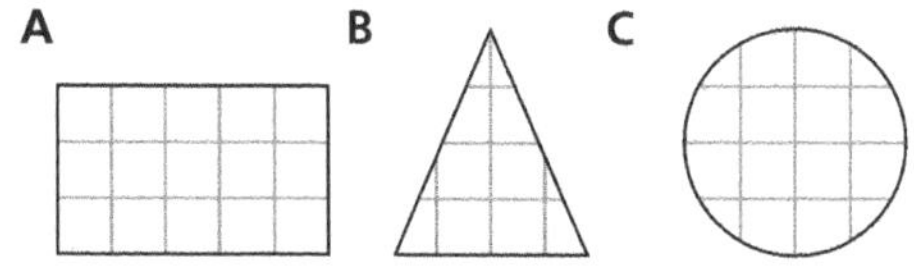

2. If "<" means "is less than", write true or false for:

a $2 \times 8 < 5 \times 4$ ____

b $35 < 3 \times 10$ ____

3. True or false?

a $3 \times 9 = 9 \times 3$ ____

b $3 \times 9 = 9 + 9 + 9$ ____

4. ● ○ ● ○ ● ○

1st 2nd 3rd 4th 5th 6th

If this pattern continues, will the 41st circle be shaded? ____

5. 6, 17, 28, ____, ____, ____
6. 100 − 15 − 15 − 15 − 15 ____

Challenge

Write number sentences of your own using < (less than) or > (greater than) signs.

____

____

____

*

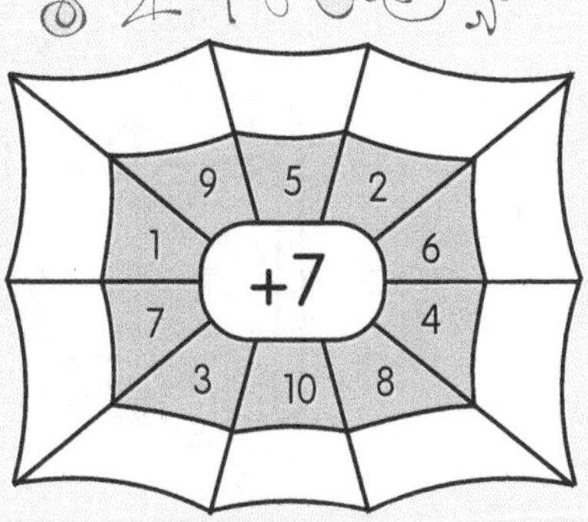

*

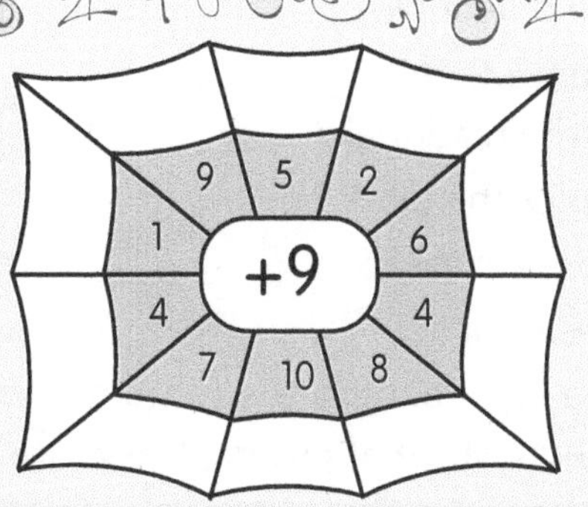

odd − even = ____

30:1 ☐ out of 16

1. 2×6 ______
2. $14 - 4$ ______
3. $16 - 6$ ______
4. $2 + 9$ ______
5. $\begin{array}{r} 19 \\ +\ 2 \\ \hline \end{array}$
6. $4 + 8$ ______
7. 10×6 ______
8. 3 lots of 5. ______
9. 2 less than 10. ______
10. $\begin{array}{r} 18 \\ -\ 6 \\ \hline \end{array}$

11. a The analogue time is ______ to ______.
    b The digital time is ______ : ______.

12. Is it likely that you will go to school tomorrow? ______
13. How many ears would 10 children have? ______

14. True or false? (< means "is less than".)
    a 3920 > 3951 ______
    b 7900 < 7852 ______
15. Round off to the nearest 10:
    a 73 ______ b 36 ______
16. 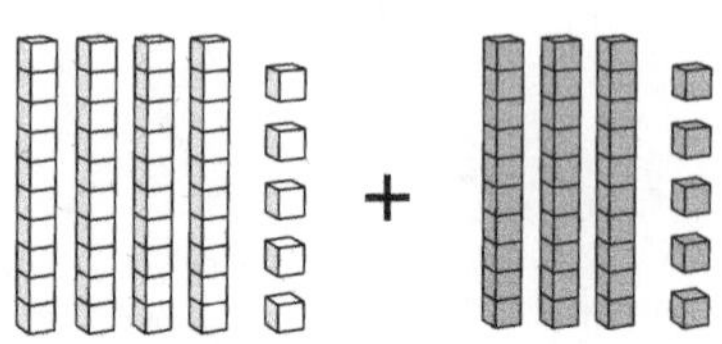

    ______ + ______ = ______

30:2 ☐ out of 17

1. $29 + 37$ ______
2. $800 - 500$ ______
3. 8×5 ______
4. 6×5 ______
5. $\begin{array}{r} 10 \\ \times\ 9 \\ \hline \end{array}$
6. 30 shared by 5. ______
7. 7 groups of 5. ______
8. $16 \div 2$ ______
9. 84 m + 17 m ______
10. $\begin{array}{r} 2 \\ \times\ 9 \\ \hline \end{array}$

11. 912, 922, 932, ______, ______, ______
12. I had 23 books but lost some. 11 are left. How many were lost? ______
13. 5 flowers in each bunch. How many in 6 bunches? ______
14. Complete this pattern.
    $\frac{1}{2}$, 1, $1\frac{1}{2}$, 2, $2\frac{1}{2}$, ______, ______
15. Order from smallest to largest.
    1692, 999, 1588 ______
16. Write the numeral for five thousand one hundred and ninety-eight. ______
17. 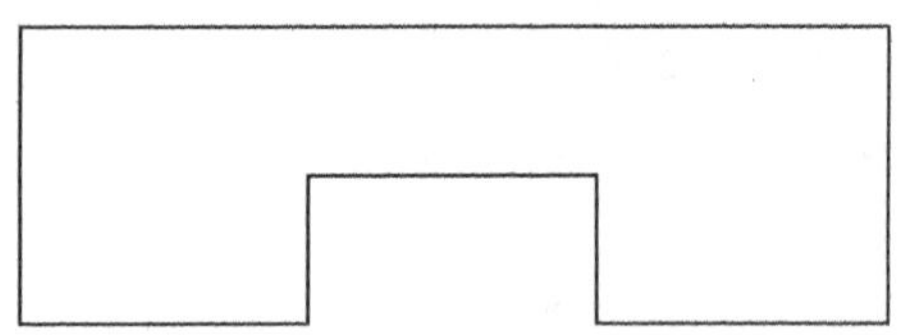

    How many place-value ones blocks are needed to cover this area?

Area = ______ blocks

Jorge must choose one object.

1. What is the chance that:
   a he will pick the black ball? ______
   b he will not pick the black ball? ______
   c he will choose a cube? ______
   d he will choose a ball? ______
2. If I add 10 more black balls to the container, will Jorge have more or less chance of picking the white ball? ______

 ISBN 978 1 4886 2183 3

30:3   ☐ out of 10

1

Tens	Ones
3	9
+ 1	4

2

Tens	Ones
2	7
+ 3	5

3 Complete the table.

First number	1	2	3	4	5	6
Second number	2	4	6			

4 99, 97, 95, ______, ______, ______

5 I own 43 stickers. This is 8 more than Rhonda owns. How many does Rhonda own? ______

6 Is it certain that if I swim, I will get wet? ______

7 137 cents in dollars. $______

8 253, 263, 273, ______, ______, ______

9 The number of these rectangles that would be needed to cover:

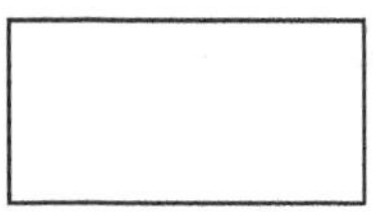

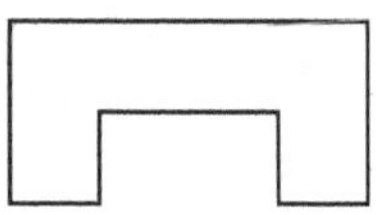

a ______   b ______

10

a 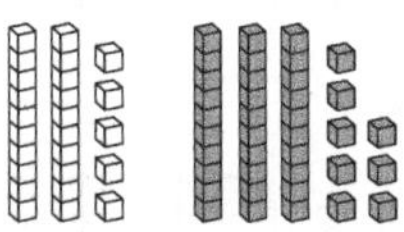

25 + 38 = ______

b 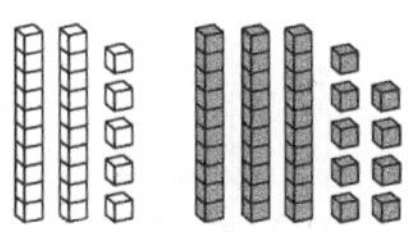

25 + 39 = ______

30:4   Extension   ☐ out of 7

1 In how many different orders can you write the letters A, B and C? (You could make a list.) ______

2 Colour three quarters of the boats.

3 Our zoo has 56 seals. Their zoo has 17 seals less. How many seals in both zoos? ______

4 How many place-value ones blocks do you need to cover this area?

Area = ______ blocks

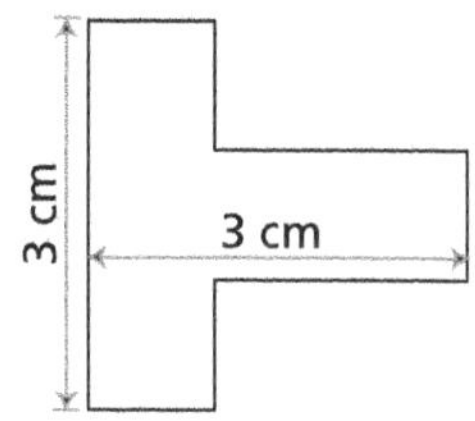

5 Which quadrilaterals have all sides equal?

______

6 If this pattern continues how many hexagons will be in row:

a 5? ______

b 10? ______

7 Jill had 50 books. She gave away 21. How many did she have left? ______

Challenge

Write a number story with the answer 42.

______

______

______

Turn to ID Card A on page 6.
Give the answers for these numbers.

(11) ______   (12) ______

(13) 6 ______ 2   (14) 4 ______ 10

(15) 8 ______ 10   (16) ______

(17) ______   (21) ______ expander

31:1 ☐ out of 16

1. 2 × 9 ____
2. 12 − 2 ____
3. 15 − 5 ____
4. 1 + 10 ____
5. 76 + 15 (vertical: 76 over + 15)
6. 40 g + 20 g ____
7. 10 + 7 ____
8. 4 + 8 + 6 ____
9. 75c + 25c ____
10. 18 − 10 (vertical: 18 over − 10)
11. If I toss a coin 10 times, am I very unlikely to get 10 heads? ____
12. Write thirty grams in short form. ____
13. Is it likely that the next school bus you see will have passengers on it? ____

14. 15 birds were on the lake. 5 flew away. How many were left? ____

15. 26 bottles, 7 broken. How many left? ____
16. Give the rule for this pattern.

20, 40, 60, 80, 100, ...

____

31:2 ☐ out of 15

1. 58 + 35 ____
2. 49 + 25 ____
3. 7 × 4 ____
4. 10 × 6 ____
5. 5 × 8 (vertical: 5 over × 8)
6. 15 shared by 3. ____
7. 3 rows of 3. ____
8. 50c + 30c + 10c ____
9. 200 g + 100 g ____
10. 5 × 4 (vertical: 5 over × 4)
11. 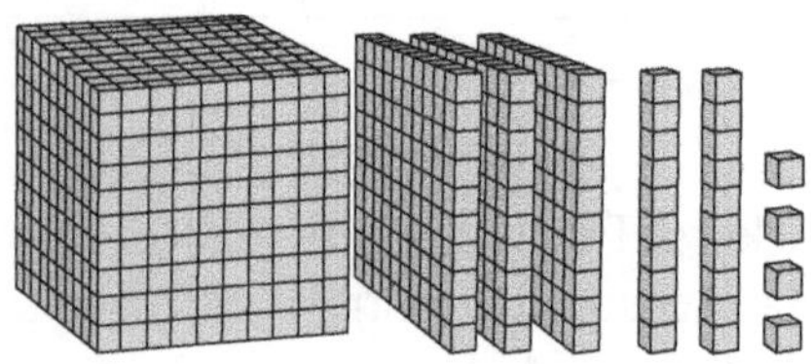

The number modelled above. ____

12. The number before 3600. ____
13. I played golf. What was my total score for these 4 holes? ____

Hole 1	8
Hole 2	9
Hole 3	7
Hole 4	10

14. Complete:

3, ____, 9, 12, ____, ____

15. 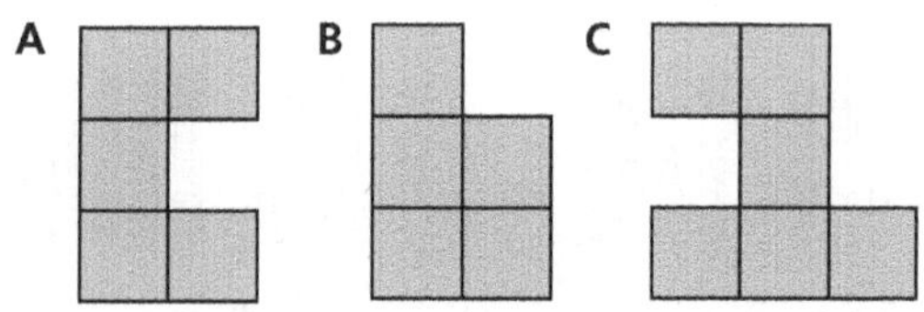

Which shape has the greatest area? ____

Writing Fractions

The part shaded is:

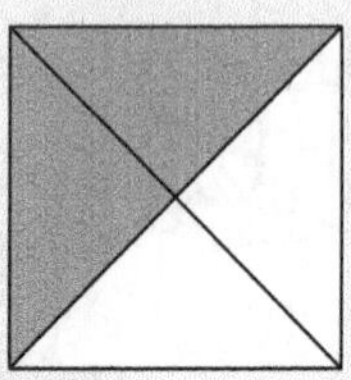

2 out of 4
or
one half
$\frac{2}{4}$ or $\frac{1}{2}$

a 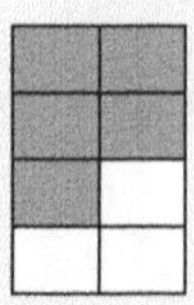 ____ out of ____ or $\frac{\square}{\square}$

b 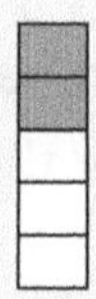 ____ out of ____ or $\frac{\square}{\square}$

c  ____ out of ____ or $\frac{\square}{\square}$

d  ____ out of ____ or $\frac{\square}{\square}$

31:3 ☐ out of 9

1

Tens	Ones
4	6
+ 3	9

2

Tens	Ones
5	7
+ 1	7

3 Write the rule that connects the second number to the first.

First number	1	2	3	4	5	6
Second number	6	7	8	9	10	11

Rule: ______

4 Write this as one numeral.

1 000 + 700 + 90 ______

5 Round off 6 482 to the nearest thousand. ______

6 A

B

C

What would be weighed in:

a kilograms? ______ b grams? ______

7 The number before 7 219. ______

8 What number added to itself gives 14? ______

9

a

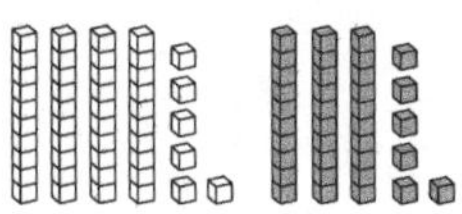

46 + 36 = ______

b

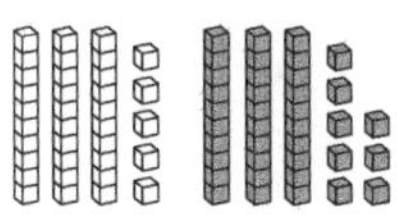

35 + 38 = ______

31:4 Extension ☐ out of 5

1 Three bricks were placed between each pair of poles.

a How many bricks were used? ______

b How many would be used if there were 10 poles? ______

2 I have 28 toys. To how many children can I give 4 toys?

______

3 Add 15 each time.

10, ______, ______, ______, ______

4

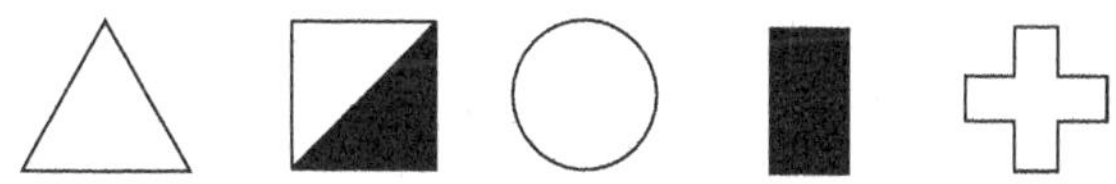

If this pattern was repeated, what would the 19th shape be? ______

5 Luke has 12 books. Kim has 3 times as many. How many has Kim? ______

Challenge

List items that would be measured in grams.

______

______

______

______

______

Near Doubling

a 8 + 9 = ______ b 16 + 15 = ______

c 7 + 8 = ______ d 24 + 23 = ______

e 20 + 21 = ______ f 35 + 36 = ______

g 32 + 33 = ______ h 13 + 14 = ______

i 16 + 17 = ______ j 26 + 25 = ______

32:1   ☐ out of 16

1. 8 + 8 ______
2. 11 − 4 ______
3. 1 × 9 ______
4. 19 − 10 ______
5. $\begin{array}{r} 13 \\ +\ \ 9 \\ \hline \end{array}$
6. 3 × 9 ______
7. 9 + 10 ______
8. 13 minus 4. ______
9. \$15 + \$50 ______
10. $\begin{array}{r} 68 \\ -\ \ 4 \\ \hline \end{array}$
11. The numeral for 700 + 40 + 6. ______
12. Place 807, 153 and 629 in order from largest to smallest. ______
13. Cross out the mistake in the pattern.

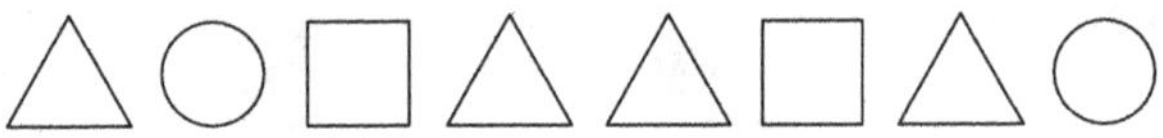

14. The value of the 4 in 4631. ______
15.

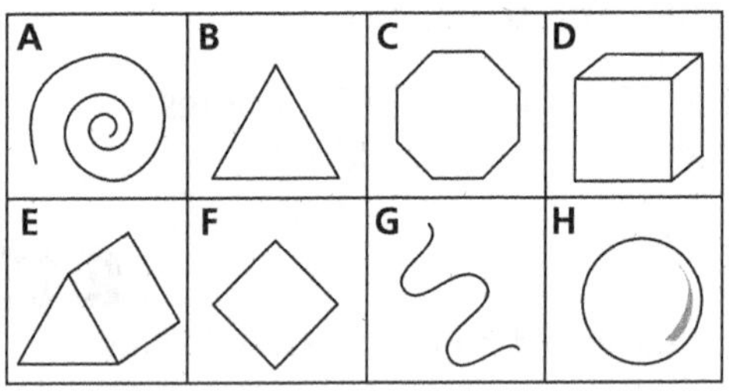

a How many angles on shape **C**? ______

b How many faces on shape **D**? ______

c Name shape **E**. ______

d Which are 2D shapes? ______

e Which are solid objects? ______

16. If there are 12 eggs in 1 dozen, how many eggs in 2 dozen? ______

32:2   ☐ out of 17

1. Double 9. ______
2. 27 + 59 ______
3. 2 × 7 ______
4. 10 × 7 ______
5. $\begin{array}{r} 2 \\ \times\ \ 7 \\ \hline \end{array}$
6. Sum of 36 and 25. ______
7. \$12 + \$8 + \$7 ______
8. 100 cents equals ______ .
9. 20 m minus 17 m. ______
10. $\begin{array}{r} 10 \\ \times\ \ 8 \\ \hline \end{array}$
11. Write sixty kilograms in short form. ______
12. Start at 26. Count by even numbers.

    26, ______, ______, ______, ______

13. If I toss 10 coins, will I always get the same number of heads and tails? ______
14. The number before 3670. ______
15. 4 books have 20 pages each. How many pages altogether? ______
16.

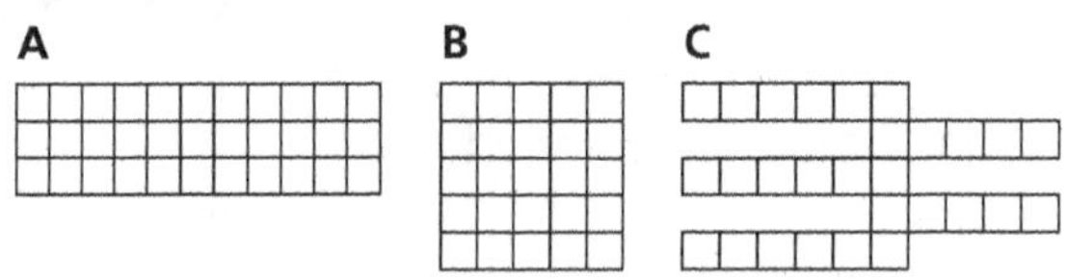

The shape with:

a the greatest area. ______

b the smallest area. ______

17. How many corners has:

a **A**? ______

b **B**? ______

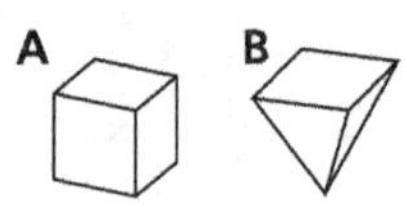

Place the letter from these boxes on the line below, in order, from *least likely* to *most likely*.

The next person to walk through the classroom door will be:

A a teacher	**B** the principal	**C** my mother
D a human	**E** a father	**F** a boy

least likely ________________________________ most likely

 • *AUSTRALIAN SIGNPOST MATHS 3 MENTALS* • ISBN 978 1 4886 2183 3

☐ out of 9

1

Tens	Ones
6	7
+ 4	5

2

Tens	Ones
3	9
+ 6	3

3 What ordinal number follows 42nd? ______

4 The day after Thursday. ______

5 If it is Tuesday the 5th, what will it be in 4 days time? ______

6 Write ten grams in short form. ______

7 4 books have 80 pages altogether. How many pages in each book? ______

8 **a** Match the similar solid using lines.

A B C

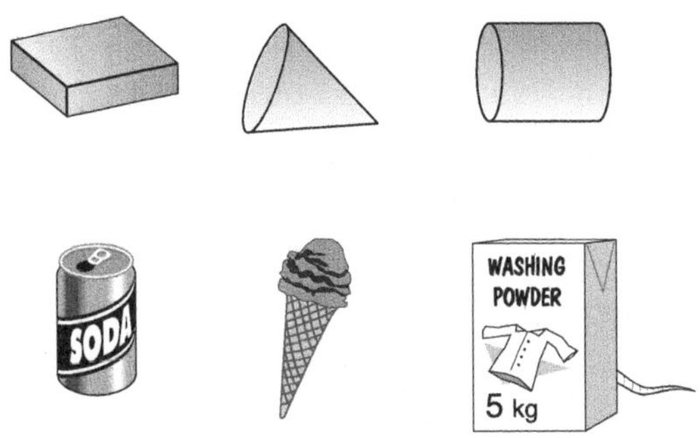

b Name solid **B** above. ______

c Do solids like **A** stack easily? ______

d Will shape **C** roll? ______

9

a 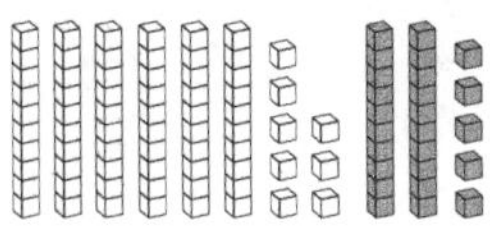

68 + 25 = ______

b 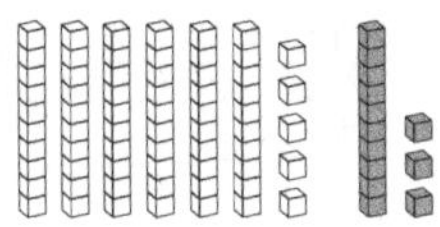

65 + 13 = ______

☐ out of 7

1 Write down each set of 3 counting numbers that have a total of 7.
(Numbers can be used more than once.)

______

______

2 70 − 10 − 10 − 10 − 10 ______

3 Ten toy soldiers were standing in a row. Between each pair there are two toy cars. How many toys are there altogether? ______

4 25 + 35 + 45 + 55 ______

5 90 − 15 − 15 − 15 ______

6 Add 17 each time.

17, ______, ______, ______

7 In a volleyball game, each team has six players on the court. How many players in 10 games altogether? ______

Challenge

Draw a 3D object. Label as many features as you can.

a 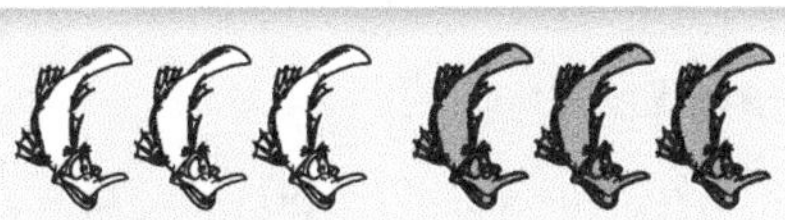

Part shaded = ____ out of 6
= ____ out of 2

b 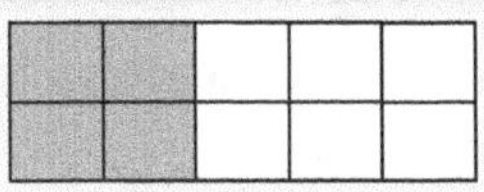

Part shaded = ____ out of 10
= ____ out of 5

c 

Part shaded = ____ out of 8
= ____ out of 4

d 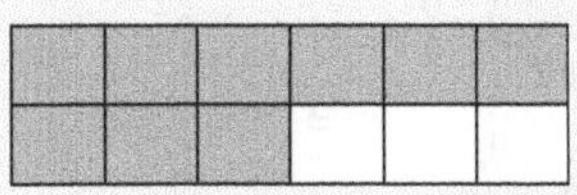

Part shaded = ____ out of 12
= ____ out of 4

33:1

out of 19

1. 11 − 1 ____
2. 4 + 7 ____
3. 10 × 9 ____
4. 18 − 8 ____
5. 55 − 3 ____
6. 2 + 10 ____
7. 4 × 2 ____
8. 3 m + 8 m ____
9. 4 + 4 + 4 + 4 ____
10. 14 + 9 ____
11. 7:30 is the same as ____ past ____.
12. Four books cost $2.00. How much for one? ____
13. Draw 5 groups of 2 flowers.

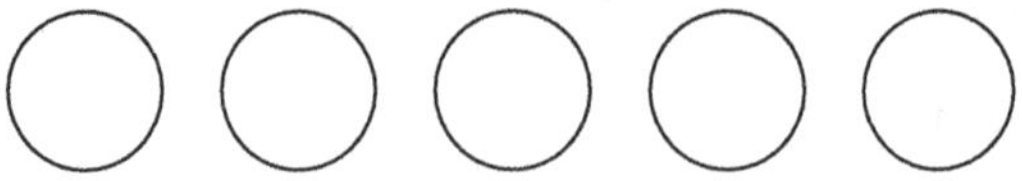

How many altogether? ____

14. Weeks in 1 year. ____
15. **a** A square has ____ angles.
    b A triangle has ____ sides.
16. How many toes on 8 people? ____
17.

	3	7	4	5	2	10	6	9
× 5								

18. Laura and Akos set up a lemonade stand for two hours.

    a How many drinks did they sell if they sold 10 each hour? ____
    b How much money did they earn if each drink was $1.00? ____
19. Use a multiplication sign to write 4 rows of 3. ____

33:2

out of 17

1. 29 + 29 ____
2. 56 + 25 ____
3. 3 × 5 ____
4. 9 + 5 ____
5. 1 × 7 ____
6. 7 groups of 2. ____
7. Ninety minus ten. ____
8. 84 subtract 33. ____
9. 40, 44, ____ ,52
10. 19 + 9 ____

11. Name this shape.

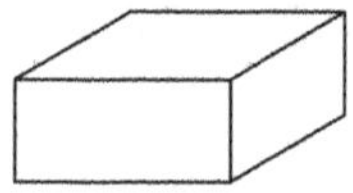

____

12. 3 less than 2 060. ____
13. Write 3 705 in words. ____
14. Name this shape. ____

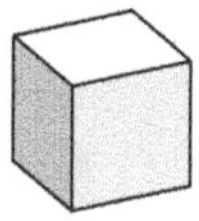

15. Colour one quarter of this group.

16. There are 5 monkeys in each cage. How many in 4 cages? ____
17. A B C D

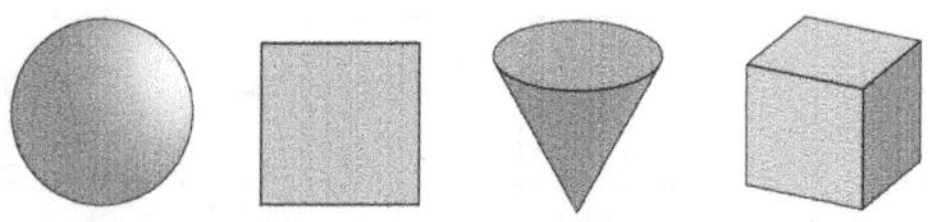

Which shape is *not* a solid? ____

Subtraction by Counting Back

a 17 − 3
b 21 − 2
c 60 − 1
d 49 − 3
e 30 − 3
f 42 − 4
g 51 − 2
h 32 − 2

 ISBN 978 1 4886 2183 3

33:3   ☐ out of 7

1

Tens	Ones
7	9
− 6	5

2

Tens	Ones
8	7
− 3	5

3 Write the numeral for the number shown. ______

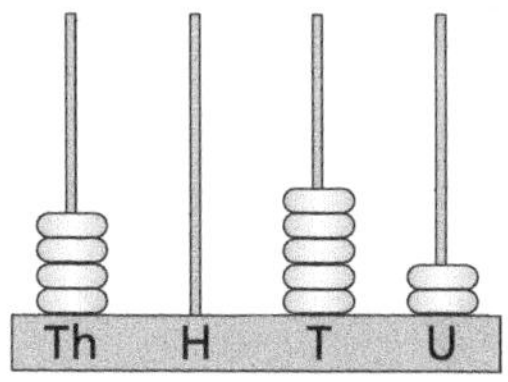

4 Colour 3 eighths.

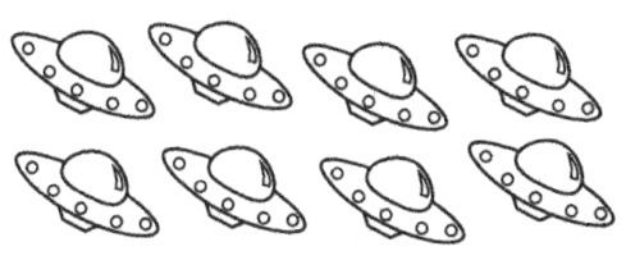

5 376, 374, 372, ______, ______

6

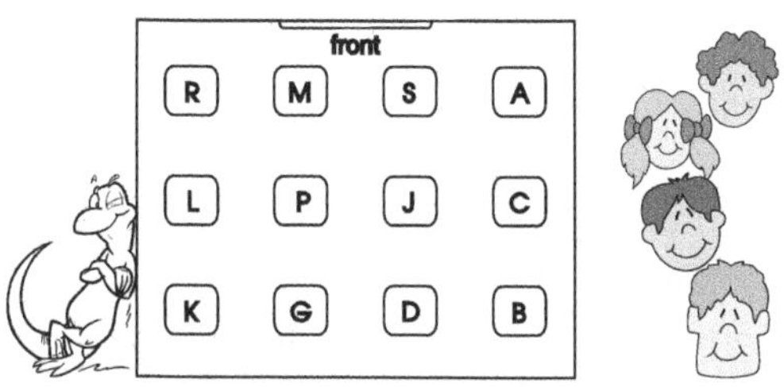

a Who sits in front of **L**? ______

b Who sits behind **S**? ______

c Who sits to the right of **G**? ______

d Who sits to the left of **P**? ______

e Who sits in the back right corner? ______

7 How many:

a edges? ______

b faces? ______

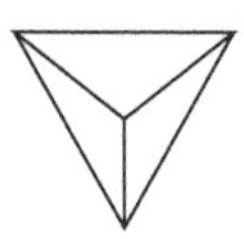

33:4   Extension   ☐ out of 5

1 How many:

a edges? ______

b faces + corners? ______

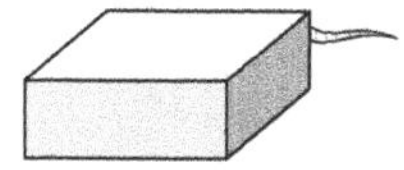

2 It takes 12 minutes to colour in one page. How many minutes will it take to colour 5 pages? ______

3 How many hexagons would be in row:

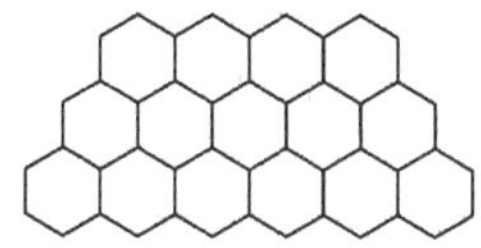

a 5? ______

b 10? ______

4 5 sheep and 3 chickens. How many legs? ______

5 50 − 20 − 15 − 10 ______

Challenge

Draw a map of a room in your home.

Draw a key to show things in the room.

Turn to ID Card B on page 7.

Give the answers for these numbers.

(2)	______	(3)	______
(23)	______	(24)	______
(25)	______	(26)	______
(27)	______	(28)	______
(29)	______	(30)	______

34:1 — out of 13

1. 19 + 4 ______
2. 17 − 9 ______
3. 3 + 8 ______
4. 2 × 10 ______
5. $\begin{array}{r} 34 \\ -\ \ 3 \\ \hline \end{array}$
6. 11 − 10 ______
7. 49 + 7 ______
8. $1.00 − 80c ______
9. 7 more than 7. ______
10. $\begin{array}{r} 62 \\ +\ \ 4 \\ \hline \end{array}$

11. How many lines of symmetry has this shape? ______

12. Which is closer to 1 metre, the height of a cat, the width of a door or the length of a car? ______

13.

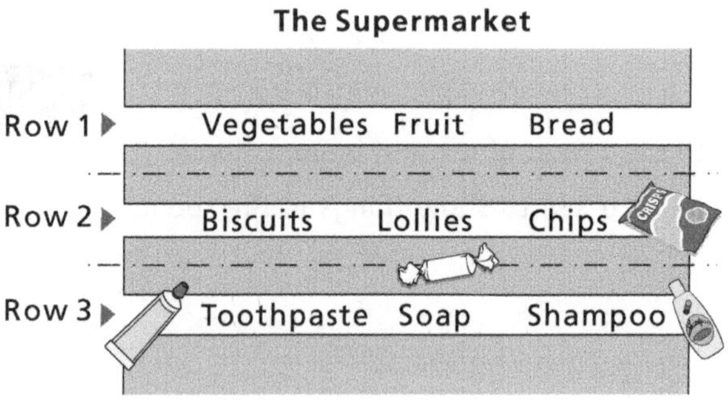

a Which row has chips in it? ______

b What is found between bread and vegetables? ______

c What is found next to the toothpaste? ______

d Which row has bread in it? ______

e What is between the biscuits and chips? ______

34:2 — out of 18

1. 29 + 52 ______
2. $96 − $33 ______
3. 29 + 7 ______
4. 34 − 21 ______
5. $\begin{array}{r} 49 \\ +\ \ 5 \\ \hline \end{array}$
6. 4 rows of 3. ______
7. 54 + 13 − 13 ______
8. 2 times 5. ______
9. 10 ÷ 2 ______
10. $\begin{array}{r} 58 \\ +\ \ 3 \\ \hline \end{array}$

11. How many 2 cm lengths could be cut from the ribbon below? ______

12. Centimetres in 1 metre. ______

13. Circle the duck 2nd from the right.

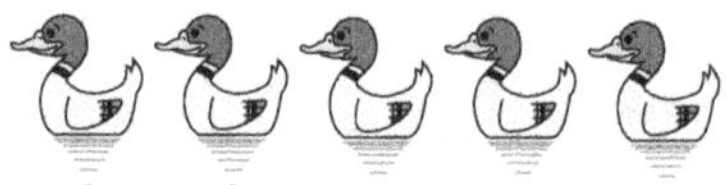

14. School days in one week. ______

15. If I can hold 11 pegs in one hand and 12 in the other hand, how many pegs can I hold in my hands altogether? ______

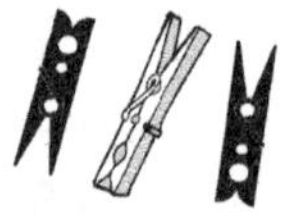

16. Which shape is the cone? ______

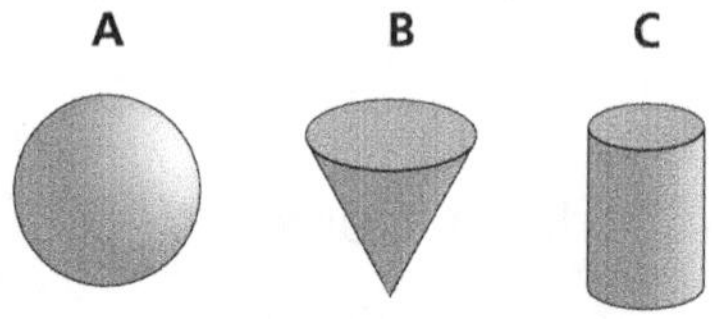

17. The numeral for two hundred and thirty-one. ______

18. 83 + 26 − 26 ______

When you play noughts and crosses, in how many different ways can you make:

a a line of three crosses? ______

b two noughts, side by side? ______

1

	Tens	Ones
	6 8	0
+	4	2

2

	Tens	Ones
	2 4	4
+	9	2

3 Draw the top view of each shape.

a 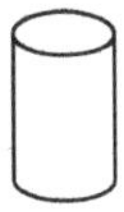

b 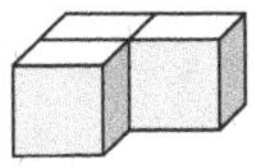

4 59 + 13 − 13 = ______

5 How long is this line: in cm? ______

in mm? ______

6 Jon is now 18. How old will he be in 25 years? ______

7 Shade 6 out of 12.

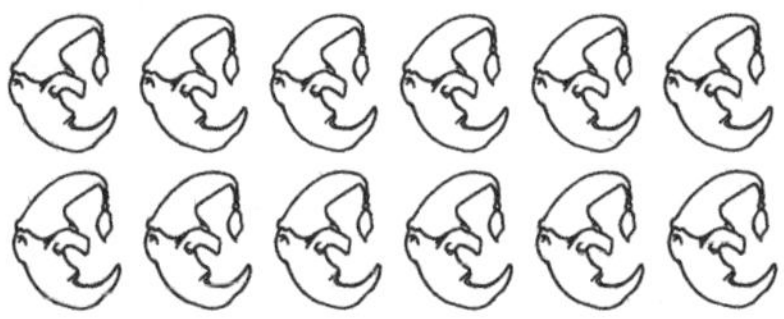

8 8th, 9th, 10th, ______, ______

9 Is this a regular shape?

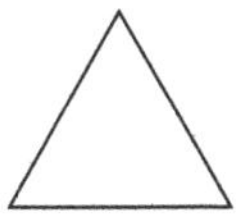

______

10 The difference between 7 and 17. ______

11 I swam 20 metres, then 30 metres and then 40 metres. How far did I swim altogether? ______

1 5337 plus 4. ______

2 How many place-value tens blocks, placed end-to-end, would reach:

a 1 metre? ______ b 2 metres? ______

3 How many different ways can you arrange these in a row?

______

4 How many lines of symmetry has a regular hexagon? ______

5 25 + 15 + 20 + 10 ______

6 80 − 10 − 15 − 20 ______

7 3 rows of 5 plus 4 rows of 3. ______

8 In 2 copies of the same game there were 32 dice altogether. How many dice were in one game? ______

Challenge

Draw a sphere and describe it.

______

______

______

Addition Linked with Subtraction

a 4 + 3 = ☐ 7 − 4 = 7 − 3 =

b 5 + 7 = ☐ 12 − 5 = 12 − 7 =

c 2 + 8 = ☐ 10 − 2 = 10 − 8 =

d 6 + 4 = ☐ 10 − 6 = 10 − 4 =

e 5 + 8 = ☐ 13 − 5 = 13 − 8 =

f 9 + 3 = ☐ 12 − 9 = 12 − 3 =

 • *AUSTRALIAN SIGNPOST MATHS 3 MENTALS* • ISBN 978 1 4886 2183 3

35:1 out of 19

1. 9 + 3 ______
2. 17 − 10 ______
3. 3 × 5 ______
4. 11 − 2 ______
5. 99 − 3 ______
6. 5 + 10 ______
7. 2 × 9 ÷ 9 ______
8. Half of $50. ______
9. Multiply 6 by 5. ______
10. 6 + 6 ______
11. What number follows 376? ______
12. The number shown below. ______

4	hundreds	7	tens	2	ones

13. Centimetres in 1 metre. ______
14. Is the length of a car closer to 2 metres, 4 metres or 20 metres? ______
15. How long is this line: in cm? ______ in mm? ______

16. 4 + 3 = 3 + ☐ ☐ = ______
17. This shape is a s______.

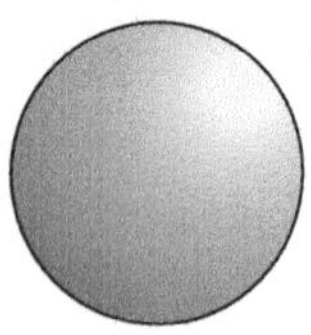

18. A stove is less than 15 cm high. True or false? ______

19. Write 5 190 in words.

______

______

35:2 out of 17

1. 98 − 35 ______
2. 47 + 36 ______
3. 25 + 25 ______
4. 16 − 8 ______
5. 28 + 5 ______
6. 4 lots of 10 kg. ______
7. $4.60 − $1 ______
8. 1 m − 40 cm ______
9. 35 ÷ 7 × 7 ______
10. 59 + 11 ______

11. 3 more than 1 999. ______
12. Write 4 020 in words. ______

______

13. 59 + 38 − 38 = ______
14. Is the length of your foot longer than 30 cm? ______
15. A B C D

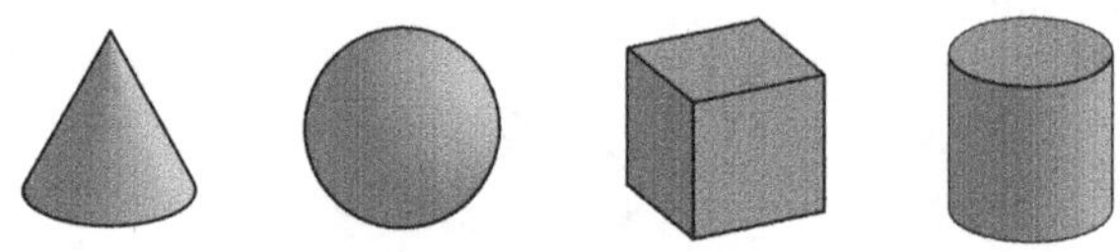

a Which object won't roll? ______

b Name shape **C**. ______

16. Would a ruler weigh less than 1 kg? ______
17. Write < or >.

a 5920 ______ 5093

b 7700 ______ 7785

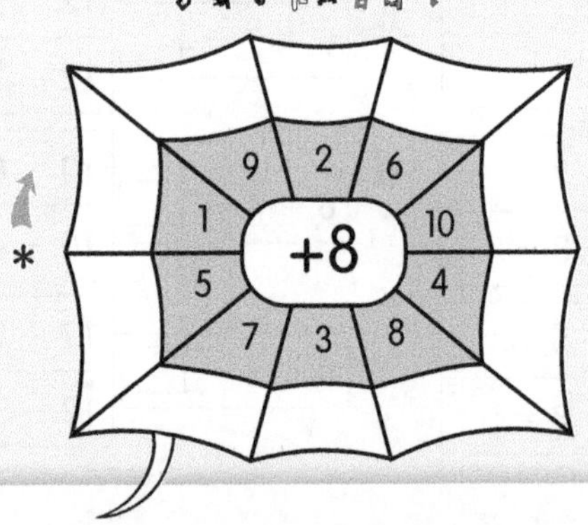

If you add an even number:
- the answer will be even if the other number is even.
- the answer will be odd if the other number is odd.

What happens when you add these types of numbers?

odd + odd = ______

even + odd = ______

 ISBN 978 1 4886 2183 3

35:3 out of 7

1.

	Tens	Ones
1	7	3
+	5	3

2.

	Tens	Ones
5	9	3
−	2	2

3. The value of the 6 in 607. ______
4. 43 + 28 − 28 = ______
5. Estimate how many rulers would fit along the length of your desk. ______
6. Centimetres in 3 metres. ______
7.

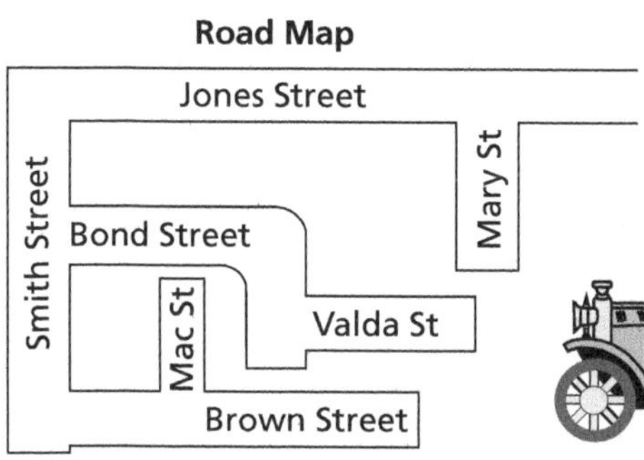

a Mac Street joins ______
b Mary Street joins ______
c Valda Street joins ______
d What Street joins Jones Street and Brown Street? ______
e What other streets do you travel on to get from Valda Street to Mac Street?

______

______

35:4 out of 5

Extension

1. a Colour one half of these sheep red.
   b Colour one quarter blue.

2. If 12 × 9 = 108, find:
   a 108 ÷ 9 ______ b 108 ÷ 12 ______
3. If 32 + 19 = 51 then:
   a 19 + 32 = ______ b 51 − 19 = ______
4. If this pattern continues, how many squares would be in row:

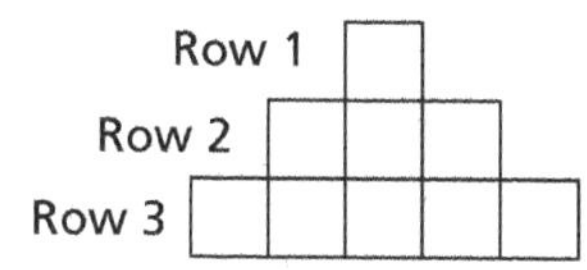

   a 5? ______ b 10? ______
5.

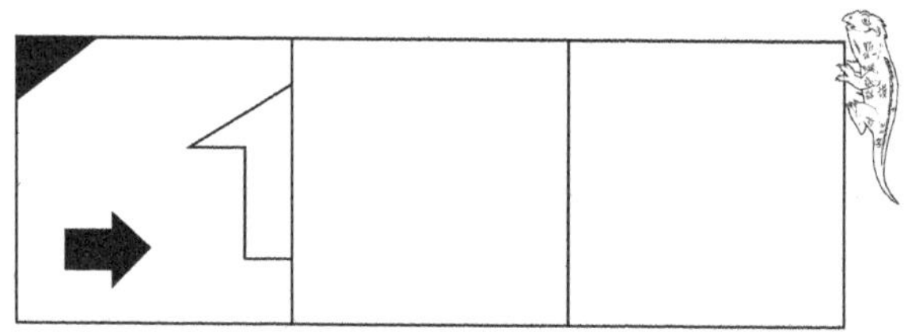

Complete this pattern by flipping each tile to the right.

Challenge

Draw your own pattern by flipping a shape or design.

Turn to ID Card A on page 6.
Give the answers for these numbers.

(11) ______ (12) ______

(18) ______ (19) ______

(20) ______ (21) ______

(22) ______ (30) ______

  ISBN 978 1 4886 2183 3

36:1

out of 17

1. 8 + 8 ______
2. 1 × 6 ______
3. 13 − 3 ______
4. 7 + 0 ______
5. $\begin{array}{r} 76 \\ +\ 2 \\ \hline \end{array}$
6. 9 − 3 ______
7. 4 × 2 ÷ 2 ______
8. Half of 8. ______
9. 3 less than 12. ______
10. $\begin{array}{r} 13 \\ -\ 10 \\ \hline \end{array}$

11. Write 7 008 in words.

______

______

12. Which of the objects:

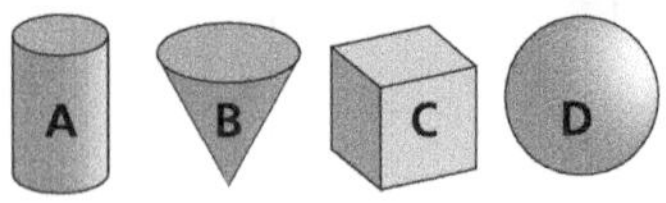

a will roll? ______
b will stack easily? ______
c has the most edges? ______
d has the most surfaces? ______

13. Is this a flip, slide or turn?

______

14. Slide this shape to the right.

15. Millilitres in 7 litres. ______
16. Write the short form for 400 millilitres. ______
17. 10 more than 3 567. ______

36:2

out of 17

1. Double 46. ______
2. 86 − 25 ______
3. 9 × 2 ÷ 2 ______
4. 8 × 5 ______
5. $\begin{array}{r} 58 \\ +\ 3 \\ \hline \end{array}$
6. 35 ÷ 5 × 5 ______
7. 7 × 5 ______
8. Digits in 776. ______
9. 37, 39, ______ , 43
10. $\begin{array}{r} 69 \\ +\ 12 \\ \hline \end{array}$

11. Centimetres in 8 metres. ______
12. Write < or >.

a 5 872 ______ 5 299
b 7 500 ______ 7 671

13. Would a horse weigh less than 1 kg? ______
14. What two shapes are used to make this model?

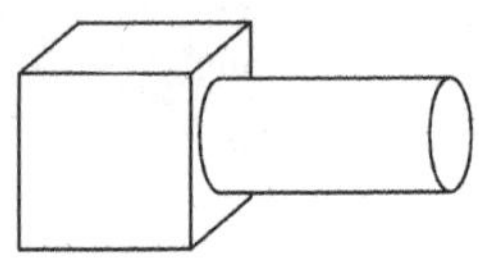

______

______

15. A B C

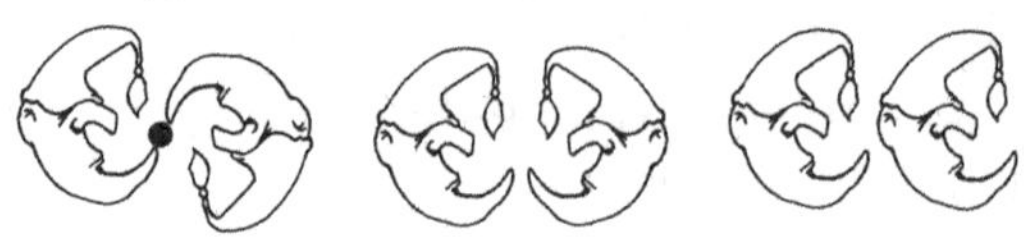

Which picture is:

a a flip? ______ b a slide? ______

16. From $10.00 take away $6.00. ______
17. Write the short form for 5 litres. ______

Turn to ID Card A on page 6.
Give the answers for these numbers.

(1) ______ (2) ______
(3) ______ (4) ______
(5) ______ (6) ______
(23) ______ graph (24) ______
(25) ______ graph (26) ______

36:3 ☐ out of 13

1

	Tens	Ones
7	4	1
+	9	3

2

	Tens	Ones
5	8	2
+	4	0

3 10 less than 5 972. ______

4 How many:

a faces? ______

b corners? ______

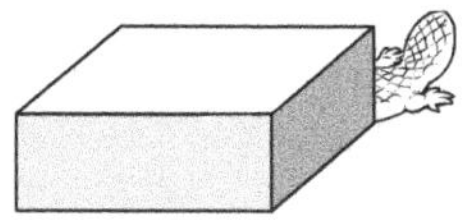

5

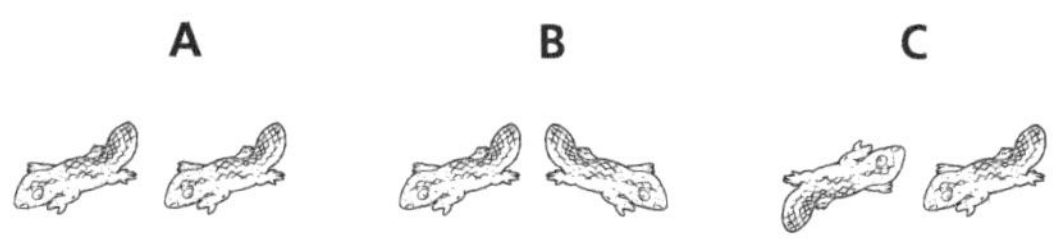

Which picture shows:

a a turn? ______ b a flip? ______

6 I had \$7.30 and spent \$1.40.

How much was left? ______

7 Litres in 2000 mL. ______

8 If 12 × 4 = 48, find:

a 48 ÷ 4 ______ b 48 ÷ 12 ______

9

The total value of the coins is: ______

10 55c + 70c + \$1.00 ______

11 How many days in July? ______

12 3, 6, 9, 12, 15, ______, ______, ______

13 How many 10c coins in \$1? ______

36:4 ☐ out of 6

Extension

1 This cylinder is 8 cm high. How high is:

a one slice? ______

b three slices? ______

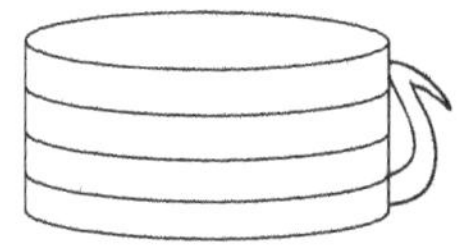

2 Number of faces plus the number of corners minus the number of edges.

______

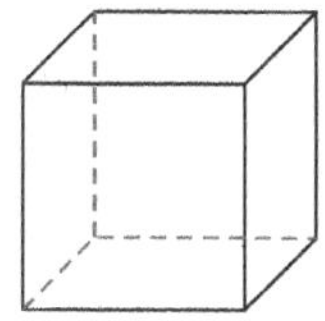

3

If this pattern continued, what would the 27th shape be? ______

4 If 26 + 28 = 54, then:

a 54 − 28 = ______ b 54 − 26 = ______

5 a 30 minutes after 7:15.

______

b 30 minutes before 7:15.

______

6 80 − 25 − 25 − 27 ______

Challenge

Draw a prism and label its attributes.

a Ten trees are planted in a line with two bushes in each space between the trees. How many bushes were planted?

______

b Ten trees are planted in a circle. Two bushes are planted in each space between the trees. How many bushes have been planted?

______

37:1 ☐ out of 17

1. 18 − 10 ____
2. 3 × 6 ____
3. 9 + 9 ____
4. 13 − 3 ____
5. $\begin{array}{r} 4 \\ +\ 10 \\ \hline \end{array}$
6. 5 × 6 ÷ 6 ____
7. 7 + 4 ____
8. 5 more than 7. ____
9. Take 2 from 8. ____
10. $\begin{array}{r} 18 \\ -\ 8 \\ \hline \end{array}$
11. Name the shape. ____

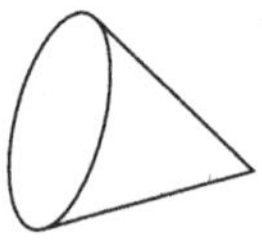

12. Is this a flip, slide or turn? ____

13. 0, 8, 16, ____, ____, ____, ____
14. Write 7 litres in short form. ____
15. **a** Digital time: ____
    b Analogue time:
    ____ past ____

16. What number is 5 less than 50? ____
17. The irregular shapes are: ____

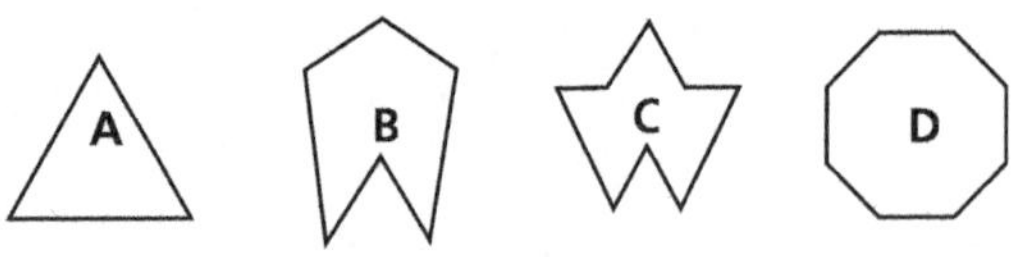

37:2 ☐ out of 19

1. 39 + 43 ____
2. 28 − 16 ____
3. 2 × 10 ____
4. 20 ÷ 10 ____
5. $\begin{array}{r} 10 \\ \times\ 6 \\ \hline \end{array}$
6. 4 groups of 10. ____
7. 37 subtract 20. ____
8. \$4 + \$4 + \$4 ____
9. 16 ÷ 4 × 4 ____
10. $\begin{array}{r} 2 \\ \times\ 8 \\ \hline \end{array}$
11. Does a cube have six faces? ____
12. A B C

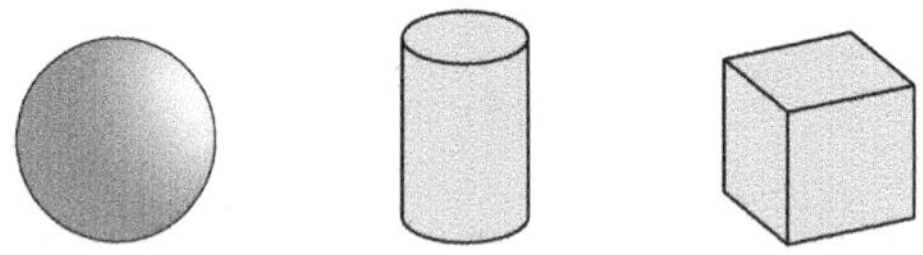

    a Which object has corners? ____
    b What is shape **C**? ____
13. I had \$8.50 and spent \$2.40. How much was left? ____
14. 100 − 25 − 25 − 25 ____
15. Litres in 5000 mL. ____
16. Name the shapes in this picture.
    ____
    ____

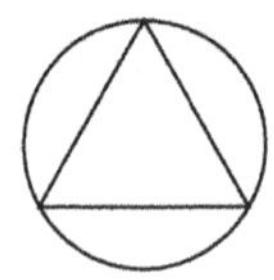

17. Centimetres in 4 metres. ____
18. The change from \$20 if I spend:
    a \$12.50 ____ **b** \$8.70 ____
19. If 596 + 357 = 953, then find:
    a 953 − 596 ____ **b** 953 − 357 ____

To round off correct to the nearest 5 cents, give the closest answer that ends with 5 or 0.

a Is 52 cents closer to 50 cents or 55 cents?

b is 97 cents closer to 95 cents or \$1?

Round off each of these correct to the nearest 5 cents.

c 63c ____ **d** 21c ____ **c** 88c ____ **f** 99c ____

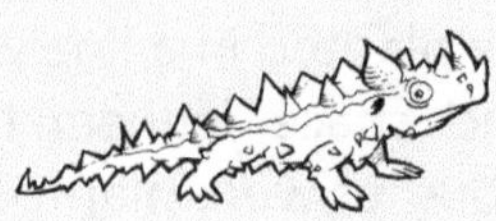

37:3

out of 12

1

	Tens	Ones
	6 9	2
+	4	6

2

	Tens	Ones
	5	3
+	1 8	2

3 I had $10 and spent $3.20.

How much was left? ______

4 Millilitres in 5 litres. ______

5 Cross out the mistake in this pattern.

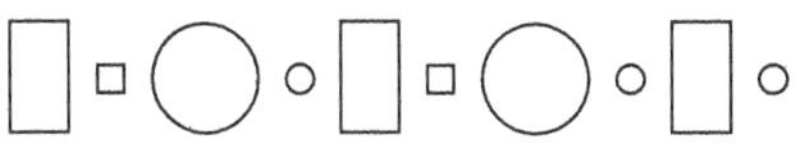

6 I had 60 blocks in a tower. 35 fell down. How many were still standing? ______

7 12 eggs = one dozen

How many eggs in half a dozen? ______

8 Use the jump strategy to find 37 + 25. ______

9 Would a cup hold less than a litre? ______

10 0, 15, 30, ______, ______, ______, ______

11 Draw the front and side view of the cube.

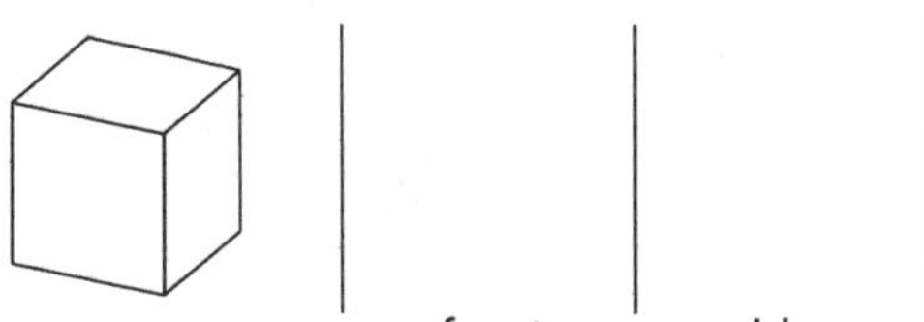

front side

12 A cube has ______ faces.

37:4

Extension

out of 5

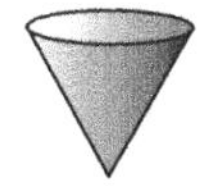

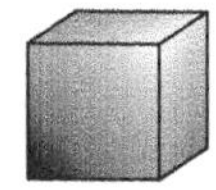

1 a The number of points on 23 cones. ______

b The number of faces on 5 cubes. ______

c The number of edges on 2 cubes. ______

2 Draw a flip and slide of shape A.

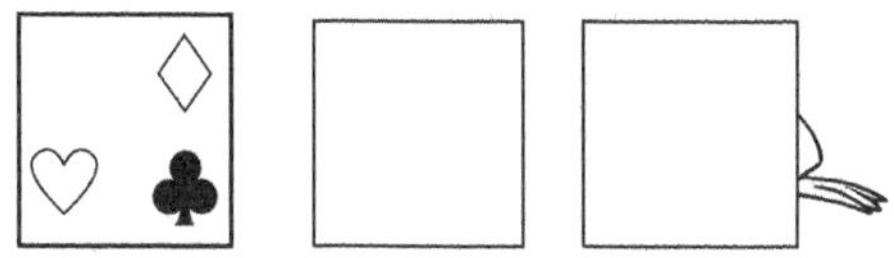

Shape A Flip of A Slide of A

3 a

$$\begin{array}{r} 60 \\ - \square \\ \hline 32 \end{array}$$

b

$$\begin{array}{r} \square \\ - 17 \\ \hline 24 \end{array}$$

4

How many legs on 3 dogs, 3 ducks and 5 crocodiles? ______

5 2 metres minus 50 cm. ______

Challenge

Make a number pattern using the rule:

a Add 25. ______

b Subtract 30. ______

c Add 9. ______

d Subtract 6. ______

e Add 50. ______

Fill out this table for the person measured in unit 1.

Name: ______ **Date:** ______

Age: ______	Mass: ______ kg	Shoe size: ______
Height: ______ cm	Waist: ______ cm	Neck size: ______ cm

How have these measurements changed since unit 1 was done?

______

How Would You Name the Lizards?

1

2

3

4

5

6

7

8

9

10

11

12

13

14

Real names:

1 Horned lizard **2–3** Bearded dragon **4** Gecko **5** Shingle-back lizard
6–11 Common garden lizard **12** Blue-tongue lizard **13** Skink **14** Frilled-neck lizard

 • *AUSTRALIAN SIGNPOST MATHS 3 MENTALS* • ISBN 978 1 4886 2183 3